WIECH

Indians Of
Southwestern Connecticut
In The
Seventeenth Century

John Alexander Buckland

HERITAGE BOOKS, INC.

· Published 2002 by
HERITAGE BOOKS, INC.
1540E Pointer Ridge Place, Bowie, Maryland 20716
1-800-398-7709
www.heritagebooks.com

ISBN 0-7884-2028-3

THE WIECHQUAESKECK
Indians of Southwestern Connecticut
in the Seventeenth Century

CONTENTS

APPENDICES

WIECHQUAESKECK REFERENCES

TYPES OF REFERENCES

The references are grouped by type to give a better understanding of their sources, and their probable validity. As much material as possible was taken from the writings of 17th century observers. These references are given a special annotation so that their sources are obvious. The types are:

17th Century Documents

These are annotated with recognizable abbreviations, such as *(Bradford)* for William Bradford, which help indicate their importance and validity. Comments about some of these authors are given in Section 6, under "European Observers of Wiechquaeskeck Life"

17th Century Maps in Chronological Sequence

These maps are annotated by the mapmaker's name. They were chosen for their historical importance, and because of specific information on them. A few early 18th century maps are included in the list.

17th Century Land Transfer Agreements

These are listed chronologically to give a time-lapse picture of the invasion of the English colonists into Wiechquaeskeck territory. Some are discussed in Chap. 8, "The First Fairfield County Real Estate Boom."

Archeological Reports

These are listed chronologically in the Wiechquaeskeck References section. They are annotated with a combination such as *(ARCH6)*. They are all professional, published reports.

Other Documents That Illuminate the 17th Century

The great amount of scholarly research and analysis that has been done in the 19th and 20th centuries has been invaluable, and is often used for illumination of the period. These references are referred to by a number from an alphabetically-sequenced listing by author. They are annotated by reference and page, such as *(27: 15)*.

Personal Communications

These are used when no other source of the information was available, and are noted in the text. The information can be verified by the author, but should be considered as opinion.

ILLUSTRATIONS

ACKNOWLEDGEMENTS

I thank the many generous, helpful people in the libraries, museums and universities that I have visited. They have uniformly been pleasant and informative. I particularly thank the following for their support and encouragement:

Dr. Nicholas F Bellantoni, Connecticut State Archeologist, University of Connecticut, Storrs, Conn.

Deborah Brinkerhoff, Bruce Museum of Arts and Sciences, Greenwich, Conn.

Chitanikapai, a.k.a. Nicholas A. Shumatoff, Jr., Bedford, NY.

Faith Damon Davison, Archivist, The Mohegan Tribe, Conn.

Dr. Walton C. Galinat, University of Massachusetts, Amherst, Mass.

Charles Gehring, New Netherland Project, New York State Library, Albany, NY.

Dr. Herbert C. Kraft, Department of Anthropology, Seton Hall University, South Orange, NJ.

Richard E. McCabe, Director of Publications, Wildlife Management Institute, Washington, DC.

John McNiff, Roger Williams National Memorial, Providence, RI.

Walter 'Silent Wolf' Van Dunk, Tribal Chief, Ramapough Lenape Nation, "Keepers of the Pass," Mahwah, NJ.

Ernest A. Wiegand, Archeology Department, Norwalk Community-College, Norwalk, Conn.

I have had considerable support, useful research and helpful suggestions, from my wife, Miram Renwick Buckland.

John Alexander Buckland

Greenwich, Connecticut

INTRODUCTION

This book honors an Indian Nation that has been popularly misnamed, and thus long forgotten by the general public. It is the Wiechquaeskeck of the Hudson River estuary region. The Wiechquaeskeck once occupied much of the Bronx, most of Westchester County, New York, and southwestern Connecticut. They were a numerous, strong, and healthy people when they first gazed at the white sails of European ships off their shores in the 16th Century. They were respected by their many neighboring Algonquian-speaking tribes, with whom they traded and intermarried, even over long distances *(24)*. They exemplified the Europeans' best ideas about Woodland Native Americans.

The Wiechquaeskeck of western Fairfield County, Connecticut, were part of a unique tribe that has not been generally recognized for over 200 years. They belonged to a large group of Native Americans called the Lenape, or Delaware. Much has been written about the Lenape in New Jersey, their heartland, and many of those descriptions can be applied directly to the Wiechquaeskeck. The Lenape were not simply in present-day New Jersey. Many were north and east of the Hudson River, and others were in Delaware and eastern Pennsylvania. They were all part of the Algonquian-speaking Native tribes who had spread from the Ohio River to the Atlantic shore and up to the Great Lakes, from Maine to the Carolinas, and all across eastern Canada from the Rockies to the Maritimes. The Delaware spoke the Eastern Algonquian language in several dialects. They spoke the Munsee dialect in Northern New Jersey and Connecticut.

The Wiechquaeskeck were friendly with the Wapping to their north. They were very close to the Manhattan who lived in what is now New York City. They regularly visited other Lenape tribes, on Long Island, in New Jersey, and in the Hudson River valley.

The life of the Wiechquaeskeck centered on hunting and gathering in the fields and forests, growing corn and vegetables, and catching and smoking fish and shellfish. They worked white and purple seashells, making wampum and jewelry. They built walled "pounds" to kill deer, and they made fish traps and nets to increase their seafood supply. They were fearful of the powerful Pequot, so they raised palisades around some villages and built many coastal "palisadoes," or small forts, to defend themselves. The construction of their palisades was not a post-Contact phenomenon. The Dutch found the Wiechquaeskeck palisades in place when they arrived (*vanderDonck*), and had little difficulty in tearing them down (*Jameson*). They were not built to withstand European guns.

The Wiechquaeskeck sank from a thriving tribe, to a decimated people, to obscurity. Because they had early contact with the Europeans, they were wasted by smallpox and other virulent diseases that had been scourging Europe at that time. As many as 90 percent may have died from imported diseases. When the remnant raised their stone weapons, the Dutch responded with gunpowder, and destroyed whole villages. The story of the overwhelming European immigration is described, because it is fundamental to the decline of the Wiechquaeskeck.

This story of the Wiechquaeskeck is about one geographical area that is populous and thriving today. The ideas about their physical conditions, the principles of technology transfer, their lifeways, and the patterns of their footpaths are applicable to most of the other Native Americans in the region, however.

Most of these details about the Wiechquaeskeck were taken directly from 17th century documents that described either them or their neighboring Algonquian-speakers at the time. There were a great many letters and reports sent by the Dutch in New Amsterdam back to Holland. Although most have been lost or destroyed, some of the remaining writings were translated in the past 200 years, first by people like John Romeyn Brodhead, who was edited by O'Callaghan in 1863, and by Jameson in 1909. New York State has funded much historical research about the times, and definitive work has been produced in the past several years by The New Netherland Project in Albany, New York. Early English settlers in eastern Connecticut and Massachusetts also wrote about the lifestyle of the Eastern Woodland Indians. Many of those early books have now been photo-reproduced and reprinted.

Information was also gleaned from the many 17th century maps that were made in The Hague, Amsterdam, and London. Some of these maps were merely copies of others, with added illumination, but they all helped to locate many tribes and features of the time. General European historical information, and professional reports of archaeological digs in the area, were studied.

As we drive around Fairfield County today, we see names like Amogerone, Keofferam, Nawthorne, Noroton, Norwalk, Ponus, and Rippowam on road signs. These were Wiechquaeskeck names that have not had vivid meanings for us for over 250 years.

Over time, the Wiechquaeskeck have been called the "Siwanoy." Siwanoy referred to their occupation, however, and was not their tribal name. Many of their artisans made sewan, or wampum, along the shore, and they were the "Siwanoy" ("oy" means people), or "makers of wampum." Other Natives, who lived on Long Island, in Pennsylvania, and even in Massachusetts north of Boston, were also called "Siwanoy."

Some of the Wiechquaeskeck took strings of wampum, as "money," to trade with the Manhattan tribe. With a shortage of European coins for trade, both the Dutch and English soon recognized wampum as legal tender, and for a time the Wiechquaeskeck had a profitable business in making strings of wampum to support local European business. They commuted to trade on a footpath which is now called "U.S. Route 1" in Connecticut and Westchester County, and "Broadway" on Manhattan Island. Thus western Connecticut residents commuted to trade their wampum on Wall Street in the 17th century. The same business routine has continued for 400 years!

The small and capable Wiechquaeskeck tribe thrived on this land where two million people now live. They trod where we tread.

John Alexander Buckland

THE WIECHQUAESKECK

INDIANS OF SOUTHWESTERN CONNECTICUT IN THE SEVENTEENTH CENTURY

CHAPTER 1

THE FATAL CLASH OF CULTURES

Many factors contributed to the decline and disappearance of the Wiechquaeskeck. A Stone Age culture was invaded by an Iron Age culture, which had writing, iron equipment and gunpowder. The earliest and greatest debilitating factor, however, was the importation of diseases from other continents.

When the Pilgrims arrived in Massachusetts in 1620, they were met by only a few Native Americans. The Algonquian tribes there had already been devastated by European pestilences, starting in the early 1500's. In addition, they were wary, because some had been attacked and even enslaved, by some traders who had arrived earlier. A few of the Indians fought the newcomers, some fled inland, and some came forward to meet them. This was the same pattern for all the coastal Algonquian in the Northeast, including the Wiechquaeskeck.

This clash of cultures, which had started in the 16th century, proved fatal to many eastern Native Americans. The Wiechquaeskeck tribe was finally utterly destroyed.

Differences Between the Cultures

There were many differences between the two cultures that clashed dramatically on the Atlantic coast of North America:

- The Indians had no immunity to the diseases that had swept across Europe, Asia, and Africa for generations. Within the century, they were decimated. Most Europeans had developed some immunity previously, and they were far more numerous.

- The Indians had a technology based on naturally-occurring materials such as bones, stone, plants, hides, etc. They had simple weapons. European iron and gunpowder easily overwhelmed them *(Chap. 9)*.

- The Indians, like all peoples, became angry when treated badly or misunderstood. When they struck out to defend their rights, however, steel met their stone, and they were shattered. When there were arguments over the meaning of land agreements, the invaders nearly always won *(Chap 8)*.

- The Indians were sparsely-settled hunters and gatherers. They had vegetable gardens near their inland villages and along the shore during the fishing and clamming months. They moved to seasonal hunting and gathering camps, but would go to their central village for ceremonies, and tribal pursuits *(ARCH14, vander Donck: 88, 96)*. When they gathered, they perceived themselves strong. They were no match for European technology, organization, and numbers *(Chap. 6)*.

- The Indians had no written language, but relied on a strong oral tradition. They could not document their tribal structure and knowledge of their surroundings. They could not prove their claims to the land, other than orally. They had no way of understanding the written English Common Law. Since they did not have a concept of "land ownership," they often signed documents without realizing the meaning of the written pages *(Chap. 8)*.

- A Native tribe had oral treaty arrangements with other tribes, agreed upon at face-to-face meetings. They visited and traded with other tribes at great distances. The people sang, danced, played games, told stories, and had seasonal celebrations. Yet, they were looked upon as wild and ignorant savages by the Europeans because they did not write or read. They simply had a different way of thinking, relating, and recording *(vander Donck: 71) (Chap. 7).*

- The Indians lived communally, with all their belongings in the open. If anyone needed clothing or a tool, they used it. They understood war and seizure, but they did not understand the restricted use of personal belongings among friends. They had no concept of the European definition of "stealing," especially from your immediate neighbors *(Chap. 7).*

- The Europeans never understood the structure of the varied Indian family and tribal organizations, and the fluidity of tribal boundaries. They often wrote agreements to "buy" land that was not "owned" by the Native signers. The Native Americans even changed their tribal groupings over time, depending on the strength, astuteness, and relationships of their sakimas. This was most confusing to the settlers *(deLaet: 45, deRasierres: 103).* Only late in the century, some surviving Indians, like Wespahin, learned how to use land agreements to their own advantage *(Chap. 8).*

Clash of Cultures – Smallpox and Other Plagues

The Native American population along the eastern seaboard succumbed to imported diseases very rapidly. Dean R. Snow *(46: 32-42)* analyzed the populations of the aboriginal cultures of New England. He concentrated on the great epidemics of smallpox, measles, and other diseases of the early 1600s. His numbers may have been conservative, but his reasoning is convincing. Snow estimates that in the drainage area of the lower Hudson River, there were from 24,800 to 51,800 Munsee-speaking Natives in the year 1600. Possibly, about 9,000 of them may have been Wiechquaeskeck. This put their population density at 90 to 190 people per square kilometer, similar to all the tribes from Boston to New York, because of the favorable climate and the migratory fish resources. After the epidemic of the early 1600s, however, there were only about 4,500 Natives (possibly 1,500 Wiechquaeskeck) left in the lower Hudson Valley, a mortality rate of 81% to 91%. The death rate was the same throughout southeastern New England.

When this disaster was followed by the devastation of Governor Kieft's War in the 1640s *(Chap. 9)*, very few Wiechquaeskeck remained. Most of the remnants died rejected, or drifted away and consolidated in refugee communities, first in Ridgefield and Kent, Connecticut, then in Springfield Massachusetts, Squakheag New York, and other towns during the late 17th century. From there they disappeared *(Chap. 10)*.

It is very likely that the devastation from imported diseases started in the late 1500s and peaked in the early 1600s. Snow felt that the early fishermen and adventurers had too small crews, and were too long at sea, to have carried the disease vectors. But neighbors of the Weichquaeskeck, the Tappan tribe on the lower Hudson (possibly 2,000 people) was destroyed by bubonic plague when visited by one small trading ship. One or more rats with infected fleas had come from Europe, and left the ship to move among the Tappan, infecting them with bubonic plague.

The Europeans, Asians and Africans, who were on the trading ships in those early contact years, were a rough mixture of people, and some had been pressed into service from the dregs of the world's seaports. They often went ashore at New Amsterdam. Plagues and pestilences were sweeping Europe and Asia at the time, and had infected many of the sailors. There was bubonic plague, smallpox, tuberculosis, measles, mumps, syphilis, and other diseases to which the surviving Europeans had developed some immunity, after they had been devastated themselves in previous centuries. The Native Americans had absolutely no immunity to these fearsome diseases. A few rats with fleas leaving the boats, a few sailors coming ashore with infections and lice, a few ill men left on the shore, and soon the dreaded pestilences spread to the unsuspecting Natives.

Jacob Frederick Stam *(Stam)* wrote in 1637: "Before the English came to inhabit at New Plimoth, Frenchmen trading with the natives for beaver fought them." Europeans were in America very early.

A distressing aspect of these plagues is that they first hit the Native tribes who had been the friendliest to the European newcomers. The Indians who most resisted the traders and settlers were slower to be infected, and were strong enough to offer resistance to the encroachment of the whites. But, the invisible disease germs soon passed to nearly all tribes in northeastern America, including the Wiechquaeskeck. The devastation was rapid, as Stam noted:

> In a short time the Plague fell on the Indians, that they died on
> heapes and lay in their houses and the living that were able to shift
> for themselves would runne away & let them dy, and let there be
> Carkases above the ground without burial.

Daniel Gookin, who collected early documents about the Indians in
New England *(Gookin: 8)* wrote about the "Narragansitts":

> . . . a very great number of them were swept away by an epidemical
> and unwonted sickness, An.1612 and 1613, about seven or eight
> years before the English first arrived in those parts to settle the col-
> ony of New Plymouth. Thereby divine providence made way for the
> quiet and peaceable settlement of the English in those nations. . . .
> Doubtless it was some pestilential disease. I have discoursed with
> some old Indians, that were then youths; who say, that the bodies all
> over were exceeding yellow, describing it by a yellow garment they
> showed me.

Many foreign diseases became pandemic all across North America. It
was not that America was disease-free before 1492. The Native
Americans already had major health problems with tuberculosis, amoebic
dysentry, influenza, and pneumonia. But, the newly introduced diseases
were rapid killers and spread everywhere. Since the 14th century, the
crowds and squalor of European cities had incubated diseases like
smallpox, Black Death, measles, typhus, and scarlet fever. Millions had
died, and the germs remained always present in European populations.
It took very few infected people to bring them to America.

In the 17th century, the European invaders little knew that they were
carrying death. They wondered in amazement as the Native Americans
died. No one had any idea what caused smallpox infection in the early
1600s, when the plague hit the coastal Algonquians the hardest. It was
not until the late 19th century that research proved the process of bacterial
infection, and the need to isolate those with the diseases.

Clash of Cultures - Stone versus Iron and Gunpowder

Another major factor in the fatal clash of cultures was the European
capabilities of warfare. The invading troops were trained and drilled.
They used guns against stone weapons. In the early 17th century, the
Indian palisades offered little resistance to these attackers.

Before European Contact, the Indians had fought each other with stone projectiles, using arrows, spears, and clubs. These were deadly, but slow, and tribes often surrendered, and became subservient to other tribes, rather than be wiped out. Van der Donck describes the Wiechquaeskeck in "Of Their Wars and Weapons" *(vander Donck: 100):*

> Their weapons formerly were bows and arrows, with a war-club hung to the arm, and a square shield which covered the body up to the shoulders; their faces they disfigure in such a manner that it is difficult to recognize one known before; they bind bands or snakeskins around the head...and thus they march onwards.

There is little archeological evidence of warfare in the region prior to the Late Woodland Period. This is partly because of the general destruction of sites, and partly because of the very thin, acid soil in the area. Certainly, the palisades around villages and the palisadoes were pre-Contact, as they were described by early Dutch and English *(Chap. 6F)* who were the first Europeans into the area. Also, ancient skeletons have been unearthed near Manhattan that had stone projectile points imbedded in the bones *(45: 17).* Obvious signs of Native warfare among the Wiechquaeskeck have been found near New Rochelle, New York. The Lenape were part of the great movements of Native peoples that routinely altered tribal boundaries, well before Contact. The Wiechquaeskeck were subservient to the Mahican, who had a history of clashing with the Mohawk. The Wiechquaeskeck fortifications were mainly defensive against Pequot, moving down the coast. Generally, however, the Wiechquaeskeck were surrounded by friendly Algonquian-speaking neighbors.

When Europeans arrived, the stone weapons proved useless against gunpowder and steel sabers. The palisadoes were smashed at will, and whole villages were destroyed by musket fire. During Governor Kieft's War, 1640 to 1645, the Dutch slaughtered hundreds of Indians near New Netherland with their overwhelming firepower. This war culminated in John Underhill's destruction of the Wiechquaeskeck village of Nanichiestawack at Cross River, New York, killing six or seven hundred of the few remaining in the tribe *(Chap. 9).*

The power of European gunpowder delivered the coup de grace to the Wiechquaeskeck. A later factor, which completely disrupted previous tribal boundaries, was the enlistment of Native Americans to fight wars beside the European factions. In the 18th century, tribes sided with the

French or the English against other Indian tribes. They joined with the intra-European conflicts, at great loss to themselves. Even a few Wiechquaeskeck were probably drawn into this fighting, since they were close to the Mahican.

J. Fenimore Cooper wrote "The Last of the Mohicans" in Mamaroneck, New York. Mamarunek was a Wiechquaeskeck sachem and an ally of the Mahican. Cooper understood how the frontier had shifted, and that some of the remaining friends of the Mahican died off in the French-English border wars *(Chap. 10)*.

Clash of Cultures - Lack of a Written Language

In the fatal collision of cultures that took place in the 17th century, the lack of a Native written language played a strong part. There was a complete misunderstanding by the intruders about the organization, intelligence, and feelings of the Native Americans. To a great extent, this was because the Indians had no written language to convey the essence of their culture, and of their land ownership, to the invaders.

In the 17th century, the Europeans called the Indians "savages" (salvages, sauvage) and felt superior to them. Since nothing was written down by the Natives, they could not explain or prove anything about their organization or their land. No one appreciated their intelligence, their complex organization, their great craftsmanship, and the strength of the oral communication among all the tribes of Native Americans. How could sitting around a council fire and smoking pipes be equal to a piece of legal paper? The Europeans simply did not understand the indigenous people.

The Puritans and missionaries in New England tried to "civilize" the Indians through Christianity and friendship *(Johnson, Heckewelder)*. They taught some of the Natives to read and write, and to adopt the European way of life, including their social and political organization. They established about 30 "Praying Towns" where Christian Indians were assumed to be living just like Europeans, owning and working their land. The Praying Towns nearly all disappeared in the 1670's, however, after the outbreak of King Philip's War. Many young Indians, who had previously been friendly with the settlers, joined with King Philip (Metacomet). Some of them came from the Praying Towns, and since all

Indians looked alike to the Europeans, most of those in the Praying Towns were also either driven out, or fled *(42: 174)*. Newer, mostly non-Puritan, settlers who were land-hungry simply grouped all Indians together. An unfortunate result of King Philip's bloody attacks was that few Indians were ever trusted again anywhere in New England, and very few got any instruction in literacy.

This attitude reached southwestern Connecticut, as they heard of the Indian attacks in Massachusetts and northern Connecticut, and were afraid. The Town Meeting minutes in Greenwich talk about erecting palisades around the meeting house, and arming the men in case the few remaining Wiechquaeskeck joined the Wampanoag uprising.

One of the last Praying Towns, where Wiechquaeskeck were taught to read and write, was Schagticoke (Scatacook) in northwestern Connecticut. It was to there that many had fled when they were pushed out of southwestern Connecticut. Some Indians, such as Occam, a minister in Schagticoke, had been well-educated and tried to organize their few surviving people. This did not last many generations, however. European traders purposely brought in rum to the struggling Indian towns, and exploited the few settled Natives there *(Chap. 10)*. These new immigrants used both legal and illegal methods to sieze the land, push out the Indians, and even kill them *(10, 41)*.

The Wiechquaeskeck in Connecticut had very few settlers near them who were interested in their welfare, or who made any effort to teach them to read and write. There are oral stories that some Indians were buried in Tomac Burying Ground in Old Greenwich, as church members. If the stories are true, it would mean that a few Indians, probably working on settlers' farms, had joined the local church. In that case, they would have been taught, at least, to read the Bible. There were similar stories throughout Fairfield County. None appear to be documented.

Clash of Cultures – Attitudes towards Land Ownership

The English settlers regularly used land transfer documents with local Wiechquaeskeck leaders to claim ownership of land. The remaining sagamores and sakimas (whom they often called "sachems") signed documents giving away their rights "legally" to specific pieces of land *(Chap. 8)*. Soon the Wiechquaeskeck had no land rights at all. Whenever

Europeans wanted land, they simply brought trade goods, drew up a document, and had it signed. After all, most of the Indians had already died off, and the few that remained could not read, and were of little concern. To make it legal under English Common Law, documents were put in front of Wiechquaeskeck leaders that were full of legal phrases. None of the Wiechquaeskeck who signed could read the documents. They were in no position to resist any offer, anyway, as most of the tribe had died from the plagues. So they went through the motions of a "land sale," accepted what they got, and were then eased off the land.

These land transfers were all quite legal to the English. Although many of the settlers could not read either, and simply marked the document with an X, the meaning was clearly understood by them. They were buying the land permanently. That concept was foreign to the Wiechquaeskeck. They thought that they were simply getting some great gifts for the use of the land, which no one "owned" anyway. The remaining Wiechquaeskeck soon found themselves displaced.

At first, some early Puritan thinkers, such as Roger Williams of Rhode Island, had insisted on formal land deals to be fair to the Indians, which gave them legal rights under English Common Law. Roger Williams *(Williamsletters: 295)* recognized the complexity of Indian property systems and insisted that title to the land rested in the hands of local sachems, who should receive remuneration from Englishmen purchasing their lands so that title claims could be completely cleared. The first Fairfield settlers were careful to keep the documents legal *(Sect. 8)*. Later settlers simply used legalisms to grab land in a way that would give them the ownership in the colonial courts of law. The Natives signed away their land under pressure. Only a few, like Chik-in Warrups and Wespahin (John Cauk), caught on to the concept, and worked it to their advantage *(Sect. 3)*.

Most of the land transactions were signed in "good faith" on the part of the early settlers. The deeds were signed with marks by the Indians, in ignorance of the details of what was happening, but also in "good faith" on their part. They were diminishing. Later settlers gave the Indians no consideration, and just took the vacated land.

The cultures had clashed, and it had proved fatal to the Wiechquaeskeck of western Fairfield County, Connecticut, the Bronx, and Westchester County, New York. In 1861, Hardy died. He was the last of the Wiechquaeskeck line known to be still living in Greenwich or Stamford at the time. He was buried in an unmarked plot on private land on lower Round Hill Road in Greenwich.

Connecticut in the 18th century – Library of Congress

CHAPTER 2

THE INDIANS AND THE EUROPEAN IMMIGRATION

A. AMERICA BEFORE EUROPEAN HISTORY

People had lived in eastern North America for at least 10,000 years before the first European sailing ships crossed the Atlantic in the 15th and 16th centuries. This summary places the Wiechqueskeck within that space and time. *(Fig. 1, Connecticut Time Line Before European History)*

The End of the Last Ice Age

The events of the end of the last Ice Age are important to the story of the Native Americans of the Hudson River Valley and Connecticut. The vast ice sheet and its final melting shaped the land *(14)*. The changing conditions of the last 10,000 years determined the lifestyle of the Natives. Great glacial lakes were formed, then they drained. Many rivers shifted significantly and shrank. For example, in the 17th century, the Norwalk Indians could paddle a large dugout canoe up to the lake at the source of the Norwalk River *(Chap. 6)*. Now the streams and ponds are smaller, and filled by sedimentation. Little has changed in the general topography of this area since 1600 AD, however. The coastal water levels are not markedly different, since many archaeological digs have found shore villages close to the present water line. The large Norwalke village clearly has been flooded by the rising Atlantic Ocean, however *(Chap. 11-A)*.

Long before the original Paleo-Indians (or "ancient Indians") moved in to hunt and gather food, the continental glaciation of the Ice Age, in the Pleistocene Epoch, had stretched down to about the level

Figure 1

Connecticut Time Line Before European History

17,000 BC The last advance of the Wisconsin III Glacier from the vast Laurentide Ice Shield. It was a mile thick, and the terminal moraine created Long Island. It shaped Connecticut. Geologically, this was the brief Holocene, or Recent, Period, with the extinction of the large animals and the rise of man.

15,000 BC The Ice Shield melted back to the St. Lawrence River. The Atlantic Ocean moved Into Long Island Sound.

10,000 BC Paleo-Indian Period. Small groups of nomadic hunters moved through the Northeast, using the Clovis fluted spear point *(Fig. 38)*.

8,000 BC Early Archaic Period. People moved in from the South as hunters and gatherers. They used large spear points *(Fig. 38)*.

6,000 Middle Archaic Period, A deciduous forest developed in a warming trend. Indians occupied many sites in Connecticut *(Fig. 39)*.

4,000 BC Late Archaic Period. Indians developed a seasonal round of subsistence and settlement patterns, and the population increased *(Fig. 39)*.

1,700 BC Terminal Archaic Period. Possibly a migration of new people through the area with a different, broad-bladed projectile point.

1,000 BC Early Woodland Period. Settlements along the coast with hunting, fishing and gathering. Fired ceramics began to be used. *(Figs. 40, 41)*.

1 AD Middle Woodland Period. A more sedentary pattern of life, possibly with the introduction of horticulture and food storage *(Figs. 40, 41)*.

1,000 AD Late Woodland Period. Corn, squash and beans from the Southwest diffused to the Northeast. Horticulture started in sedentary villages. Some Indians traded over great distances. Fortifications were erected *(Figs. 41, 42)*.

1,497 AD Contact Period. John Cabot reached the Great Banks, and took the news of the cod back to Europe. European history began in northeastern America.

1,520 AD Cod fishermen, fur traders and opportunists started to land along the coast of New England, and interacted with the Native Americans.

1,600 AD European settlements were attempted in New England.

1,620 AD First permanent settlement in New England at Plymouth, Massachusetts.

1,637 AD English and Dutch settlers started to move into southwestern Connecticut

Adapted from Wiegand (52)

of New York City. It is called the Laurentide Shield, and it covered all of Canada and the northern part of the United States. The final stage of this immense glaciation is called the Wisconsin glacial drift *(14)*. It deposited a terminal moraine that created Long Isand. When the ice sheet melted back, it receded from Connecticut and Massachusetts, some 15,000 years ago.

The ice sheets that covered the top of the world sheared off the earlier mountains in this area and carved out today's river valleys. They left some rock formations that became rock shelters for wandering hunters. They left sand and gravel drumlins and moraines that had been formed by the ice. The runoff water left alluvial deposits and deltas which later made agricultural fields. Some of these became Indian village sites. Posts could be placed into the soft soil, and the land could be tilled. The drainage was excellent.

As the ice drew back, the whole land was saturated with the water that poured from the huge melting glacier. The water had tremendous force, and it was loaded with sand and rock, scouring out the land and reshaping it. On a tiny scale, in some places, the sand-water flowed as from a nozzle directly onto soft sedimentary rock. It swirled out perfectly round and smooth depressions called "potholes." If these were near an Indian settlement, some believe they could have been used for either storage or cooking. Cooking would have been accomplished by filling them with water, then dropping in heated rocks before the food was added. Otherwise, the Natives used skin-lined holes or bark containers for this purpose. A small, fine example of a pothole can be seen on the west side of the junction of Cold Spring Road and Stillwater Road in Stamford. Some people look at potholes and think they were carved out by Natives because they are so perfectly round. They were formed naturally.

Connecticut today still shows the striations of the great ice sheet that had ground down the mountains. The many broken stone ridges and exposed rocks running north and south, and the stony soil, are marks of the ice action. The result dictated the shape of future settlement and farming areas.

About 12,000 years ago, the land was not unlike the far north of Canada today. It was wet tundra with sparse vegetation. Animals could move in to forage close to the ice front. These were animals such as the huge woolly mammoth *(Mammuthus primigenius)*, musk-ox *(Ovibos moshatus)* and caribou *(Rangifer)*. Paleolithic people from the south may have followed to hunt them. Further south, in the scrubby subarctic forests of Connecticut, there were mastodon *(Mammuthus americanum)* and animals like the stag moose, giant beaver (*Castoroides)*, elk, peccary, deer, and bear. The land was wet and harsh.

In 1979, Ernest Wiegand, of Norwalk Technical College (now Norwalk Community College), led a dig where some mastodon bones had been found in a swamp at Lake Kitchawan, in Pound Ridge, New York. Bones had fallen into the anaerobic (oxygen-free) mud of the swamp and had been preserved there for up to 10,000 years. A single mastodon molar was found that was almost as large as a child's head. This was a fascinating find because most bone remains of animals in Connecticut last only a few decades. The acidic soil normally destroys the bone calcium. Many lithic (stone) fragments of Native handcraft have been found from early periods, but very few bones. Most bones in Connecticut decompose over the years in the acid soil. The mastodon bones were only preserved because they had lain over the millenia in non-acidic mud *(51)*. There were no marks of stone weapons on the mastodon bones, which could have been evidence of interaction between them and the Paleo-Indians. The Wiechquaeskeck had not yet arrived in the area.

The First People – The Paleo-Indian Period (10,000 to 8,000 BC)

Probably by 10,000 years ago, Paleo-Indians started to move into northeastern America. These first people were groups of hunters who probed north after the melted water from the great ice sheet had dropped sufficiently to allow passage over the boggy land. This period of great change lasted from about 10,000 BC to 8000 BC.

A Paleo-Indian site in Litchfield County, Connecticut, dated at 8240 BC, has been studied and reported. Their findings are described by Robert Moeller in **6LF21 - A Paleo-Indian Site in Western Connecticut** *(32)*. It is probable that this site is representative of all southwestern Connecticut toward the end of the Paleo-Indian Period.

These early Native Americans hunted with both spears and arrows, and used the superb fluted Clovis projectile point, as they pursued both large and small animals *(Fig. 38)*. There is evidence that "warm" plants,

Figure 2

Dundee Rockshelter, Old Greenwich, Connecticut
circa 2000 BC

Illustration by Bryan K. Buckland

The Dundee Rockshelter is in Edward R. Schongalla Park in Greenwich, Connecticut. Stuart Fiedel made an archeological study there in 1985 (ARCH14). He found that it was visited most frequently between 2500 to 1700 BC. The sketch is of the existing rockshelter. It was much longer in Archaic times. Pothunters and vandals have damaged the site.

like white oak, hickory and shrubs had begun to grow across the region *(32, 46)*. The Natives probably found ways of cooperatively hunting caribou, bear and elk. They subsisted on little animals and fish, however.

The Paleo-Indians were nomads, who only sparsely populated this region. Possibly they operated from base camps, from which parties of hunters pursued deer, while others foraged, and caught fish and smaller animals. There was rockshelter occupation *(Fig. 2, Dundee Rockshelter, Old Greenwich, Connecticut)* with quarries, workshops, and killsites, which have been found *(51)*.

It is possible that they could also have hunted the last of the huge prehistoric animals that still roamed the continent, but that is only speculative in Connecticut. The mastodons and other animals that grazed on the new scrubby woodlands were very big, and there is no archeological evidence that any were killed by stone projectiles in this area. The Mashantucket Pequot Museum depicts a group of caribou being herded past a simple killing site, which is probably a good representation. There were certainly many "deer pounds" *(Sect. 6C)* in Wiechquaeskeck territory by the 16th century.

In looking at the Connecticut countryside today, it is interesting to remember that it is in the very last throes of the Ice Age. We easily see the ice-scoured hillsides and rocks. The soil is still full of miscellaneous rocks and boulders, which had been pushed along for many miles by the great Ice Sheet. But, the ice-melt water in the ground has now almost dissipated. Streams that flowed full and fresh from melting ice for the Wiechquaeskeck are now shallow and sluggish. The Tankiteke could paddle a 20-foot dugout canoe up the Norwalk River to Ridgefield in the 17th century *(Chap. 6B)*. That would be impossible today.

The Archaic Period (8,000 to 1,000 BC)

The Archaic Period is divided by archaeologists into the Early, Middle, Late, and Terminal Archaic, each about 2,000 years long *(Fig. 1)*. This Period started as largely a pine and spruce forest, but deciduous trees slowly moved in as the climate warmed. The sea level gradually rose to close to its present level, as the great ice sheet continued to melt in the North. Long Island Sound changed from a glacial lake to salt water, when the Atlantic rose and surged in. A few sites have indicated that the Indians were gathering oysters in the Hudson River area. As time went by, the climate allowed a deciduous forest to develop, and the Indians had a much greater variety of plants and animals to use. Seasonal patterns began, such as spring fishing camps, fall hunting camps, and coastal summer shellfishing camps. Rockshelters were still in use. The technology of projectile points changed markedly. Soapstone in the area was used to fashion cooking containers *(51)*.

Elsewhere around 6,000 BC, many of the Natives of southwestern America and Mexico had begun to farm, developing their main food source. Their population density thereby increased. Their farming methods slowly diffused to the Northeast. Diffusion is the very slow process of the transfer of technologies by person-to-person and tribe-to-tribe contact. The northeastern Native Americans remained semi-nomadic hunters and gatherers until about 1000 AD, when they also started to learn the techniques of farming.

The Woodland Period (1,000 BC to European Contact)

The Woodland Period has been divided into three parts, Early, Middle, and Late Woodland. Each was about 1,000 years long. People became more settled, and there was enough time for them to develop their own domestic products, such as bowls, pots, and personal ornaments. Knowledge of clay manufacture moved by diffusion across the continent, from the south. Skin garments were used, but some weaving began.

In the Early Woodland Period (1,000 BC-1 AD), fired clay vessels gradually replaced the more cumbersome soapstone pots. Hunting, fishing, and gathering continued, but seashore camps were occupied in the summer, to gather and store shellfish and fish *(ARCH16, ARCH18)*.

In the Middle Woodland Period (1-1000 AD), there is evidence of a more settled pattern of life, because large pits for food storage have been found. Horticulture began in this period, indicating longer occupation of their summer camp sites.

In the Late Woodland Period (1,000 AD- Contact), the Native Americans began to have permanent year-round villages with horticulture *(Chap. 11)*. There were also temporary sites used for seasonal hunting and fishing, and probably for gathering shells for wampum making. The villages often had fortifications on high, defensible land. There is evidence of violent death, and warfare among the Indian tribes, in this period *(45)*, possibly caused by increased populations and a limited resource base. Large shell middens were created at the coastal camps. Numerous features have been found by archeologists, such as hearths, refuse pits, earth ovens, and human and dog burials *(Chap. 11)*.

Little direct evidence of horticulture has been unearthed in Connecticut, largely because of the quick deterioration of organic remains by the acidic soil. Indirect evidence has been found, such as mortars and pestles for grinding corn, and buried baskets for grain storage. The earliest Europeans wrote of extensive agriculture by the Natives, however.

The Woodland People

We do not know how many waves of different Native immigrants moved into this area in the past three thousand years. In the first thousand years BC, we call them the Early Woodland Culture. These were possibly the first Algonquian people. Some had come down from Siberia and Alaska to spread over the continent, while some probably evolved from earlier peoples already here. Archaeologists have found that there were many changes in tools and living habits over the centuries. Some changes could have come from new waves of immigration by other tribes, and some could have been simply technology transfer among indigenous groups. There were sufficient differences for archaeologists to give names to Periods of time *(Fig. 1)*, however, to indicate clear distinctions between their findings in the different archaeological horizons.

In the first thousand years AD, the distinctive culture is called the Middle Woodland. The population density increased along the fertile seacoast, with its ready supply of seafood. There was trading with other tribes, probably over great distances. This was a time of considerable diffusion of ideas about early farming methods, tools, and technologies. We have some information about their life from archaeological digs *(Chap. 11)*, but we cannot be sure who they were, as there was appreciable inter-tribal movement over the centuries. For example, Adena-like projectile points were found in Rye, New York, indicating possible movement from mid-America *(ARCH17)*.

It was during this time that the technology for making ceramics came north from the southern tribes. The techniques of handling and firing clay, and using grit and shell to temper it, became well known. Many potsherds have been found in archaeological sites. Geometric designs were commonly incised in the clay *(Chap. 11C)*.

There is much more archaeological information about the next thousand years, and it can be correlated with other data obtained throughout North America. There were early movements of the great Algonquian-speaking Woodland people. Agricultural methods and many basic technologies were shared and transferred, slowly but steadily.

Throughout the Lenape (Delaware) area there was communication among the bands during this Period. Before European contact, the Wiechquaeskeck worked closely with many other Native tribes in the lower Hudson Valley area *(Chap. 3)*. In about a fifty-mile radius, the Munsee dialect of the Algonquian language was spoken. This meant that there were close relationships from Long Island to Pennsylvania and from central New Jersey to the Poughkeepsie area. The Wiechquaeskeck traded with all these bands, and, possibly, sometimes supported them in fighting intruders. They also intermarried with them. Young men went out to other bands, and either returned with a wife or stayed in their wife's village. This made for many supportive tribal relationships.

During the 16th century, the Wiechquaeskeck lived a relatively stable existence for the times. They had a temperate climate, sufficient farm land, and abundant fish and game supplies. In the Protohistoric Period, before European Contact, however, they had to build crude palisades around their villages, and outlying guard posts, because of incursions by the Pequots and possibly even the Mohawks. They knew what a flotilla of large canoes meant when it landed on their shores. On the other hand, they were normally surrounded by friendly Munsee-speaking tribes with whom they traded and visited.

They had the time to build large fish traps and deer pounds to increase their supply of food *(Chap. 6)*. They worked together to burn down trees *(Fig. 16)* and to laboriously fashion dugout canoes from the logs *(Fig. 17)*. In historic times, they had a summer industry along the shore making wampum. The women worked tirelessly in the gardens, tanned hides for clothing and prepared food for winter use. The men carefully knapped the projectile points for hunting, and made the hooks and nets for fishing. They hunted and fished singly and in groups. The young men sometimes took long trips to visit other tribes *(24)*. They gathered at the central villages and played vigorous sports to prepare themselves for possible fighting. An early lacrosse-type game was probably popular.

Then, in the early 1700's, the Europeans arrived in their large boats with billowing white sails, firing mysterious guns. The Native world was utterly disrupted as the Historic Period began. It is noteworthy that the Wiechquaeskeck were not afraid of the Europeans coming in their huge boats with sabres and gunpowder. Even when the Europeans devastated their villages, they did not flee in the face of that extraordinary power. When the 17th century explorers arrived, some would even paddle to an armed vessel in their dugout canoes shouting, and shooting stone-tipped arrows. Van Meteren quotes Henry Hudson (*vanMeteren: 7*): "In the lower part of the river they found strong and warlike people."

B. THE EUROPEAN DISCOVERY OF AMERICA

There are many stories, and some archaeological finds, that lead people to dream of explorers who came to America from Europe and Asia before Columbus. Legends and histories abound. We know that the Norsemen lived in their Vinland colony on Greenland from 800 to 1400 *(33: 102)*. The Norse also had a colony at L'Anse aux Meadows on the northern side of Newfoundland. Some believe that the Norse Sagas read that they came into Long Island Sound, where they would have interacted with the Wiechquaeskeck. However, it was Christopher Columbus who truly "discovered" America for the rest of the World in 1492. Columbus' discovery was mapped and reported for any following mariner to read. His findings were published throughout Europe. Others followed quickly in his wake. Cabot reached the northern Algonquian people in 1497. Some Wiechquaeskeck saw Verrazano's ship in Long Island Sound in 1524 *(Fig. 4)*. A continuous stream of explorers, fishermen, adventurers, traders, and settlers came to the New World in an unbroken line. Enough other European visitors came past the mouth of the Hudson through the 1500s that the local warriors were quite unafraid when Henry Hudson arrived among the Wiechquaeskeck in The Half Moon in 1609, to explore what was first called the River of Mountains, later the Mauritius River, and now the Hudson River.

The Routes of the European Explorers

Thus, the interaction of the Wiechquaeskeck with the European invaders did not start with the settlers moving into the Hudson River area in the early 1600s. For a century before, a great many fishermen, traders, explorers and adventurers had sailed into Long Island Sound. They had come from Europe for fish, furs, minerals and timber. The famous explorers, who came later, had heard the stories, and they often simply mapped well-travelled routes.

Generations of Wiechquaeskeck had thus seen sailing ships off their shores, and some had made contact with the strangers *(Fig. 4)*. Henry Hudson was the first to record, in 1609, their familiarity with European ships. By 1645 there were ships from 18 nations moored in what is now New York Harbor, and some Wiechquaeskeck visited there regularly.

Figure 3, **The Routes of the European Explorers**, illustrates the process by which European nations came in contact with the Native Americans in the 16th century. European navigators had globes of the world showing lines for both latitude and longitude marked for 360 degrees, in degree increments *(53)*. They knew that the world was round. They crossed the ocean by "latitude sailing" *(33: 34)*, so that after they left Europe, they arrived in the New World at about a known latitude, when they so planned. Explorers could map the Connecticut coast, and others could sail to specific places there.

Columbus sailed west from the Azores, and he arrived at an island in the Bahamas. In his subsequent three voyages, he headed further south to explore the Carribean and South America. Most of the Spanish and Portuguese explorers, who later followed Columbus, only touched the southern part of America, far from Connecticut and the Wiechquaeskeck. Other Europeans soon heard of Columbus' voyage. John Cabot sailed by a northerly latitude route *(Fig. 3) (33: 177)*. This put him straight through the vast school of codfish that were on the Grand Banks, and directly towards Newfoundland. There were so many codfish that they slowed the passage of his ship in the water. He explored a large Algonquian area that is now eastern Canada and took the news back to England and France. Columbus had found gold, silver, and maize to take back to Europe. Cabot found codfish and furs. It would later be beaver, furs and timber that opened the Hudson River to the European settlers.

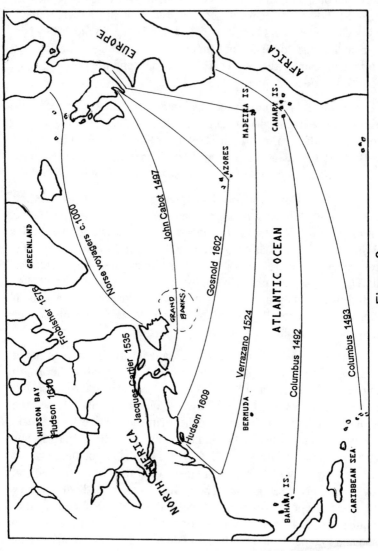

Figure 3
The Routes of the European Explorers

In 1524, Giovanni da Verrazzano sailed for France. He generally took a northerly Trade Wind route across to America, because there were Spanish warships patrolling the lower latitudes. On reaching northern Florida, Verrazzano turned up the coast of America, looking for a Northwest Passage to Cathay. He noted the Virginia and Delaware Capes. He wrote *(Verrazano: 135):*

> All along *(the coast)* we saw great fires because of the numerous inhabitants; we anchored off the shore, . . . and because we needed water we sent the small boat ashore with xxv men. . . We saw many people on the beach making friendly signs.

As he passed New Jersey, he described the coast as "green with forests." Next came the first European meeting with the Wiechquaeskeck in the Age of Discovery. "After a hundred leagues," Verrazzano continued *(Verrazzano: 137):*

> . . we found a very agreeable place between two small but prominent hills; between them a very wide river, deep at its mouth, flowed out into the sea; and with the help of the tide, which rises eight feet, any laden ship could have passed from the sea to the river estuary.

That description fits New York's Lower Bay, at the mouth of the Hudson River. It was the local Natives' first view of Europeans in an amazing ship, and many came out to see the strangers. Verrazzano anchored in the Narrows, which are now spanned by the Verrazzano Bridge. He noted:

> Since we were anchored off the coast and well sheltered, we did not want to run any risks without knowing anything about the river mouth. So we took the small boat up this river to land which we found densely populated *[This area was probably the very large village of Nayack or Wichquawanck, the Rockaway neighbors of the Wiechquaeskeck, in what is now Brooklyn].* The people were almost the same as the others, dressed in birds' feathers of various colors, and they came towards us joyfully, uttering loud cries of wonderment, and showing us the safest place to beach the boat. We went up this river for about half a league, where we saw that it formed a beautiful lake, about three leagues in circumference *[This was probably the Upper Bay of the Hudson estuary, the area of the Raritan, Manhattan and Wiechquaeskeck people].* About xxx of their small boats ran to and fro across the lake with innumerable people aboard who were crossing from one side to the other to see us. Suddenly, as often happens in sailing, a violent unfavorable wind blew in from the sea, and we were forced to return to the ship,

leaving the land with much regret on account of its favorable conditions and beauty; we think it was not without some properties of value, since all the hills showed signs of minerals.

It is very likely that some Wiechquaeskeck visiting the Manhattan Indians were part of the group who met the Europeans for the first time in 1524. They were wearing large feathers on their heads. Verrazzano called them "garlands of birds' feathers." Some of the early pictures show them arranged vertically in a head band, but we do not know how they were fixed *(Fig. 4)*. The Indians were bare except for "skins of small animals and narrow belts of grass." It was a joyous time for the local Munsee-speaking Natives. It was not to be happy for long, however, as traders and fishermen would soon arrive, then settlers and armed troops, and their land would be changed forever.

The Vanguard of the European Migration

European settlers did not come to America until long after commercial contacts had made a strong beachhead. Literally thousands of fishing and trading boats followed John Cabot's northerly route across the Atlantic, throughout the 16th century, to catch the cod and to trade for furs *(33)*. They came from the fishing ports of France, England, Holland, Spain, and Portugal. Some of them came ashore in Newfoundland, Nova Scotia, and Maine to prepare and dry their cod, allowing them to take more home. There, they met Algonquian-speaking Natives and traded with them. Some ships wandered down the eastern seaboard of America, probably as far as Connecticut. At least, word of their presence in the New World would have passed down the coast.

Although some 16th century Europeans traded as far down the coast as New York, it was not until the early 17th century that Wiechquaeskeck lands would be carefully explored. They were then charted more accurately than Verrazano had pictured them in order to allow later ships to sail the coast with confidence *(Appx. B)*.

Swedish traders and settlers generally took the most northerly route across the Atlantic *(Fig. 3)*, to the southern tip of Greenland. From there, they sailed south down the American coast. Most of the early Swedes started settlements on the Delaware River, near the present sites of Wilmington and Camden. Some of them moved into Wiechquaeskeck territory on the Hudson River.

Admiral Samuel Eliot Morison wrote an excellent analysis of the early history of exploration in *"The European Discovery of America, The Northern Voyages A.D. 500-1600" (33)*.

This period marked the beginning of modern European influence on northeastern America. The Wiechquaeskeck soon had frequent contact with the Europeans. As the 17th century started, coastal mapping had begun. Figure 4, **A European Ship in Long Island Sound**, is a 19th century artist's view of what a European coastal mapping expedition may have been like. This view could well have been drawn where the local Natives stood at the end of Shippan Point, in Stamford, and watched the Europeans arrive. The ship stood offshore because of the fearsome "archipelago" of small islands and sunken rocks close to land. A large rowboat would have brought the surveyors to the land.

Soon a few Dutch settlers arrived, and farmed in the New Amsterdam area, often among the Wiechquaeskeck. Serious immigration began to Connecticut soon after the Pilgrims survived at Plymouth in 1621. In 1643, the Great Migration started from England on the northern route. The floodgates opened later in the 17th century, and thousands of other Europeans swarmed expectantly across the Atlantic. They completely displaced the few remaining Wiechquaeskeck.

When Henry Hudson sailed up the Hudson River for the Dutch in 1609, the Wiechquaeskeck had fearlessly surrounded his ship, even after some were shot. They had seen European ships before and knew that ordinary men were on them, even if they did have guns. About that time, however, imported, invisible epidemics started to strike the Wiechquaeskeck. Their mortality rate was high, and the European invaders soon occupied their deserted lands.

C. EUROPEAN MIGRATION TO WIECHQUAESKECK TERRITORY

The Dutch Migration

Soon after Hudson's voyage, the Dutch moved into the New York area to trade for furs, particularly beaver, and to harvest timber, often for ship's masts. A few colonists moved in. About 1640, they

Figure 4

A European Ship in Long Island Sound

"Indians standing on shore looking at small boat approaching from ship." Woodcut above the Introduction to Sears, *History of U.S., illustrated.* Reproduced from the Collections of the Library of Congress. USZ6-844. 917872.

This could have been drawn almost anywhere on the western Connecticut shoreline, but it looks very much like Shippan Point, Stamford, with the Wiechquaeskeck watching one of the early mapping expeditions, such as Cornelius Hendricksen, 1614.

started to establish plantations in order to supply the colony and to grow foods for export. (A "plantation" meant a plantation of farmer-settlers, not the planting of specific crops). New Amsterdam was the best harbor on the eastern seaboard. It had deep water, was close to the ocean, had few hazards, and had good places to land. There was a large protected mooring area. There was plentiful fresh water, forests of timber for repairing the ships and for taking back to Europe, and good farm lands. The Native Americans, including the Wiechquaeskeck, proved reasonably friendly in the beginning. Figure 5, **Earliest View of New Amsterdam,** shows New York Harbor after the fort was built, some settlers had arrived, and many trading ships came among the Natives. Long Island is in the background. Staten Island is to the right.

Traders came to New Amsterdam from all over the Old World, including Africa and Asia. The Wiechquaeskeck met many of them. Only half of the Dutch troops used for port protection came from Holland. The others were from England, France and Spain. Nicolaes van Wassenaer wrote numerous letters, assembled as "Historich Verhael," starting in 1609 *(Wassenaer: 67)*. In 1624, he said:

> . . . the River Montagne, now called Mauritius, *[later called Hudson River]* is navigable full fifty leagues up, through divers nations, who sometimes manifest themselves with arrows, like enemies, sometimes like friends; but when they have seen the ships once or twice, or traded with our people, they become altogether friendly.

Van Wassenaer describes the powerful Maikan *(Mahican)* in the area that is now Albany. South of them were the Wiegagjock *(Wiechquaeskeck)* and a dozen other tribes.

Figure 6, **Earliest Map Showing the Wiechquaeskeck** was drawn about 1614/16. This Cornelis Hendricx map shows the "Wikagyl" *(Wiechquaeskeck)*, "Manhattes" and Tappans correctly placed. That spelling of the name of the Wiechquaeskeck is commemorated today in the Wikagyl Country Club of New Rochelle, New York.

Van Wassenaer describes the voyage of the first Dutch settlers:

> A ship was fitted out under a commission from the West India Company, and freighted with families, to plant a colony among these people *[a "plantation"]*. But to go forward safely, it is first of all necessary that they be placed in a good defensive position and well provided with forts and arms, since the Spaniard, who claims all the country, will never allow anyone to gain a possession there.

t' Fort nieuw Amsterdam op de Manhatans

Figure 5
Earliest View of New Amsterdam

This picture appeared in the earliest edition of *Beschrijvinghe Van Virginia, Nieuw Nederlandt, Nieuw Engelandt,* . . .,published in a little book by Joost Hartgers, Amsterdam, 1651. In that book it was engraved in reverse, and has been corrected. The original drawing was made much earlier. Reproduced from the Collections of the Library of Congress. USZ62-17525. 915413/CO.

Figure 6
Earliest Map Showing the Wiechquaeskeck

This Cornelis Hendricx (Cornelius Hendricksen) map of 1614/16 shows the "Wikagyl" (Wiechquaeskeck) correctly placed in Westchester. The name of the Wiechquaeskeck is commemorated today in the name of the Wikagyl Country Club of New Rochelle, New York. The "Manhattes and the "Tappans" are also shown.

Reproduced from the Collections of the Library of Congress, Geography and Maps Division, of a map of the Hudson River area submitted by Cornelis Hendricx to the States General of the Netherlands, 1614/16. LC 915610.

This explains why Fort Amsterdam was built on the lower tip of Manhattan Island. It was to defend against Spanish, English, or other European attacks from the sea. The English did attack and take Fort Amsterdam later, in 1665, with a strong fleet. Fort Amsterdam was not built to defend against the Indians, but to defend the fur trade against Old World enemies. The Dutch were outnumbered and could not really control the Indians, in the fore of whom were the Wiechquaeskeck. They tried for some local control of the Natives by building a wooden wall on what is now Wall Street, hence the name.

In 1628, van Wassenaer *(Wassenaer: 88)* wrote:

> Governor Minuict . . .went thither from Holland on January 9, Anno 1626, and took up his residence in the midst of a nation called Manhates, building a fort there, to be called Amsterdam, having four bastions and faced outside entirely with stone . . . The population consists of two hundred and seventy souls, including men, women and children. They remained as yet without the fort, in no fear, as the natives live peaceably with them...
>
> These strangers for the most part occupy their farms. Whatever they require is supplied by the Directors. The winter grain has turned out well there, but the summer grain which ripened before it was half grown in consequence of the excessive heat, was very light. The cattle sent thither have thriven well, and everything promises increase, as soon as the land is improved, which is full of weeds and poor.

Note that they had brought their own European grains with them - wheat, barley, and oats, and these needed time to find strains adapted to the new conditions. They grew poorly at first. The English in New England did much better by adopting the Indian maize (corn) immediately, and learning to like succotash and cornbread. The maize had already become adapted to the climate by hundreds of years of Native horticulture *(Chap. 6D)*.

Thus, in the early 1600s, the Dutch took the long southerly route across the Atlantic *(Fig. 3)*, built Fort Amsterdam, and had a most profitable trade in furs in the Hudson, Connecticut, and Delaware River Valleys. At that time they still existed relatively peaceably with the Wiechquaeskeck, who still had furs to trade. But people wanted to move to the new land, and the Dutch rulers soon found that it was highly profitable to encourage such plantations, as they produced farm goods, timber, and minerals for export *(27)*. The Dutch West India Company managed New Amsterdam and the fur trade, but they gave out great parcels of land to the "patroons" (proprietors of manorial estates) to manage as plantations. These large estates created serious problems with the Wiechquaeskeck in the 1640s.

Most of the patroons were Dutch, such as David de Vries, who had been a captain sailing around the world with the Dutch East India Company. In 1640, he started a large plantation roughly where the Bronx Zoo is today *(deVries: 205)*, among the Wiechquaeskeck. He wrote:

> I began to make a plantation, a league and a half or two leagues above the fort *[Fort Amsterdam on Manhattan Island]*, as there was there a fine location, and full thirty-one morgens *[a morgen was about 2.1 acres]* of maize-land, where there were no trees to remove; and hay-land lying all together, sufficient for two hundred cattle, which is a great commodity there. I went there to live, half on account of the pleasure of it, as it was all situated along the river.

This was just like the land that the English settlers found as they came into western Connecticut at the same time. There was open farming land, and in Wiechquaeskeck territory. That year, deVries went in his sloop up the Hudson River and wrote:

> Opposite Tapaen lies a place called Wickquaesgeck *[today's Dobbs Ferry]*, where there is maize-land, but all stony or sandy, and where many pine trees grow. We generally haul pine masts from there. The land is also mountainous. *[Note that the Westchester hills looked like mountains to the Dutch, from their flat homeland.]*

In 1641, deVries was enjoying his farming and had a good relationship with the local Indians. This was all disrupted when all the Munsee-speaking Lenape started to fight the settlers. Governor Kieft's War began to explode throughout New Netherland *(Chap. 9)*.

Figure 7, **European Sailing Ships of the 17th Century**, shows some of the common types of ships that came to Connecticut's shore. The larger ships were generally similar to the well-known reproduction of the *Mayflower*, which today is moored at Plimoth Plantation. The Dutch ships on the Atlantic Ocean in Figure 7 were drawn on Willem Blaeu's map of 1635. They came in different sizes with different rigging. There were ships, barks, frigates and pinnaces *(33: 572)*. In any fleet, there would have been one or more heavily-armed warships to protect the other ships from piracy or from the warships of other countries.

Two bark-rigged sailing ships of the 17th Century
with coastal shallop, a small sailboat, and a large rowboat.

Dutch ships on the Atlantic Ocean.
(from Willem Blaeu's map, 1635)

Figure 7
European Sailing Ships of the 17th Century

The upper ships in Figure 7 are two bark-rigged sailing ships of the 17th century. Note that calling a ship a "bark" referred to the number of its masts and the rigging of them. They came in different sizes. Many ships in those days carried *tuns*, or double-hogsheads, of wine. Tun became a measurement of carrying capacity, and was the original "marine ton." Around New Amsterdam in the 17th century, the tuns usually held rum from the Caribbean. The rum caused considerable problems among the Native Americans. A great deal of rum was imported, and some was used by land-seeking Europeans to incapacitate the Natives.

Among the group of ships in Figure 7 is a coastal shallop. This would have been the sort of ship seen most often by the Wiechquaeskeck. A shallop could be as long as 30 feet. The name *shallop* comes from the French *chaloupe en fagot*, which refers to the way it was stored in pieces on a ship to be brought across the Atlantic. A shallop had one or more masts and could have had at least one halfdeck, which was helpful for the settlers who came down the Connecticut coast from New Haven and Boston. A shallop sailed well and could easily be handled in Long Island Sound. Evidently, the Abenaki of Maine had sufficient furs to trade with which to acquire some shallops. They learned to sail them, just as the Indians of the coast were all accomplished on the water in their dugout canoes.

Large rowboats were also carried on the sailing ships. The Europeans soon discovered the numerous hidden rocks and islands on the Connecticut shoreline. They called it an *archipelago* on their maps *(see Fig. 47)*. They, therefore, kept their ships well out in the Sound, and sent rowboats ashore to survey and to talk to the Natives *(Fig. 4)*. The small sailboat shown in Figure 6 would have been a work boat, and used for fishing.

The English Migration

The first successful plantation of settlers by the English in New England was in 1620, at Plymouth, Massachusetts, although there had been earlier attempts *(33)*. Word of the success of Plymouth traveled swiftly in England, and there was a tremendous surge of emigration to America. The people coming over were not only Puritans looking for religious freedom, but were all types of people looking for a new life, and not all of them fit the Boston mold. This was The Great Migration of 1625 to 1643.

The first wave of immigrants, from 1625 to 1633, numbered about 3,000 and were mainly educated Puritans. They had been farmers or tradesmen. In the next ten years, 17,000 more came, mainly in organized family groups or "company" groups that were ready to establish a whole town together. They soon outnumbered and overwhelmed the Native Americans along the coastline, who had been the first to be decimated by the diseases brought in by earlier traders. Some of this great wave of settlers did not fit well with the theocratic towns of coastal Massachusetts, and the best land there had already been taken. Therefore, they pushed either inland in Massachusetts or north and south along the coast. Others agreed with the Boston Church, but moved on simply to find better available land.

In 1633, people from three Massachusetts towns left as a group to get better farming land, and to found settlements around the Hartford area in Connecticut. They set up an equally autocratic government in Hartford, although it was freer in terms of citizenship and landholding. Within seven years, some of them moved south into Wiechquaeskeck land (such as the Wethersfield Men's Plantation in Stamford), looking for more space as the colony grew *(Chap. 8)*.

Such movements lead to competition among the settlers coming into western Fairfield County *(Chap. 8)*. Some had allegiance to Hartford (the Connecticut Colony), some came from Quinnipiac (the New Haven Colony), and others came from Massachusetts (the Bay Colony). The groups moved quickly to the areas they wanted, and made offers of trade goods to the Wiechquaeskeck for land. The Colony of Connecticut came together as an entity in 1665. By that time, most of the western Fairfield land had been taken over by settlers. The remnant Wiechquaeskeck had mostly drifted north.

The political shifts in Connecticut had an effect on Governor Kieft's war against the Wiechquaeskeck. The English towns were busy, and none would help the Dutch, even when asked. The Greenwich settlers, who felt threatened by rampaging youngWiechquaeskeck, could not get military aid either from any English colony, so they threw in their lot with the Dutch and gave Kieft's troops free access to Greenwich and Stamford. This base was then used to attack the Wiechquaeskeck stronghold of Nanichiestawack in New York *(Chap. 9)*. Capt. John Underhill, the English commander of the Dutch troops in that attack, had been living in Stamford, because he had been asked earlier to help in its defense.

English settlers still kept moving into southwestern Connecticut.

The French Migration

French migration to the New World had been principally to Canada in the earlier years. Those settlers were nearly all Catholic, and some were active missionaries to the Algonquians in the north. A different group of French settlers came from La Rochelle, in France, to settle in New Rochelle, Westchester County. They arrived in 1688 as the Wiechquaes-keck were diminishing. They were the Hugenots, the Protestants of the western coast of France, and they took over vacated Wiechquaeskeck lands. Some of them later moved up to Greenwich and Stamford.

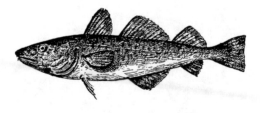

Codfish

Coastal Shallop of the 17th Century

CHAPTER 3

THE WIECHQUAESKECK AND THEIR NEIGHBORS

The Wiechquaeskeck were a strong tribe in a bountiful land. They had palisaded villages *(vanderDonck: 80, vanWassenaer: 80)*, outpost forts, good hunting forests, fertile farming land, and abundant coastal fisheries. They were surrounded by many friendly tribes, although they were occasionally invaded by the Pequots from the east. Snow estimated that there were about 9,000 Wiechquaeskeck in the early 16th century *(46: 33)*. They were Algonquian Woodland Indians who spoke the Munsee dialect *(19)*. This made them related to all the Munsee-speaking Native Americans from the mid-Hudson valley to central New Jersey and from Long Island to the Delaware River. They can all be called Lenape, or Delaware, Indians. The Munsee-speaking bands around the New York City area in the early 17th century are shown in Figure 8. They communicated with each other, traded widely, and intermarried.

When the Europeans arrived, the Wiechquaeskeck occupied most of the area that is now The Bronx and Westchester County, New York, and western Fairfield County, Connecticut. In the early 1600's, they were friendly to the European invaders. By 1640, there had been frequent arguments. Some were killed, and they had killed some settlers *(34)*. Finally, the Dutch were enraged and crushed them *(Chap. 9)*. In the early 17th century, they were devastated by epidemics brought over from Europe. When the 17th century ended, they had been destroyed. The hundred or so remaining Wiechquaeskeck scattered to the winds *(Chap. 10)*.

More than two million people now live in the land that the Wiechquaeskeck occupied in 1600 AD. Most of their area is now paved over and built upon, although some parks remain in a state that they might recognize. Some of their sites have been unearthed by archaeological digs *(Chap. 11-A)*. Most of their sites have been obliterated by construction.

U.S. Route 1, New York State Routes 9 and 22, and Broadway Avenue on Manhattan Island, were formerly major Wiechquaeskeck footpaths *(Fig. 11)*. Today, there are few named geographic points that recall the Wiechquaeskeck. One of them is Wicker's Creek in Dobbs Ferry, New York, where the tribal village of "Wickquaskeck" once stood on the Hudson. One of the largest Wiechquaeskeck villages was near New Rochelle, and the "Wikagyl" Country Club commemorates them. There are many street and place names in the area which keep alive the names of individual Wiechquaeskeck and some of their bands.

The Wiechquaeskeck on Early Maps *(Appx. B)*

1613/1614. The Adriaen Block map printed the first mention of New Netherland. It placed the Mahican astride the Hudson River, but did not note other local tribes. When Block sailed up Long Island Sound, through Hells Gate and the East River, he saw a thousand Indian fires along both shores, smoking fish and shellfish for their winter use.

1616. The Schipper Cornelius Hendricx map showed the Mahattes (Manhattans) and the Wikagyl (Wiechquaeskeck) north of them. The Mahican were shown further up the Hudson *(Fig. 6)*.

1635. The Willem Janszoon Blaeu map, *Nova Belgica et Anglia Nova,* *(Fig. 44)* showed the Manatthans occupying all of the Wiechquaeskeck area. Since the two tribes were very close, that is understandable. This map became a basic source for many other maps in the 17th century, but the Wiechquaeskeck name, which was omitted, seldom appeared on other maps of the time.

1655. Nicolaum Visscher's map, *Novi Belgii - Novaeque Angliae Nec Non Partis Virginiae Tabula* was an excellent development of William Blaeu's map of 1635. It showed numerous villages and forts (palisadoes) on the Hudson River and Long Island Sound. These forts fit into the story of the New Netherland War that involved the Wiechquaeskeck *(Chap. 9)*, and with the stories about Pequot raids.

1656. The Adriaen van der Donck map of New Netherland depicted the 1616 period *(Fig. 45)*. It showed the Manhattan, Siwanoy, and Pachami, and the Wiechquaeskeck villages of Sinsing, Alipkonck (Tarrytown), Wickquaskeck (Dobbs Ferry), Saeckkill (Yonkers), Nanichchiestawack

(Cross River), and Betuckquapock (Mianus) in Wiechquaeskeck territory.

1663. The Gulielmus Hack map showed the area as "The Monhegans Country," with the villages of Wickquaskeck and Seekill on the Hudson River, and Marenuck (Mamaroneck), the name of a sachem, on Long Island Sound.

1671. The Arnoldus Montanus map, *Novi Belgii*, showed the Manhattan and Pachami in Westchester and the Siwanoy in Connecticut, identical to the Blaeu map.

1675. The Jer. Sellers & Chas. Price map, *A Chart of ye Coast of New England, etc.*, showed the "Wisquaskeck" on the "Hudsons River" with the Haverstraw tribe shown close beside them, instead of the Sint Sing, as on other maps *(Fig. 46).*

1676. The John Speed map, *The Theatre of the Empire of Great Britain*, copied the earlier village names of Sinsing, Alipnock, Wickquaskek, and Saech Kill on the Hudson River, and Nanichiestawack inland *(Fig. 47).* It shows the Native palisado, Betuckquapock, but calls the area "Siwanoys," and has the Manhattan occupying the Wiechquaeskeck lands.

1685. The Nicolaum Visscher map, *Novi Belgii Noavaeque Angliae, etc.*, was obviously drawn by historians in The Netherlands *(Fig. 48).* The map was obviously drawn to celebrate the Restitution of New Netherland to the Dutch. It gives several Dutch names for the Groote Rivier (Hudson River), and lists all the Native villages along the Hudson River, including "Wickquaskeck." The sites were mostly the fur-trading villages. It also showed Naniechiestawack and Betuckquapock, but located the Manhattans and Siwanoys in Wiechquaeskeck territory.

There was nothing on the early maps that showed the location of the Wiechquaeskeck tribal boundaries. The maps, however, clearly showed the location of what are probably many of their villages and palisadoes. It is hard to be sure on some of the maps whether the mapmaker is depicting an Indian palisado or a European building. Most of the maps were drawn either in The Hague, Holland, or London, England.

The Wiechquaeskeck in Early Documents

In 1624, Nicholaes van Wassenaer *(vanWassenaer: 67)* described the people on "the River Montagne, now called Mauritius" (later called the

Hudson River) as follows:

> Below the Maikans *[Mahican]* . . . on the east side; Wiegagjock *[Wiechquaeskeck]*. . . Two nations lie there lower down at Klinckersberg *[location?]*. At the Fisher's hook *[Montauk Point]* are Pachany *[Pachami]*, Warenecker, Warrawannankonckx. . . The Manhates *[Manhattan]* are situate at the mouth.

In the letter of Isaack de Rasieres *(deRasieres: 103)* in 1628, he described Long Island: "where many savages dwell, who support themselves by planting maize and making sewan, and who are called Souwenos *[Siwanoy]* and Sinnecox."

Jameson, the translator, added in a footnote, "The Siwanoys lived near Pelham; The Shinnecocks at the east end of Long Island." Evidently the "Souwenos" were simply those who make sewan (wampum), and there were Souwenos (Siwanoy) on both sides of Long Island Sound. He also notes: "The tribes are held in subjection by and are tributary to the Pyquans *[Pequots]*." This helps to explain why the Wiechquaeskeck coast of Connecticut was so heavily fortified with palisadoes. The Pequots were never far away.

In the journal of David Pietersz de Vries *(deVries: 206)* on May 25, 1640, his entry said:

> Opposite Tapaen lies a place called Wickquaesgeck *[site of Dobbs Ferry]*, where there is maize-land, but all stony or sandy, and where many pine trees grow. We generally haul pine masts from there. The land is also mountainous." *[The writer is from flat Holland!]*

J. Franklin Jameson's translation of the Journal of New Netherland *(Jameson: 213)* talked about the Native problems in the area and said that, in1638, "he of Witqueschreek living northeast of the island Manhatans, perpetrated another murderous deed" *(Chap. 8)*. Later (1642), the massacre of the "Witquescheck" at Pavonia is described, and in 1644, the village in Cross River, New York is called "Witquescheck." The Dutch clearly knew that the Wiechquaeskeck were all over the area from Manhattan to Connecticut.

In 1642, David de Vries *(deVries: 213)* wrote: "About the same time a harmless Dutchman, named Claes Rademaker, was murdered by a savage. . . It was on the Wickquasgeck Road over which the Indians passed daily" *(Chap. 9)*. The Wickquasgeck Path ran the length of Manhattan Island *(5, 20)*. It was used by the Natives to trade, first with the Manhattan, then with the Dutch at Fort Amsterdam. In later colonial times, it was called the Albany Post Road. It followed the route of Broadway from the Battery, on the southern tip of Manhattan Island, to its junction with St. Nicholas Avenue in Harlem. It then rejoined Broadway in northern Manhattan. From there, it was the same route as U.S. Route 9 up to Albany, New York.

This murder was the turning point in the Dutch relations with the Wiechquaeskeck. De Vries continued:

> The Commander sent to them and made inquiry in Wickquasgeck why this Dutchman had been so shamefully murdered. The murderer answered that, while the fort was being built, he came with his uncle . . . bringing beavers, in order to trade with the Dutchmen . . . some . . . took away from his uncle his beavers, and then killed him. He was then a small boy, and resolved that, when he should grow up, he would revenge that deed upon the Dutch.

This act of revenge kindled the final Dutch attack against the Wiechquaeskeck, which ended in their annihilation *(Chap. 9)*.

The Journal of New Netherland *(Jameson: 281)* told of Governor Kieft's forces in their first foray against the Greenwich area in March, 1643 *(Chap. 9)*. They went first to Stantfort (Stamford). They landed at Tomac Cove, and marched to Cos Cob, where:

> The old Indian captured above having promised to lead us to Wetquescheck, which consisted of three castles. . . found them empty . . . our people burned two. .

These were probably palisadoes near the mouth of the Mianus River that are shown on the Visscher map and other maps. They were eighteen miles from "Wetquescheck," which was Nanichiestawack, near Cross River, New York. The Dutch killed the few Natives in the cluster of wigwams at Petaquapen (Cos Cob) *(Chap. 9)*.

Relationships Between Native American Tribes

The Native American tribes had few defined boundaries for their territories, and inter-tribal relationships were frequently in flux. Those who spoke similar dialects, and had similar histories, generally worked together. Affairs were often decided by leaders meeting around council fires.

There were, of course, natural boundaries such as rivers, lakes, and mountain ridges, but there were no "lines drawn in the sand" to indicate property or ownership. They had no maps and no written agreements, until the Europeans arrived. They simply occupied farming and hunting areas. It is not accurate to draw maps of ancient tribal areas with solid line boundaries. Dotted line boundaries, if any, are more descriptive of the reality.

Native Americans, particularly young men, but sometimes family groups, visited and traded with other tribes at great distances. Hyde *(24: 94)* tells stories of Delaware Algonquians visiting both Hurons in Ontario and other Algonquians in Ohio. He notes that, at one time, Delawares traveled regularly past Lake Champlain, and traded with the Algonquians in Quebec. They were cut off from that route when the Mohawk expanded their area across Lake Champlain. There is no record of how far young Wiechquaeskeck men travelled in those days, looking for trade, wives, and adventure. We know from the archaeological record *(Chap. 11)* that the Wiechquaeskeck enjoyed the same technological advances in weaponry, farming, and household items that were used in a radius of a thousand miles.

The easiest tribes for young Wiechquaeskeck to trade and work with, and to look for wives, were naturally those who spoke a similar language. Even if the dialect was different, they could communicate. The Wiechquaeskeck were Algonquian speakers of the Munsee dialect. They were related to the great group of Native Americans that stretched across much of Canada, down the eastern seabord to the Carolinas, and in the Ohio and upper Mississippi valleys. They all visited and traded with each other *(24)*. We know little of their tribal areas before 1600, although their oral history would indicate that they had been substantially in the same areas for hundreds of years before the Europeans arrived. On the other hand, we know that groups like the Cree, Iroquois and Pequots forcibly changed many tribal boundaries, both before and after Europeans arrived.

A millennium before the 17th century, the amazing Adena Culture, on the Ohio and Mississippi Rivers, had an effect on the northeastern Algonquian up to about 200 AD, both in religious concepts and material cultures. It created a peaceful trading hub that radiated far beyond their area. The Adena Culture probably had much to do with the rapid diffusion, or technology transfer, of the agricultural products and methods of the Southwest across the mid-continent. It also encouraged the spread of the use of copper from the great native copper pits on the

Keewatin Peninsula on Lake Superior. The early explorers found that the Wiechquaeskeck and their neighbors had some copper objects. Kraft believes that Adena-related Indians visited the Munsee area in the sixth to fourth centuries BC, bringing copper artifacts made with a high degree of technical skill *(27: 150)*. He notes that some copper was mined in New Jersey, also, but metallurgical analysis has shown that many of the objects were made from the Lake Superior copper.

Archeological studies have shown that there was much long-distance trading. In 1964, Powell *(ARCH9)* found two artifacts near Norwalk that could indicate trading over hundreds of miles. One was a bright green plasma (quartz) artifact that probably came from Alabama or Georgia. The other was a design on a hematite paintstone that could have been a motif of a southern cult. In 1988, Fiedel *(ARCH17)* found some Orient Fishtail points in Rye, New York. These broad spears matched nothing else in the area. He noted that they resembled the Adena type, suggesting "some kind of participation by northeastern populations in the Adena interaction sphere."

Thus, the Wiechquaeskeck of the 17th century were truly "American" in the modern sense. They used some products, agricultural methods, and manufacturing techniques that had diffused from other parts of America. If a useful new projectile point (arrowhead or spearhead) was developed anywhere on the eastern half of the continent, it would probably have reached the Wiechquaeskeck. Pottery making and design methods were clearly learned from others. This diffusion of technology is of great help to archaeologists in dating the materials they find in local digs. If they have a date elsewhere for a certain technology, then they can sometimes assign a date to their findings in Wiechquaeskeck archaeological digs *(Chap.11)*.

Most of the Wiechquaeskeck did not have to travel far for their trading and experiences, however. Speaking Algonquian, they easily conducted business with many neighboring tribes. Much of their trade, and their search for wives, would have been within about a 50 mile radius of their territory, with occasional forays of another 50 miles. This included all the Munsee-speaking bands of the Lenape (Delaware) Indians. Figure 8, **Some Munsee Bands in the early 17th Century**, shows the Munsee-speakers that were close to the Wiechquaeskeck. There were many other Munsee-speakers in northern New Jersey.

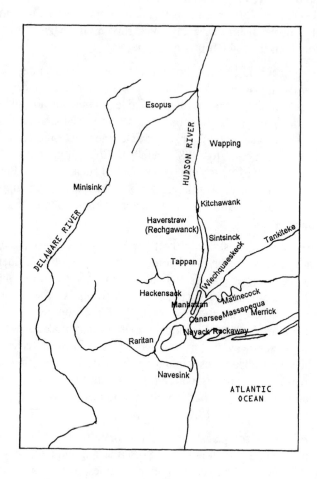

Figure 8
Some Munsee Bands in the Early 17th Century

Adapted from Paul Andrew Otto, **New Netherland Frontier . . .
1524-1624** *(25),* and Oliver A. Rink, **Holland on the Hudson**,
Cornell University Press, 1986.

Goddard *(19: 236)* noted that Munsee has been spelled Monsey, Munsey, Munsy, and Minsi. It means "person from Minisink," which is in northern New Jersey. "As a linguistic term Munsee includes all groups of any period that spoke dialects of the language spoken by the Munsee group" even though not all were Munsees in a political sense. He believed that the eastern boundary was the Five Mile River in Darien *(19: 214)*, which means that it did not include the Tankiteke. He put the Canarsie, Wiechquaeskeck, Esopus, Tappan, Hackensack, Minisink, and other smaller groups, in the Munsee area. Paul Otto *(Fig. 8)* added more tribal names. The Nayack and Rockaway might have been grouped under the Canarsie, as also others. The Wiechquaeskeck could easily speak to many heighboring groups.

The only clear tribal boundaries of the Wiechquaeskeck were the Hudson River and Long Island Sound. There were undefined transitions between the Wiechquaeskeck territory and that of the Manhattan to the southwest, the Sint Sing, Pachami, and Wapping to the north, and the Tankiteke and other Paugussett Indians to the east. When the Europeans arrived with their legal descriptions, compasses, and measuring devices, tribal lines were drawn on maps for the first time.

The European invaders had little idea about the complexity of the inter-tribal relationships, because no agreements between Native tribes were written down. To make matters more confusing, the oral agreements sometimes changed, depending upon who was sitting around the council fire. Salwen *(41: 166-168)* said that Indian political groups can be thought of as relatively flexible multivillage alliances. The village was the basic sociopolitical unit, but individuals could easily change village affiliation. The Dutch only learned about Native federations when they attacked one tribe and others rose up to retaliate.

The Manhattan

The Wiechquaeskeck had a close relationship with the Manhattan, on Manhattan Island, and the Canarsie, in what is now Brooklyn, on Long Island. As noted earlier, there was even a Wiechquaeskeck Path down the middle of Manhattan Island "over which the Indians passed daily" *(deVries: 213 and Chap. 5)*. When Verrazano's ship sailed into New York Harbor, there were certainly some Wiechquaeskeck among the celebrating Native people in the canoes, because the Wiechquaeskeck mingled with both the Canarsie and the Manhattan. We can be certain that Verrazano's description of the welcoming Natives in their feathered finery can be applied to the Wiechquaeskeck.

At the beginning of the 17th century, it is likely that the important Wiechquaeskeck manufacture of sewan (wampum) caused an increase in the traffic down U.S. Route 1 and the Weichquaeskeck Path on Manhattan Island. The Dutch and English were both accepting wampum as trading "money," as there was insufficient other currency *(Chap. 4)*. There were a great many traders converging on New Amsterdam and Manhattan Island from all over the world. There were few coins in circulation, and wampum was needed as legal tender. It was soon commercialized by the Europeans. It must have been fascinating to the young Wiechquaeskeck to go down to the New Netherland docks and see the big sailing ships and the different people from all over the world.

Later in the 17th century, the Manhattan tribe faded away. Grumet *(20: 25)* discusses the problem of determining the extent of the Manhattan tribal area and their relationships with the Rechgawanck, who were said to have then been in the Bronx. The difficulty is that, in the 17th century, the remnants of whole tribes were being displaced from their earlier lands, and moving to the shelter of friendly tribes. Grumet notes that the Rechgawanck have been associated with the Hackensack and Tappan groups and may have been the Haverstraw. The Rechgawanck in The Bronx may have been pushed earlier out of the higher Hudson Valley by Mohawk and Mahican movements, then absorbed into the Manhattan. Time has erased the details.

The Manhattan were also close to the Canarsie, who may have occupied part of Manhattan Island as well as Brooklyn. It appears that the Manhattan, whose name is now legendary, were simply squeezed off their island by the European settlers, and their dramatic losses to disease. They just disappeared from the area. The few remaining people probably dispersed to other tribes, including the Wiechquaeskeck, since the two tribes had been very close.

The Wapping

It was formerly thought that the local Native Americans (Wiechquaeskeck) belonged to a "Wappinger Confederation" in the lower Hudson River Valley because of 19th century writings, such as by

Ruttenber *(41)*. It is doubtful that such a confederation ever existed as a political entity, however. Anthropologists and linguists have long questioned it. In the Smithsonian's **Handbook of North American Indians, Vol, 15, Northeast** *(19)*, Ives Goddard said that "there is no evidence that a 'Wappinger Confederacy' extended from the Hudson to the Connecticut." T. J. Brasser *(7: 203)* suggested "that the Mahican forced all Indian groups along the east side of the Hudson to acknowledge Mahican rule" in the early 17th century. By 1675, the Wappinger and Housatonic were divisions of the Mahican confederacy. Bert Salwen *(42: 173)* saw no positive evidence that there was a great Delaware-speaking Wappinger-Mattabesec Confederacy. (The Mattabesec were west of the Connecticut River, and included the Norwalke, who were Paugussett.) There was a Wapping tribe of Algonquian speakers who occupied the highlands of the eastern side of the Hudson River Valley. Brasser *(7: 204)* said they were called the "Highland Indians" and were under the Mahican. They are memorialized today in the name of Wappingers Falls, a town in Dutchess County, New York. They have disappeared as a people.

The earlier belief that there was a "Wappinger Confederation" probably came from Jameson's translation of the Narratives *(Jameson: 284)* in the 19th century. The bodies of "twenty-five Wappingers"were found among the Wiechquaeskeck when Nanichiestawack was devastated. Wapping men would naturally have been among the Wiechquaeskeck, however, because there was a trail between the tribes that went both ways. It was similar to the Wiechquaeskeck visiting among the Manhattan, with a trail between them that was "used daily."

The word "Wappinger" probably came from the British and northern European use of the possessive suffix "er." Someone simply added an "er" to Wapping to show that they possessed the "Confederation," and the name was picked for the tribe. (This would mean that the Hudson Valley town of Wappingers Falls, where the Wapping Tribe once lived, has a double possessive ending.)

The name "Wapping" appears in records in several museums and libraries in Westchester and Fairfield Counties. A good example is in the records vault of the Town of Greenwich, Connecticut, where there are 18th century copies of many original 17th century documents. One of these is a land transfer deed, dated 1686 *(Sect. 8)* which includes the statement: "Given unto my hand to be ye Truth by me ye above sd

Wesskum, who am a sagamore of Wapping" (with his mark).

Wesskum also stated that he was "four score years old" in 1686, so he had lived through the contact with the Europeans and had seen the devastation of his people by disease and war. He was representing a tiny remnant of a once-strong tribe. Wesskum actually belonged to the Wiechquaeskeck tribe in the Greenwich area in 1686. A likely explanation could be based on Driver's finding *(12: 226)* that many Native Americans did not marry close relatives up to second cousins. De Rasieres wrote *(deRasieres: 108)* in the 17th century, among the Mahican, "they must not have intercourse with those of their own family within the third degree," or second cousins. The Lenape were expected to marry outside their own phratry, or clan. This meant that the young men went away from their village to search for mates, because they generally lived in family groupings. They sometimes brought their wives back to their own villages. At other times, because the wigwam "ownership" was usually matrilocal, it was a good idea to stay in the wife's family village. Such a man was Wesskum, who stayed in fertile Greenwich with abundant seafood, but always remembered his highland home with the Wapping tribe.

The Wiechquaeskeck young men had many different opportunities to look for mates. They could easily go in any compass direction to find tribes that spoke Munsee. It was not so for the Wapping, however. North of them stood the Mahican, who felt superior to them. East of them were thinly-populated miles of mountains, and the Paugussett, who spoke the Quiripi dialect. West of the Hudson River camped tribes that were perilously close to the Mohawk. But, south to the Wiechquaeskeck territory, and its neighboring Munsee friends, was an easy trip, and they were welcomed. Thus, many Wapping men moved south, but they still loved their highlands and remembered that they were Wapping. This is why the name "Wapping" appears a number of times in Westchester and Fairfield County archival records.

The tribal name, Wapping, is not completely understood. Some authorities say that it means "opossum", because of the linguistic similarity *(19: 238)*. The trouble with that idea is that there were no opossums north of the Hudson River in the 17th century. Opossums had been driven south many years before by the Laurentide Ice Shield. Authorities at The American Museum of Natural History believe that opossums did not cross the Hudson River, coming back north, until the early 19th century. A more likely meaning of Wapping would therefore be a variant of "eastern light" or sunrise. This meaning is preferred by some modern Wampanoag.

The Mahican (Mohican)

The Mahican (Mohican) were a powerful tribe that held the upper Hudson River Valley around Albany *(13)*. In early documents, they have been called Mahican, Mohican, Mahikander, Muhheakunn, and many other variations. The tribe's name was derived from *Muhheakunnuck*, describing the tidal water of the Hudson River *(19: 211)*.

The Mahican should not be confused with the Mohegan of eastern Connecticut. They have different histories and spoke different dialects. Part of the confusion is because both names resemble the Algonquian word for "wolf." The early French referred to the Mahican as *Loups*, or wolves *(19: 24)*. According to the oral tradition of the Mohegan, however, when the Mohawk drove the Mahican from the upper Hudson River valley, a small band travelled southeast and joined with the Mohegan in Connecticut, after many years.

In an earlier century, the Mahican held the whole Hudson valley to north of Lake Champlain, and they traded with their fellow Algonquian speakers in Quebec and Ontario. Much has been written about them *(7, 13, 19, 42)*. The Mahican were the undisputed rulers of the lower Hudson River valley in the late 16th century, and they exacted tribute and support from all neighboring tribes, including the Wiechquaeskeck. In no sense was this a "confederacy" of tribes. The Mahican were the masters. They often visited their subordinate tribes and sat in on their councils *(Jameson)*.

Thus, when the Dutch made treaties with the Indians around New Netherland, Mahican leaders would sometimes take part. For example, when peace was made in 1645 after the New Netherland War, the Mahican sachem Aepjen (also called Skiwias, Eskuyias, and other variations) signed the agreement for the "Wappinger, the Weichquaes-kecks, the Sinsink, and the Kitchawank" tribes along the east side of the Hudson River *(Brodhead, 13: 169) (Chap. 9)*.

The Wiechquaeskeck acknowledged Mahican rule in 1649, when they were willing to sell part of Manhattan Island, and made "promise to induce their Rulers on the North River to take the matter over."

This was not an unacceptable arrangement to the Wiechquaeskeck and to other Munsee-speaking tribes along the Hudson. It protected them from frequent ravages by the Mohawk. The Mahican stood at the top of the rich Hudson Valley like a stone curtain. The lower Hudson was thus held by the Mahican, working with the Lenape who supported them. The Mohawk, and their other Iroquois allies, walked at will down the Tuscarora Trail to the Carolinas, taking booty from some Pennsylvania Delaware tribes along the way. They walked east on the Mohawk Trail, killing and looting the Massachusetts tribes. They struck down the Connecticut River Valley almost to Pequot territory. But, they did not come down the Hudson River valley until the Dutch upset the balance by giving more guns to the Mohawk for beaver pelts than they had given to the Mahican.

Because they were not written down, there were few understood arrangements between the many Native tribes. For example, the Mahican ruled the Hudson River Valley, but they apparently had a mutual agreement with the Paugussett bands in the Housatonic River Valley, who were under pressure from the Pequot in the east. The Housatonic River tribes are grouped with the Mattabesec Confederation, which included most of the tribes on the west side of the Connecticut River.

The Tankiteke

The Tankiteke band of the Norwalk River Valley had a very close relationship to the Wiechquaeskeck. They certainly were friendly neighbors. Their "boundary," the Five Mile River in Darien, was easily crossed. The Visscher map shows that the palisadoes, erected for protection against the Pequot, were built on every river mouth along the coast. It is possible that the Tankiteke were also Lenape, but it is more likely that they were Paugussett, and spoke the Quiripi dialect. Norwalk historians *(38:11)* could not determine whether the Tankiteke belonged to the Wappinger (Mahican) or Mattabesec (Paugussett) federations. They worked on friendly terms with both. They needed to fit in with the coastal fortifications of the Wiechquaeskeck, as well as with the river protection of the Mattabesec tribes living between the Housatonic and Connecticut Rivers. Goddard *(19: 214)* notes that the Quiripi-speaking Housatonic groups were close to the southwestern Connecticut Indians, but that the "proper designation for the Sound-Shore Indians of Fairfield remains obscure." Salwen *(42: 173)* says that the boundary between the

Munsee-speaking Delaware (such as the Wiechquaeskeck) and the Quiripi-Unquachog-speaking Mattabesec was probably somewhere between the Housatonic River and the present Connecticut-New York border. The Tankiteke were right on this boundary, close to the Norwalk River, and probably were closest to the Paugussett tribes along the Housatonic.

The "Norwalke" group of the Tankiteke occupied a desirable river valley. The navigable stretch of the Norwalk River from its mouth was longer than that of the other rivers in western Fairfield County, which gave them more arable land. It was heavily populated, and there have been many archaeological finds along it *(Chap. 11)*.

David deVries had a story about how the Tankiteke tribe tried to get friendly with the Dutch when the Dutch were fighting with the Wiechquaeskeck and the Raritan. *(deVries: 211)* He writes that in 1640:

> The 2d of November, there came a chief of the savages of Tankite-kes, named Pacham, who was great with the governor of the fort. He came in great triumph, bringing a dead hand hanging on a stick, and saying that it was the hand of the chief who had killed or shot with arrows our men on Staten Island, and that he had taken revenge for our sake, because he loved the Swannekens (as they call the Dutch), who were his best friends.

Earlier in that same year, Roger Ludlow, representing the English colonial government in Hartford, had concluded a deed of sale with the Norwalke Indians *(Chap. 8)*, and started colonization there. Evidently, the Tankiteke were satisfied with the deal and were just trying to be friendly with both the Dutch and the English. They, too, had been decimated by disease and were struggling to live relatively peaceably with the new Hartford settlers. A similar land deal had been made in Greenwich that same year with some Boston settlers. It was only ten miles away, but there was no peace there *(Chap. 9)*. The Greenwich residents had asked for protection from the Dutch, as they were being constantly harrassed by roving young Wiechquaeskeck men. The Tankiteke did not report to the sachem at Naniechiestawack. Therefore, they were not involved in the harrassing of the settlers, or in the final destruction of that village.

The Pequot

The Wiechquaeskeck's relationship with the Mahican sheltered them from the ravages of the Mohawk, but gave no protection from incursions by the equally-ravenous Pequot. The Mohawk attacked other tribes by walking along trails through the wilderness. The Pequot were blocked from walking along the Connecticut coastline by the wide Thames, Connecticut, Quinnipiac, Housatonic, and Saugatuck Rivers. They were stopped from walking east through the strong Narrangannset tribe's territory by the Providence, Sakonnet, and Fall River Bays. They therefore took to the water in fleets of dugout canoes *(Sect. 6B)* and ruled Long Island Sound.

John W. DeForest *(10:37)* reports:

> But the Indians had maritime as well as land battles, making expeditions, not through the forests only, but along the rivers and on the open sea. Roger Williams once saw a fleet of thirty or forty canoes, filled with warriors, engaged in desperate battle with another fleet of almost equal size. He has not informed us who the combatants were; but probably one party consisted of the Narragansetts, of Rhode Island, and the other of their fierce and encroaching enemies, the Pequots of Connecticut.

> The Pequots now found themselves in possession of a large extent of country . . . completely surrounded by enemies . . . Their war-parties caused terror and trembling . . . and swept with the resistless force of a tornado over the slender tribes . . . on the west.. . . Advancing along the seacoast, the Pequots conquered it as far as the bay of New Haven.

> On the south they sailed across the Sound in canoes, conquering . . . Block Island, and extorted tribute from the eastern inhabitants of Sewan Hacky, or Long Island.

Roger Williams observation, mentioned above, in **A Key Into the Language of America** *(Williams: 100)*, reads:

> I have known thirty or forty of their Canowes fill'd with Men, and neere as many more of their enemies in a Sea fight.

Daniel Gookin *(Gookin: 7)* wrote:

> "The Pequots . . . were a people feared in the most southerly bounds of New England. . . Their chief sachem held dominion over divers petty sagamores; as over part of Long Island, over the Mohegans, and over the sagamores of Quinapeake," *[New Haven is only about 35 miles east of Wiechquaeskeck country]*

Johnson *(Johnson: 114)* describes:

> "a barbarous and bloudy people called Peaquods . . . facing the English fort built on the mouth of the River (Canectico) in their large Cannowes, with their Bowes and long Shafts"

The Pequot canoes were evidently as pictured on the Blaeu Map, *Nova Belgica et Anglia Nova (Fig. 44)*, and repeated on many subsequent maps. The long bow shafts were probably rams to overturn an enemy's canoe by striking it broadside, or to hook onto the other canoe as they ran along the shaft and boarded it with battle clubs. *(Chap. 6B)* There is no direct evidence of this, but John Mason *(Mason)* talks about "the Beak Head of one of their Canoes," and Williams *(Williams: 178)* talks about them being used in a "Sea-fight."

A Pequot marine force must have looked formidable to the Wiechquaeskeck, when they came in their huge canoes up the Mianus, the Rippowam, or the Five-Mile Rivers. Since they came from a fertile area and were a numerous tribe, there would have been no way for other tribes to match their flotilla of canoes. The Wiechquaeskeck must have learned their lesson from earlier Pequot attacks and from talking to their Mattabesec neighbors before the Contact period. They put a great deal of effort into building coastal fortifications to resist becoming vassals of the Pequot *(Chap. 6F)*.

The Visscher map of 1685 *(Fig. 48)*, which was charted in 1635, clearly showed forts along the southwestern Connecticut shoreline, then called the East River. In Greenwich, the map showed five forts protecting the Mianus River and backed up by "Betuckquapock." The map is not detailed, and one of the palisado forts may have been near the Rippowam River in Stamford. The palisadoes would have been marked roughly in ships' logbooks. When they were transferred to actual maps in Amsterdam, or elsewhere, there would have been little verification of their location. The fort named Betuckquapock *(Fig. 25)*, however, is identified in its correct location on several of the early maps. These forts watched the paths leading from the coast to Naniechiestawack in Cross River, New York, the main Wiechquaeskeck village in the area. There was another group of forts near the mouth of the Norwalk River, which was probably the most densely-populated area in the region. These were Tankiteke forts, and they probably cooperated with the Wiechquaeskeck forts *(Chap. 6F)*. All the forts were evidently built before European Contact to protect the Wiechquaeskeck from unfriendly tribes, who were clearly either the Pequot or the Mohawk.

When palisadoes (defensive forts) were shown on the early maps, they must have been substantial and obvious. We have no idea how successful these forts were in deflecting strong Pequot raids. One reason they were useless against the Dutch and English guns was that there were wide entrance openings at the back, and the Europeans simply fired through them.

In 1637, in eastern Connecticut, a colonial British force destroyed the main Pequot village at "Mystick," Connecticut *(Mason: 1)*. They called it a "palizado," since it was a palisaded village. There were several skirmishes with other bands of Pequots soon after Mystick was burned. Mason writes that after the fight, "The greatest body of them went towards Manhatance" (Manhattan). The English pursued them down the coast. This would indicate that they were familiar with the territory towards Manhattan.

After the Mystick fight, the pursuing English first skirmished with the fleeing Pequot near New Haven Harbour, "then called Quinnypiag" *(Mason: 15)*. Finally, they surrounded them in a swamp near Southport, in Tankiteke territory, close to the Wiechquaeskeck. A few Pequot were killed in the fighting, and about 200 were captured. The Mystik battle and the Great Swamp fight ended the Pequot threat against the Wiechquaeskeck, as well as against the settlers.

Some Native American Leaders in the 17th Century

The names of these noteworthy Native Americans come from the Land Transfer Documents (Chap. 8) and local histories. Some were called sachems and sagamores by the English scribes.

The titles "sachem" and "sagamore" have been used in various ways in popular writings of the last three hundred years. These names were used on the land transfer documents by the settlers from Massachusetts, because they had learned them among the northern Indians. The Lenape actually used the word "sakima," not "sachem." Van Wassenaer *(vanWassenaer: 80)* said that there was "a chief in time of war, named a Sacjama." De Rasieres *(deRasieres: 103)* said that "the Manhatans called their chiefs Sackimas." The Algonquian-speaking Indians of the Northeast coast probably did not have a fixed definition for the terms. They were positions of honor, and the degree of honor varied with the individual and with his level of control as a leader. In general, however, **sachem** or **sakima** (the words can be used interchangeably) was the chief of a confederation of clans, families, or bands. A **sagamore** was a subordinate chief over one or more families or bands. In Patrick's purchase of Greenwich in 1640, some of the minor leaders were called "sachems," but this was probably another early misunderstanding on the part of the English clerks. The title "sagamore" was used most frequently for the local leaders in subsequent land transfer documents. Among the wider Wiechquaeskeck tribe, there appear to have been several sakimas at any one time. Each probably had at least one of the large palisaded villages, which the Dutch called "castles," scattered over the area of Westchester County and The Bronx.

Amogerone

AMOGERONE was one of the two "Sachems of Asamuck" in the 1640 land transfer to Capt. Daniel Patrick. Asamuck Brook flowed down from what is now called Palmer Hill on the east of Sound Beach Avenue, then into Greenwich Cove *(close to Fig. 37-19)*. It is probable that Amogerone was a sagamore. His village may well have been on the present site of Riverside Commons Shopping Center on U.S. Route 1. A village was located there, since the Ferris family found many Indian artifacts on their farm on that site *(personal communication)*. Below the village, on the brook, was Hassake (marsh) Meadow.

Amogerone is memorialized by the Amogerone Fire Company in central Greenwich and by a street name. Rare Indian bones were found in a dig in Amogerone's territory *(ARCH5)* on the corner of the old Indian footpath that is now Putnam Avenue, the former Boston Post Road, and Laddins Rock Road, which follows a headwater of Asamuck Creek.

Catoonah (Katonah)

From 1680 to 1708, CATOONAH (KATONAH, CATONA, and other variants) was the sakima over the remnants of the Wiechquaeskeck in the Bedford area and western Fairfield County, Connecticut. CATOONAH is memorialized today by a stone in the Town of Katonah, New York. He was first mentioned in 1680 as the "sachem" of a Native settlement near Bedford, New York *(40)*. This is not far from Cross River, where the village of Nanichiestawack was destroyed in 1645.

CATOONAH signed his mark on at least twelve sales of land in Westchester County and neighboring Connecticut between 1680 and 1708. In a major land transfer document in 1701 in Stamford, "CATONA, Sagamore," confirmed the old 1667 deeds of PONHASE, PENEHAY, and NOWATONEMAN, as well as the deed made to Capt. Turner in 1640 *(Chap. 8).* Catoonah was the sakima who led the last survivors of the Wiechquaeskeck out of their ancestral lands into the Ridgefield area for a few years, where they were called the Ramapoo Indians. On October 10, 1708, Catoonah and his clan sold their Ridgefield lands, under duress, to settlers from Norwalk and Milford, and they scattered. Catoonah died soon afterwards. Another of the Ridgefield signers in 1708 was WASPAHCHAIN, who was "JOHN CAUK" from Greenwich *(see WASPAHING below).* Grumet *(20)* says that "local tradition regards a hanging boulder in the town of Katonah as the tomb of KATONA and CANTITOES, his wife."

Mayn Mayanos

MAYN MAYANOS is considered to have been the sagamore of the Petaquapen clan in the Cos Cob area of Greenwich *(Fig. 37-2),* although he did not sign any existing documents. The long wigwams on Strickland Plains were destroyed by the Dutch in late 1644, but only young women and old people were killed there *(Chap. 9).* Figure 9, **Mayn Mayanos, Leader of Petaquapen, in 1643**, is artist Bryan Buckland's concept of this great leader, as he sat near the palisado Betuckquapock *(Fig. 25)* in the area now called North Mianus on the Mianus River. Mianus means "to gather." Mayanos was spoken of in 1644 *(Jameson, Journal: 281):*

> . . . a fierce Indian, who, alone, dared to attack, with bows and arrows, three Christians *[Dutch soldiers]* armed with guns, one of whom he shot dead, and, whilst engaged with the other, was killed by the third, and his head brought thither. *[Fort Amsterdam]*

This happened in Stamford, the port town. It is probable that Mayanos had gone to Stamford when he was terribly enraged by the Dutch winter attack on the helpless old people, women, and children at Petaquapen. ("Petaquapen" is linguistically similar to "Betuckquapock," and they may be considered as the same village complex, using the same Munsee word. The village stretched from Cos Cob to North Mianus.)

Figure 9

Mayn Mayanos, Sagamore of Petaquapen, in 1643
(Cos Cob, Connecticut)

Illustration by Bryan K. Buckland

An artist's conception of Mayn Mayanos, the Sagamore of the Petaquapen Band of the Wiechquaeskeck. In March, 1643, he had just learned that Dutch soldiers had attacked and burned the long wigwams in Petaquapen (Cos Cob), killing about 20 old people, young women and children who were staying there for the winter. Furious, Mayn Mayanos is about to rush to Stamford to confront the 80 Dutch soldiers alone with his bow and arrow. He killed one Dutch soldier before another soldier shot him.

Mayn Mayanos is memorialized by the Mianus River, North Mianus (an area near the ancient site of the Betuckquapock palisado), a school, and several businesses. His name is also remembered by the Mayn Mayano Tribe of The Improved Order of Redmen, a Greenwich fraternal organization.

Oruns (Aurems)

ORUNS was a woman who survived with her "papoose," mentioned in the 1686 document, as the settlers pressed in on her corn fields in Cos Cob. There was a major land transfer on February 1, 1686, that created the Horseneck Plantation (Greenwich) in the lands between the Mianus River and the Byram River. It was signed by sagamore WESSKUM and six other men. It deeded the whole area, but retained about 30 acres of planting field in Cos Cob (Indian Field) for the lives of the signers plus "ye four pappooses who are to enjoye ye above mentioned planting land during their lives and then at their decease . . .to be returned to ye towne." *(Chap. 8)*. This small clan died off or wandered away in the next 17 years. In 1703, the settlers pushed in on the rich land that was then being little used. There appears to have been only three Wiechquaeskeck adults left, WASPAHIN (also called "JOHN CAUK"), AUREMS, and PAXCANAHIN. AUREMS (ORUNS) signed this final land transfer deed with a cross, "her mark." It is likely that Oruns then followed the remaining individuals to the Ramapoo area in Ridgefield, to stay with a support group.

Pacham

PACHAM was a Tankiteke, a strong leader of the Indians in the Norwalk area. He evidently travelled widely, making and repairing relationships. In the early 1630s, he was among the Mohican, trying to get support against the Dutch. Then, English settlers started to move into his area, his tribe was depleted by disease, and he decided to take the side of the Europeans even as his Wiechquaeskeck friend, PONUPAHOWHELBSHELEN, was letting his young men harass both Dutch and English settlers. Pacham may well have been won over by Roger Ludlow in 1640 *(Chap. 8)*, and realized that there was no point in further enmity. Pacham visited New Amsterdam, declared his friendship with Governor Kieft, and joined the Canarsee of Long Island in attacking and killing a few Raritan *(Chap. 3, Tankiteke)*.

Ponupahowhelbshelen

PONUPAHOWHELBSHELEN was the Wiechquaeskeck sakima in the remote village of Nanichiestawack on Cross River, near Pound Ridge, New York, at the time of the New Netherland War (1640 to 1645). He was acknowledged as sakima by the Wiechquaeskeck in the western Fairfield County area. He quite possibly was the sakima of the Tankiteke in the Norwalk area, also, because by the end of the century the two groups had combined in Ridgefield. He was killed in the attack led by John Underhill in 1645. "Nanichiestawack" meant "fort" or "place of safety," but it could not stand against the Dutch muskets *(Chap. 9)*.

PONUPAHOWHELBSHELEN was a sakima at about the same time that MAMARUNECK was also a Wiechquaeskeck sakima in the present area of Mamaroneck and New Rochelle. Both of them seemed unaware of the strength of the Dutch forces, and they taunted them, allowing young warriors to attack the settlers.

Ponus

PONUS was one of the more famous Wiechquaeskeck in the 17th century. His name means "one who has been released." Some writers conclude that he became the sakima of the area as the ranks of the Wiechquaeskeck thinned in the late 17th century. Capt. Nathanael Turner's purchase of Stamford in 1640 was signed by "PONUS, sagamore of Toquams." It was also signed by OWENOKE, "Sagamore Ponus's Son." The 1667 land transfer in Stamford was signed by TAPHASE, son of PONASE (PONUS). It is likely that the villages of Toquam and Rippowam were both on the Rippowam River, fairly close to each other, and that Ponus was the leader of the whole Rippowam Valley at the time.

A ridge, a school, and some streets are named after Ponus. In New Canaan, there is a Ponus Monument erected by the Historical Society. It marks "the home and the traditional tomb of "Ponus Sachem of Rippowams." The Ponus Tribe No. 31 of the Order of Red Men in New Canaan commemorates him in their name.

Waspahing, alias John Cauk

WASPAHING (also WESPAHING, WASPAHILN) alias JOHN CAUK (CAK) is famous for having brokered CAUK's (or COOK's) Purchase in 1696 in Greenwich. He was not one of the "true and only proprietors," but was simply a witness to the land transfer of a large parcel lying between the Byram River and King Street (on the Greenwich border with Rye). In the second land transfer in 1701, he signed his name WASPAHING, as one of the granters. Then, in 1703, as one of the handful of remaining Wiechquaskeck in Greenwich, he signed away one of the last tracts of land along the Mianus River. The other signers were AUREMS, a woman, and PAXCANAHIN.

Some of the land transfer agreements are listed in Chapter 8. They were all made in the field, or in a house, and written down by one of the few settlers who could write. The spelling of the Indian names was simply what the scribe heard phonetically, so they differed with different scribes. It was often many years before the Town Clerk got the document and entered it into the records. He may have even rewritten some of the documents when he recorded them. Thus, the spelling of the names of particular Native Americans appeared differently on different documents. Men who learned the workings of the English system of law, like PONUS, WASPAHING, CHI-KIN WARRUPS, etc., got their names on many different documents, with different scribes and clerks recording them. The name "JOHN CAUK," which was favored by the settlers, apparently comes from the name of the village or the area in southwestern Greenwich that was called SIOASCAUK, meaning "covered at high tide." This was likely somewhere in the Byram area at the shore.

By the early 1700s, the Wiechquaeskeck of the area were beginning their flight northward. Their first move was to Ridgefield, joining with some Tankiteke in the Ramapoo area. It is probable that one of the signers of the "Deed to the Proprietors of Ridgefield" in 1708, WASPAHCHAIN, was the same JOHN CAUK.

Chi-Kin Warrups (Chickens)

CHI-KIN WARRUPS was variously known as CHICKENS, WARRUPS, CHICKENS WALLUPS, SAM MOHAWK, and other variations. He was probably a Tankiteke rather than a Wiechquaeskeck, but the two tribes were very close by then. The story of his moves, and the different names he was given, represents what was happening to all the Indian survivors in the late 17th century.

Warrups lived at what is now Greens Farm. He was a colorful character, and there are some great legends about him *(4, 23, 31)*, which he probably encouraged. "Chickens" first appeared on the record in

1679. At that point, he was 19 years old and was complaining that his land had been sold without his consent in the 1661 land deal, when he was a papoose *(Chap. 8)*. They thereupon gave him and his friend, CRECONOES, something to induce them to sign off on the deal. He was given the hundred acres in Redding on which he lived until 1749. At that time, he exchanged his one hundred acres in Redding to John Read for two hundred acres at Schaghticoke in the town of Kent, near a reservation. To make the exchange, he had to receive permission from the Connecticut Assembly. He died in Kent in the 1760s, which means that he reached 100 years of age.

Chi-Kin Warrups was only close to the Wiechquaeskeck, but his story is typical of the way the Indians were moved away from the fertile coastal lands. His name variations were also typical, but he had more nick-names than most Indians, probably because he did a lot of trading with the European settlers.

Wiechquaeskeck Villages or Camps

Along the coast, and for a few miles inland, there were a number of villages of families or clans led by leaders at the sagamore level. There was nothing standard in the definitions of villages, camps or clans. It all depended upon the capability of individuals and agreements worked out with family groups. There was sometimes more than one sagamore in a given clan area. The following is not a complete list, but are those villages mentioned in the land transfer agreements that we still have *(Chap. 8)*. Some of the known villages or groups, and their sagamores, in western Fairfield County in the middle of the 17th century, going from west to east *(Fig. 13)*, were:

- HASECO, between Byram River and Rye, led by WESPAHING.

- ARMONCK or COCKAMONG, at top of Byram River.

- MIOSSEHASSAKY, central Greenwich, between Brothers Brook and Byram River, led by WESSKUM. "Hassaky" means "swamp", or "meadow", or "coastal wetlands."

- SIOASCAUK, southwestern Greenwich, meaning "covered at high tide." This was probably where WESPAHING got his English nickname "John Cauk."

- PETAQUAPEN, between Mianus River and Brothers Brook in Cos Cob, led by MAYN MAYANOS *(ARCH3)*.

- BETUCKQUAPOCK, palisado on the Mianus River. It controlled the main east-west Native path *(Fig. 25)*. Means "round pond." The linguistic similarity with PETAQUAPEN indicates they were the same village area. The two are essentially the same word in Munsee.

- CASSACUBQUE, probably Diamond Hill in Cos Cob. Meaning could be "high rocks." The first syllable means either "sharp" or a "rock suitable for whetstones." This could indicate that there was a quartz vein there that could be used to make or sharpen projectile points. It was probably a palisado. The name is probably the origin of "Cos Cob."

- MONAKEWEGO, a summer camp on Greenwich Point used for gathering and smoking seafood. Could mean either "plenty of meat" or "deep at the end." A major archeological dig was made there in 1956, when it was called "Manakaway" *(ARCH1)*.

- ASAMUCK, a village in western Old Greenwich, led by AMOGERONE and OWENOKE *(ARCH5)*.

- PATOMUCK, a village in eastern Old Greenwich, led by RAMOTTHONE and NAWHORONE.

- RIPPOWAM, a village on the lower Rippowam River in Stamford, led by PONUS.

- TOQUAM, a village on the upper Rippowam River in Stamford, also led by PONUS.

- SHIPPAN, a village in Stamford, led by WASCUSSUE. Means "where the sea begins."

- SHEHAUGE, a village east of Westcott Cove in Stamford. The land was reserved for Indian planting grounds in the 1640 land transfer. The corn fields probably extended into modern downtown Stamford, meeting the Rippowam fields.

- MATAUBAUN, high land in North Stamford. May mean "dawn has come."

- RUNCKINHEAGE, (Ronkenhegue, Roukanhaige), a village on modern Darien land between Five Mile River and Pine Brook. Means "at the boundary place." This village was on the boundary between the Wiechquaeskeck and the Tankiteke.

- ROATON (Norsaton), a village in modern Rowayton and Noroton, led by PIAMIKIN. Means "creek almost dry at low tide."

- NORWALKE, a village in modern Norwalk, led by MAHACHEMO.

- NARAMAKE, a village in Norwalk, led by NARAMAKE (ARCH10).

- SACUNYTE, in Norwalk. Means "path along the shore."

- SASQUA, (Sasco, Sasquenaugh), a band in Southport, also sometimes led by MAHACHEMO. Means "a marshy swamp." It is famous for the Pequot's Great Swamp fight in 1638. The Sasqua band was a large group at one time.

CHAPTER 4

SIWANOY - THE PEOPLE WHO MAKE SEWAN (WAMPUM)

The Origin of the Name "Siwanoy"

Siwanoy means "the place of sewan-making," or "the people who make sewan at this place." Sewan means "wampum," or "shell beads." Oy, ois, or og means "place." There were Siwanoy all along the shore on both sides of Long Island Sound, in Delaware and in Massachusetts, north of Boston, when the Europeans arrived.

Prindle *(37)* notes that shell beads had been made in the Northeast for thousands of years. The early beads were large, and are now uncommon, since drilling was difficult with rough stone points, and few have survived. In the Middle and Late Woodland Periods (beginning around AD 200), the beads had a robust shape, about 8 mm in length and 5mm in diameter, with larger stone-bored holes of more than 2mm. When the Europeans arrived with metal awls, the Natives could soon drill holes of just under 2mm. Many beads then measured about 7 mm in length and 5 mm in diameter. The Europeans adopted sewan (wampum) as a medium of exchange, because they did not have enough small metal coins. The manufacture of wampum then increased dramatically.

Robert Bolton, in *History of . . . the County of Westchester*, New York, 1881, quotes from Cornelius van Trinhoven in O'Callaghan's *History of New York*. He says that the whole County of Westchester was called, in the Munsee dialect, "Laapawachking," which meant "the place of stringing beads," and dates it as 1609. He said the tribe there was called the "Weecquesqueecks," and they were "under the Mohegan (Mohican) Indians." He also labels the north shore of Long Island, where the Matinecock tribe lived, as **Sewanhacky**, which means "sewan land" or "sewan meadows," similar to **Siwanoy**. It is a misnomer to refer to a **Siwanoy** tribe, or band, in western Connecticut. There were Siwanoy people, the people who made sewan (wampum) all along the East coast from Delaware to Maine.

The name **Siwanoy** did not appear on the earliest maps, such as that of Willem Janszoon Blaeu in 1635, although Blaeu did identify the Manatthans (Manhattans) and the Makimanes (Mahican) in the area. *(Chap. 3).* The first mention of **Siwanoy** was on the Adriaen van der Donck map of 1656. He made the map in Amsterdam from the memory of his visit in 1645. Siwanoy was then repeated on two more maps. One was the 1671 *New World* map by Arnoldus Montanus in Amsterdam, the other was the 1671 *Novi Belgii* map by Ogilvie. These were obviously copied from van der Donck, who had himself used the 1635 Blaeu map, ufor its base information. The name Siwanoy was repeated again on subsequent maps *(Appx. B).*

It is very probable that, about 1630, someone charting the shore asked the people there the name of their tribe, through an interpreter. The two languages were vastly different in grammar and structure, and the question was understood as "who are you?" The answer was simply "Siwanoy," the people who make sewan.

Use of the name **Siwanoy** was not unique to the north shore of Long Island Sound in early accounts. Johan de Laet *(deLaet: 53)* mentioned the Sawanoos on Long Island in 1609. Adraien Block's 1614 map of northeastern Massachusetts has Sywanois there. That simply means that they also made wampum on Long Island and in northeastern Massachusetts. The name also turned up on maos of Delaware. Various early spellings of **Siwanoy** included: Sewonkeeg, Siwanoos, Siwanois, Sywanois, and Siwanog.

Clearly, the 19th century translators of 17th century documents had access to the 1656 van der Donck map that depicted the 1645 period in New Netherland. That map, and some subsequent maps, noted a Siwanoy band of Native Americans. The maps had been drawn in Amsterdam and were in error, but the name "Siwanoy" was accepted in southwestern Connecticut for nearly three hundred years. More recent translations of the early documents have shown that the name was not correctly applied.

It is understandable that writers of the 19th century picked up on the name Siwanoy from the later 17th century maps and thought that it applied to a tribe. The translators and historians, such as Edmund Burke O'Callaghan in 1863 and J. Franklin Jameson in 1909, did not have the advantage of the vast resource of translations of the Dutch writers of the 17th century that exist today. In the last thirty years, **The New Netherland Project** in Albany, New York, has produced a rich trove of translations of original writings by participants in the early immigration from Europe. They have used people skilled in Old Dutch to make the fresh translations.

Thus there were **Siwanoy** people, the people who make wampum, all along the shorelines of New England. They were excellent craftsmen, whom the Dutch tried to copy. They belonged to many different tribes of Native Americans.

Wampum in the Early 17th Century

Figure 10, **Wampum (Sewan)**, shows a wampum belt, strings of wampum, and the shells from which wampum was made in the early 17th century.

One of the first records we have of Wiechquaeskeck wampum in the 17th century is in the writings of Samuel Purchas *(Purchas: 593)*. Henry Hudson's boat was in the Hudson River, above Manhattan, and they were trading "Bevers skinnes, and Otters skinnes" which they bought for "Beades *[probably Dutch blue glass beads]*, Knives, and Hatchets." He then said:

> But some of them came again, and brought stopes *[strings]* of Beades: some had Sixe, seven, eight, nine, ten; *[wampum beads]*…and brought Tabacco and more Beades, and gave them to our Master, and made an Oration, and shewed him all the country around about.

Isaak de Rasieres, writing to Samuel Blommaert in 1628, *(deRasieres: 106)* said:

> As an employment in winter they make **sewan**, which is an oblong bead that they make from cockle-shells, which they find on the sea-shore, and they consider it as valuable as we do money here, since one can buy with it everything they have; they string it, and wear it around the neck and hands; they also make bands of it, which the women wear on the forehead under the hair, and the men around the body; and they are as particular about the stringing and sorting as we can be here about pearls.

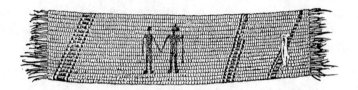

The Belt of Wampum given to William Penn's sons
at the signing of the "Walking Treaty" of 1682.
From the Collections of the Library of Congress
LC-USZ62-86486.

Quahog *(Mercinaria)* shell
used for purple *(Suki)* beads

Whelk *(Buccinum)* shell
used for white *(Wompi)* beads

Strings of wampum
used in trade.
(about 4 feet long)

Figure 10

Wampum (Sewan)

They have a marriage custom amongst them, namely: when there is one who resolves to take a particular person for his wife, he collects a fathom or two of sewan . . . and comes to the nearest friends of the person whom he desires . . . he agrees with them how much sewan he shall give her for a bridal present.

In writing about a visit to Buzzards Bay in the Cape Cod area, he said *(deRasieres: 110):*

All travellers who stop overnight come to the Sackima *[Sachem]*, if they have no acquaintances there, and are entertained by the expenditure of as much sewan as is allowed for that purpose . . . Here also they have built a shallop *[a small, open sailboat for use in coastal waters]* to look after the trade in sewan.

In writing about eastern Long Island, de Rasieres *(deRasieres: 103)* described the area, and said:

. . . it has several creeks and bays, where many savages dwell, who support themselves by planting maize and making sewan, and who are called Souwenos *[Siwanoy]* and Sinnecox *[Shinnecocks]*. . . . The tribes are held in subjection by, and are tributary to, the Pyquans *[Pequots]*.

Telling about 1640, David de Vries *(deVries: 208)* wrote:

. . . the troop brought the brother of the chief a prisoner, for whom Van Thienhoven had been surety before in eighty fathoms of zee-wan, otherwise he . . . must have been put to death.

In 1642, de Vries *(deVries: 215)* further noted the use of sewan to settle arguments, saying:

. . . one of their Indians, who was drunk, had shot a Dutchman . . . they would give one or two hundred fathom of zeewan to the widow if thereby they would be at peace.

In 1643, in a discussion about the Dutch killing Indians, even those they had begotten, an interchange *(deVries: 231)* about the talk of peace was ended:

The speaking now ceased and they gave to each of us ten fathoms of zeewan - which is their money, each fathom being worth four guilders.

On the second of John Josselyn's "Two Voyages to New England" *(Josselyn: 101)* in the 1660s, he describes their wampum on jewelry and clothing:

Their Merchandize are their beads, which are their money, of these there are two sorts, blew Beads and white Beads, the first is their Gold, the last their Silver, these they work out of certain shells so cunningly that (no one) can counterfeit, they dril them and string them, and make many curious works with them to adorn the persons of their Sagamours and principal men and young women, as Belts, Girdles, Tablets, Borders for their womens hair, Bracelets, Necklaces, and links to hang in their ears. Prince Phillip *[King Philip or Metacomet]* a little before I came for England, coming to Boston had a Coat on and Buskins set thick with these Beads in pleasant wild works and a broad Belt of the same, his Accoutrements were valued at Twenty pounds. The English Merchant giveth them ten shillings for a fathom *[six feet of beads]* of their white, and as much more or near upon for their blew Beads.

The Use of Sewan (Wampum)

The Native Americans along the Atlantic seaboard used wampum extensively. They became very good at its manufacture. The Long Island Natives were especially noted for making sewan, probably because they had a huge supply of large, thick quahogs and other shells washed in from the Atlantic. Making wampum was a time-consuming and labor-intensive process which required much patience and dexterity. A fathom string of sewan, or even up to ten feet, however, could be made and strung by a skilled worker in one day. Initially, lengths of wampum were not used among the Native Americans as money, but as tokens of relationships. The relationships could vary widely:

- Wampum belts would be exchanged between tribes as recognition of deals or agreements. One famous wampum belt had a pattern representing the union of four eastern tribes: the Penobscot, Passamaquoddy, Malecite, and Micmac. There were four tribal teepees (such as used by the Northern tribes) and a peace pipe. The Iroquois had been among the first to use representative pictures on wampum belts in this way, and the idea came back to the Atlantic coast. The coastal bands had previously made irregular designs.

- In the earlier days, from the Iroquois to the Lenape, wampum belts were used for documentation and for record keeping of significant events. They were also used to remind speakers of events that had taken place. At a council, a leader would hold up a wampum belt and use its beads to remind the people of the happenings that needed to be remembered by the tribe. Since they had no written language, the wampum belt became a mnemonic for a story to be told.

- There are several famous wampum belts that recorded major events with the Europeans. For example, when Native Delaware chiefs signed the famous "Walking Treaty" with the sons of William Penn, ceding a large area in eastern Pennsylvania, a special wampum belt was prepared to commemorate and seal the occasion *(Fig. 10)*.

- Wampum belts, clothing, and jewelry could be bestowed upon an admired leader as recognition of fealty, and then used by him to show off. Josselyn's description of King Philip's wampum *(Josselyn: 101)* is a fine example. Lesser leaders would also gather some wampum ornamentation. Much of it was beautifully worked onto garments.

- Wampum jewelry could be given by a suitor as a proposal of marriage, particularly if the woman was high-placed in the clan, such as the daughter of a sagamore *(deRasieres: 106)*. It was used similarly to the way men in other nations gave their brides a dowry or special jewelry.

The English and Dutch recognized, soon after they arrived, that the supply of wampum was limited, and that it was considered valuable by the Natives. Since it was easily measureable, they realized it could be used as a medium of exchange. There was a shortage of European coins in both the Dutch and English colonies. They soon started to use the idea of a "fathom of wampum" as currency. This was a single six-foot string of wampum beads. It was about the height of a man, so it could be held up when making a deal. The Dutch equated a fathom of wampum with four guilders *(deVries: 231)*. In small businesses around New Amsterdam, they would even use handfuls of loose wampum, counting out a few beads for a small item.

When the Native Americans found that the Europeans valued wampum, and used it as medium of exchange, they began making as much as they could. The Indians learned this quickly, because wampum was a currency that was not too different from their traditional ideas of barter. They learned how to make better wampum beads by using tiny drills made from broken pieces of tempered saw blades that had been offered in trade. This improved their manufacturing process. They evidently learned that their old, irregular, mnemonic patterns were less attractive to Europeans than a belt with a repeated pattern, such as a formalized flower or other picture. As a result, later belts have more European designs. Wampum items became valuable in trade, and were exported.

The popularity of wampum with the Europeans proved to be a triple-edged sword. First, it did help the Natives to obtain more trade goods. Second, however, it became too attractive as a product. Powerful neighbors, such as the Pequot, would come and take the wampum from the sewan-making tribes as tax or tribute. Third, the Europeans wanted to increase their profits, and, in 1627, started to produce counterfeit wampum in the Campbell factory in New Jersey, and other factories in New Netherland, using European tools. It was always recognizable, however, because it was made rapidly and coarsely without the painstaking polish of the Natives. It was not considered to be as valuable as real wampum.

In the early 1700s, Manhattan was the port where all the trading ships came, and it was famous for its high-quality wampum, which was called "Manhattan wampum." The poor quality Dutch-made wampum soon flooded the market, however, and the Director and Council of New Netherland became alarmed. The counterfeit wampum became such a problem that they passed an ordinance on May 30, 1650 *(Jameson, Journal)*:

> Whereas, we have by experience, and for a long time seen the decline and daily depreciation of the loose wampum among which are circulating many with no holes and half finished; also some of stone, bone, glass, muscle-shells, horn, yea, even of wood and broken beads, together with the manifold complaints of the inhabitants that they cannot go to market with such wampum, nor obtain any commodities, not even a small loaf of white bread or pot of beer from the traders, bakers, or tapsters for loose wampum . . . in order hereby to prevent the further importation of all lump and unperforated wampum, so as in future to obviate all misunderstanding, the Hon'ble Director and Council aforesaid, do ordain that the commercial shall pass and be good pay as heretofore, to wit, six white or three black for one stiver; on the contrary, poor strung wampum shall pass eight white and four black for one stiver. *[about a penny at the time]*

The Europeans brought in glass beads as trade items, particularly blue, and a variety of jewelry. These were most attractive to the Indians and were good for trade, but the real wampum remained the accepted medium of exchange. The Indians appreciated the glass beads and European brass items as jewelry. Herbert Kraft *(27)* describes the finding of Contact Period Indian graves in New Jersey. The man's body had a necklace of both conch shell beads and glass beads. The woman's body had been "sumptiously attired with tiny glass beads adorning her clothing, an elaborate collar of conch shells, a necklace of faceted blue glass beads," and a variety of brass European jewelry and wampum beads in her jewel box.

The Making of Sewan (Wampum)

Tara Prindle *(37)* notes at http://www.nativetech.org/NativeTech /wampum/war, (1998) that shell beads have long been used by Native Americans of Southern New England. A few large beads, called proto-wampum, have been dated at 4500 years old. Large wampum from the Middle Woodland period (about 200 AD) has also been found. It is about 8mm long and 5mm in diameter. Finely-pointed stones were used to bore the holes which could be about 2mm in diameter. By the mid-1600s, the Indians had small metal drills obtained by trading with the Europeans. Afterwards, wampum was made about 5mm long and 4 mm in diameter with 1 mm drilled holes.

Prindle *(37)* says that the word "wampum" comes from the Narrangansett words "wompi" for white, and "wompam" for white shell beads. The white beads were made from the center pillar of the Whelk *(Buccinum undatum)*. In other areas of America, different shells were used. The "sewan" worker broke the outside shell away, cut the central columnar pillar into pieces, and ground them smooth. It was possible to drill a central hole with simple pointed tools.

Figure 10 shows two kinds of shell from which wampum was made by the Wiechquaeskeck. These included the whelk and the quahog, or hard shell clam. It also illustrates the way wampum was packaged for trading in "strings," and how the two colors were intermixed to make patterns on the ceremonial "wampum belts."

The more valuable purple and black wampum was more difficult to make. It was made from inside areas of the shell of the hard shell clam, or quahog *(Mercenaria)*. The name "quahog" comes from the Narragansett word "poquahock." They were particularly abundant at the end of Long Island because they thrived in the cold Atlantic sands. These shells needed much more grinding to make beads than did the whelk because they were taken from a flat piece of shell rather than from a columnar piece.

The sewan maker would first chip at the whelks and quahogs he had gathered, to make bead-sized pieces. He would then use small pointed stone drills to make a tiny hole. European-supplied steel tools, from which smaller drills could be made, proved very useful.

After drilling, the bead would have been "tumbled," or polished, to an attractive size and shape. No observer appears to have described the wampum-making process, but from knowledge of shell and gem polishing that has been consistent through the ages, it is possible to assume how it was done. A good worker could make a fathom of beads in one day, which was several hundred. To make the beads needed for a fathom in a day, it would be impossible to polish one bead at a time, so it is probable that they used a tumbling type of polishing. They could have put many small, rough, drilled beads, with a handful of sand as an abrasive, into a leather pouch or tight-woven basket, and then have shaken them for an hour or two. This would have given a good polish and appearance. Several hundred beads could have been polished at one time in this manner.

This type of polishing technology was common in many parts of the world, and there is no reason that it could not have been learned by the Native Americans in this area. In the 1700s, Europeans were polishing gem stones in small barrels rotated by hand. By 1730, the Dutch were fabricating large quantities of wampum in factories such as the Campbell wampum factory in New Jersey *(37)*. Their wampum never looked quite the same as the Native work, possibly because the rotating polishing barrels produced a shape that was different from the shape of beads in the hand-shaken pouches. Campbell wampum was sold until the early 20th century.

Some reports say that after the Natives acquired grindstones, they strung wampum beads and held them against the grindstone with wood, rotating them until smooth. This would appear to be very difficult for such a small bead, but it may have been tried, since it was reported *(37)*. Some reports also talk about the "intense hardness" of the shell material, but such is not the case. Shell is a soft material. It is easy to cut, work, and polish, simply because it can be abraded by other materials. That is why it could be worked by hand. On Moh's Scale of Hardness, where a diamond is a 10 and talc is a 1, shell ranks with calcite at a 3. Shell is a very soft material that is quite amenable to cutting, smoothing, drilling, and polishing.

Strung beads were called *wampumpeage*, or simply *peage* or *peak*. Beads were usually strung in a length of one fathom (six feet) on fibers that had been stripped from milkweed, flax and nettle plants, and twisted into threads. A fathom contained anywhere from 240 to 260 beads *(37)*. For more valuable beads, the "fathom" was less than six feet. Sometimes, several strings of wampum were tied together as a bundle to help close a deal *(Fig. 10)*. At other times, the strings were woven into bands from one to five inches wide to make a belt. The colors of the beads were deftly arranged to make designs in the belt. An important wampum belt contained thousands of beads. That made for a lot of chipping, drilling, and polishing. They were called belts, and were sometimes worn as a girdle, but they were also worn as a sash or around the neck as a scarf.

Wampum belts have been preserved in museums, but little wampum is found in archaeological digs of campsites *(Chap. 11-A)*. Wiegand reports finding several beads at the Bear Rock Shelter in Stamford *(ARCH14)*, but only a few others have been found in the area. This is partly because each bead had value, so it was carefully handled when made. Also, many of the village sites were later destroyed, and the ground was cleared and graded. Wampum is occasionally found in grave sites, where there were ashes that made the soil basic, preserving the shell. There are only a few such sites in Connecticut *(Sect. 11)*. Connecticut soil is notoriously acid (from the underlying siliceous rock), and quickly decomposed the calcium carbonate of bone and shell.

In the early 1600s, the Wiechquaeskeck were active in the business of making wampum, and the land was truly Siwanoy, "the place of sewan." They collected whelks and quahogs in the summer. After they removed the edible portions and smoked them for the winter, they gathered the shells, possibly carrying them in a large basket. They took the shells to either the old folks' winter village, such as Petaquapen, or to the central tribal village of Naniechiestawack. In the winter months, they whiled away their time making wampum beads. In the spring, they would take their wampum strings down the Weichquaeskeck Path to trade in Manhattan.

As early as 1640, however, there was trouble and discontent in New Netherland owing to the manufacture of counterfeit wampum by the Dutch, and unfinished wampum from the Natives. People complained that payments were made in the rough unpolished stuff, while the good polished beads were exported, concealed, or simply not available *(Jameson)*. This affected the Wiechquaeskeck's livelihood.

By 1645, after the New Netherlands War, the Wiechquaeskeck had none of their great villages left. These had been where they had made most of their wampum beads in the winters. They had been further hit by diseases, and there were many fewer people. They were being pushed off their coastal lands by the immigrants *(Sect. 8)*. By 1680, the remnant had lost their fish traps, and their access to the shore was quite limited. It is doubtful that the Wiechquaeskeck made more wampum after 1680. The southwestern Connecticut coast was no longer "Siwanoy."

CHAPTER 5

MAPPING THE ANCIENT SETTLEMENTS

NASA has carried out research on Native footpaths and settlements in North America, using infrared photography from airplanes. Their findings can help fill in the gaps of the network of the ancient settlement complexes and footpaths in Wiechquaeskeck territory. We can assume that optimum footpath network designs were the result of least effort, combined with tribal protection methods, which had diffused across the continent in earlier times.

The tribal village complexes of Native Americans reflected many local relationships, and there was commerce and visiting that extended hundreds of miles in all directions. Trading took place along footpaths and waterways.

There were particularly well-trodden footpaths in the Lenape region, especially between the villages of the Munsee-dialect speakers. In all the Land of the Lenape, traders could understand the dialects, and there was relative peacefulness. Visitors would be greeted as friends many miles from their home village. Young men looked for wives in other villages, and it was helpful to visit tribes that spoke the same dialect. Some of these communicating footpaths are illustrated in Figure 11, **Some 17th Century Footpaths Used by the Wiechquaeskeck.**

The Native footpaths always followed the best walking routes across the terrain. When the colonists arrived, they followed the same Indian routes with their horses and cattle. As the years passed, roads were built on those paths for horse-drawn carts. Later, the roads were improved, then were paved for autos and trucks. American roads remained essentially on the same Native American paths until the Interstate Highway System was developed, cutting straight across the land.

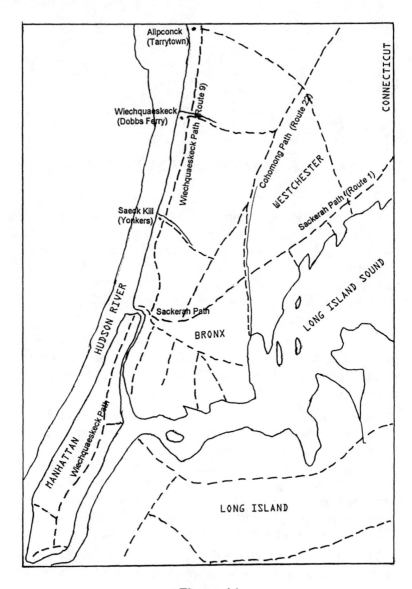

Figure 11

Some 17th Century Footpaths used by the Wiechquaeskeck

See also Robert Grumet, **Native American Place Names** . . . *(20)*

Some commuters from Connecticut and Westchester to New York City now drive their cars along U.S. Route 1 and along New York State Routes 9 and 22. These closely follow ancient Wiechquaeskeck footpaths that they also used for commuting to the lower end of Manhattan Island. Cars wait in line to pay tolls to cross the Harlem River Bridge. The Natives waited in the Bronx for their turn to cross the same river, at the same place, by dugout canoe. On the Harlem River, below the Henry Hudson Parkway Bridge, there is a sheltered cove with flat shores. There were once numerous dugout canoes pulled up on those shores, waiting to ferry Native American commuters back and forth. And those Indians were often going to lower Manhattan to trade. They were carrying wampum to Wall Street!

Native Footpaths in the Northeast

Native footpaths in the northeast of America were not well marked, unless they were regularly used, like the Wiechquaeskeck Path down Manhattan. They were paths of convenience, and the Indians knew their location by memory as much as by footprint marks. The Indians were either in bare feet or in mocassins. They did not hack at bushes and blaze trees, as the settlers liked to do. Even important footpaths were hard for Europeans to follow. When Underhill went from Greenwich to attack the village of Nanichiestawack, although it was a well-used trail, he needed a local Indian guide *(Chap. 9)*. There were no obvious trails.

There was no standard size of footpath. In **Mourt's Relation** *(Mourt: 34)*, he describes a well-marked path, "So we light on a path, but saw no house, and followed a great way into the woods." On the other hand, Johnson, in **Of Sions Saviour, in New England** *(Johnson: 82)*, says:

> Yet farther to tell of the hard labours this people found in Planting this Wildernesse . . . their farther hardship is to travell, sometimes they know not whether . . . they sadly search up and down for a known way, the Indians paths being not above one foot broad, so that a man may travell many dayes and never find one. . . . a servant maide, who was trevelling about three or foure miles from one Towne to another, loosing her selfe in the Woods. . . for the space of three dayes.

Many segments of Native footpaths in the Northeast are known from historical land records and oral history. Harral Ayres *(3)* describes eastern Connecticut and Massachusetts footpaths, and details *The Great Trail of New England* from Boston to Hartford to New Haven to New York. The route of the trail is close to a popular route for travellers going from Boston to New York on superhighways today. From Boston, the Great Trail went to Framingham, then Webster, Massachusetts, east to Windsor, Connecticut, and south to Hartford. That route stays within a few miles of present Routes 90 and 84. The Trail to New Haven went down today's Route 5. From New Haven to New York, the path was along today's Route 1, through 35 miles of the coastal "Siwanoy" area of Wiechquaeskeck territory.

The Great Trail of New England followed Native footpaths through the forests. When it began to get heavy use by settlers and traders, it became well marked. It was called Ye King's Highway in the 18th century. In western Connecticut, it was called the Post Road, and that name is still used, because the Great Trail was the road along which the modern United States Postal Service was inaugurated in December, 1672, by Governor Francis Lovelace in New York City. The first post rider started on January 22, 1673 over 225 miles of wild country with his packets of mail *(3)*. The post rider was "to goe monthly . . . and back againe" between New York and Boston, through the Wiechquaeskeck area. That first rider went with instructions and letters to provincial officials. It became the model of the postal service that we have today.

The start of the Postal Service is of interest here, because it is probable that some of the few surviving Wiechquaeskeck in the 1670's actually stood near the Post Road (the old Sackerah Path) and saw those first postal couriers. Much of the meaning would have been lost to them, however, as most still did not understand a written language.

For the western end of Wiechquaeskeck lands, R. P. Bolton *(5)* drew maps in 1922 of the main **Indian Footpaths in the Great Metropolis**, covering the five Boroughs of New York City. The Native footpaths going north joined with the principal Wiechquaeskeck footpaths. Bolton's diagrams can be seen at The Museum of the American Indian, Heye Foundation, New York. They can be followed block by block throughout New York City. For convenience, some were reproduced on a small scale by Robert S. Grumet in **Native American Place Names in New York City** *(20)*. Information from two of Grumet's maps of Manhattan and The Bronx were included in Figure11 because they tie directly into the Wiechquaeskeck footpaths.

Figure 11 shows the Wiechquaeskeck footpath connections to the Rechgawank and Manhattan in the south, to the Mahican and Wapping in the north, to the Tankiteke and other Paugussett in the east, and to the rest of the Wiechquaeskeck and to other Munsee-speakers in the west. Native Americans walked between tribes and between their own tribal villages on those footpaths. The paths followed the obvious routes, with the least grade, that skirted hills, lakes, and swamps. They are still in use today.

NASA Research on Native Footpaths

From oral history and old town records, we have known only a few pieces of the many footpaths. We can logically assemble a reasonable network, however, by studying the NASA research on Native footpaths and settlement complexes in the Southwest. The assumption is that all Native Americans had similar uses for their footpaths. Trading visitors would then take home the ideas for successful patterns of footpaths. Thus, we can use the known southwestern models, and then analyze Wiechquaeskeck footpath patterns.

NASA did their research in the Southwest and Central America *(49)* because large areas exist there that have not yet been paved over, plowed under, or built upon. Such photographic research cannot be done in the Wiechquaeskeck area, which has been disturbed by construction, and is now covered by asphalt and concrete.

Using infrared photography from planes to look below the ground surface, NASA researchers determined the Native footpath patterns and figured out why they were in those patterns. Similar ancient patterns would have existed in the Northeast, whenever such technology showed a real advantage to the Native Americans.

Figure 12, **NASA Photo of the Lower Hudson Valley**, is a high-altitude aerial photo that shows the landmarks of the lower Hudson. It is an excellent picture of Wiechquaeskeck territory to see clearly the relationships of the Hudson River, Manhattan, and Long Island Sound. This photo gives an idea of the topography of the area, as we consider where the Wiechquaeskeck road networks and settlements were. NASA also took low altitude aerial photos of Westchester and Fairfield Counties. When the two types of images are combined, there can be an analysis made of the topography, and the probable footpath locations.

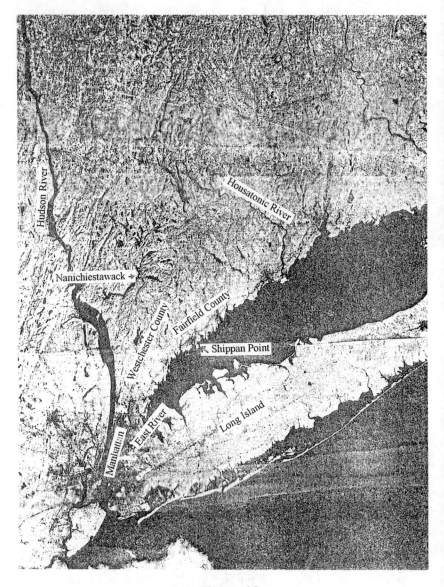

Figure 12

NASA Photo of the Lower Hudson Valley
N039-301   W072-001
Shows that Fairfield County is part of the Hudson River Estuary

Charles Trombold, in **Ancient road networks and settlement hierarchies in the New World** *(49)*, said that, "Roads are the focus of landscape archeology because they are the only tangible evidence of prehistoric settlements occupying geographical space." Trombold distinguishes between formal and informal roads. In Central America, there was a more advanced centralized civilization, and some formal roads were planned, engineered, and maintained. In the Northeast, however, the communicating paths were all informal. They were "highly irregular in layout owing to their avoidance of natural obstacles," and "the form of the routes is greatly influenced by their use." Trombold said that we consider the function of a path on the basis of what it connects.

Timothy Earle, in Trombold's book *(49)*, views the Wiechquaeskeck type of footpath pattern as a local group with high population density where, "Extensive interfamily and intergroup relationships are established for marriage, exchange, security, and . . .military alliance," which includes "frequent interaction and intergroup ceremonialism." This well describes the regular interaction of people in the Wiech quaeskeck bands.

This is a very brief introduction to the modern theory of Native footpaths that were used by tribes such as the Wiechquaeskeck. Footpaths were built for reasons that were economic, social, political, and religious.

Nicholas Short, in *The Landsat Tutorial Workbook (44)*, describes NASA's methods of remote sensing of objects or materials located at the Earth's surface. It is a textbook that, for the interested reader, gives a technical overview of the way aerial photography can be used to make maps and to define ground features, such as long-buried footpaths. There have been Landsat pictures taken that even distinguish, in color, between corn, soybeans, forest, barren land, and so on, in a remarkable way. Remote sensing has many uses in archaeology, around the world.

The remote sensing that has been most useful to find ancient Native footpaths has been infrared aerial photography from aircraft at an altitude of about 10,000 feet. Aerial photography has the advantage of being relatively close to the ground compared to satellites, and of giving excellent resolution that can pick up narrow footpath lines. Infrared sensing is used because it can pass through ground vegetation and dense tree foliage, and even penetrate six feet underground. Payson Sheets, an archaeologist from the University of Colorado, and Tom Sever, a remote sensing technologist with NASA, went to the Arenal Region of Costa Rica to excavate prehistoric village complexes covered with layers of volcanic ash *(43)*. When they found linear features by remote sensing photography, they confirmed their findings by excavation and dating techniques. They found patterns of footpaths which behavioral archaeologists could interpret. They said, "footpaths can be utilized as a window into the culture's religious, economic, political and social organization. They leave behind them the record of their presence, in the form of erosional footpaths. . . to understand the dynamic interrelationships among people, their cultures, the climate, and the biotic and physical environment."

Few Wiechquaeskeck footpaths can be viewed by remote sensing today. The remains have been dug up, built upon, and paved over. But, Sheets' and Sever's findings of Native footpath patterns have been confirmed by other major projects, including Chaco Canyon, New Mexico, by Margaret S. Obenauf *(49)*. Chacoan roads show as a large network of footpaths, which follow similar patterns on the photos. It was very likely that footpath design was another technology that was transferred across America. It was simply the path of least resistance and best use, based on a model of several central tribal villages. This matches the observations we can make in Wiechquaeskeck territory.

Wiechquaesgeck Footpaths Rediscovered

There is thus a model for the study of the Wiechquaeskeck social and political interactions. If we look at the few Native footpaths that have been remembered by both documented and oral history in New York and Connecticut, we can piece together the Wiechquaeskeck communications network of the 16th century by following the principles noted in the NASA studies. We can reasonably say:

- One of the main villages of the Wiechquaeskeck, near Connecticut, would have been Nanichiestawack (Cross River, New York). Many footpaths would have gone out radially from it.

- In the classical pattern, there would have been a ring footpath around that central village from which other footpaths would go out in all directions. The topography of the Cross River and Pound Ridge area allowed such a path plan.

- There would have been reasonably direct footpaths to the main perimeter fortifications. There obviously was such a path directly to Betuckquapock, on the Mianus River, and many paths to other palisadoes. The known paths, now roads, around Bedford, New York, point to this pattern.

- The footpaths leading to outlying Nanichiestawack settlements and camps would have been dendritic (branching) to all related encampments. Our knowledge of a few segments of such paths agrees with this, but there would have been a great number. It is not possible to now find most of the little-used footpaths.

- There would have been main footpaths to all related central tribal villages, such as to Alipkonck, Wiechquaeskeck, and Saeck-kill on the Hudson River. The starts of these footpaths are noted on some modern maps of Bedford history.

- Passing through the local network of footpaths would have been main inter-tribal footpaths, such as the Sackerah Path through the Bronx and Westchester, which approximates U.S. Route 1. There were also footpaths that are close to Routes 9 and 22 through Westchester, on the line of the roads today.

From such analysis, Figure 13, **Some 17ᵗʰ Century Wiechquaeskeck Footpaths and Camps**, shows the probable location of some of the main footpaths used for communication among the Wiechquaeskeck and their neighbors before the Europeans arrived. In this area, they were centered on the main village of Nanichiestawack, but there were connections to other large villages in all directions. Many of these were not even obvious in the 17ᵗʰ century, as the Dutch and English could not readily follow them in the winter.

These footpaths give us some idea of the road network and settlement hierarchy for the local Wiechquaeskeck before the Europeans arrived

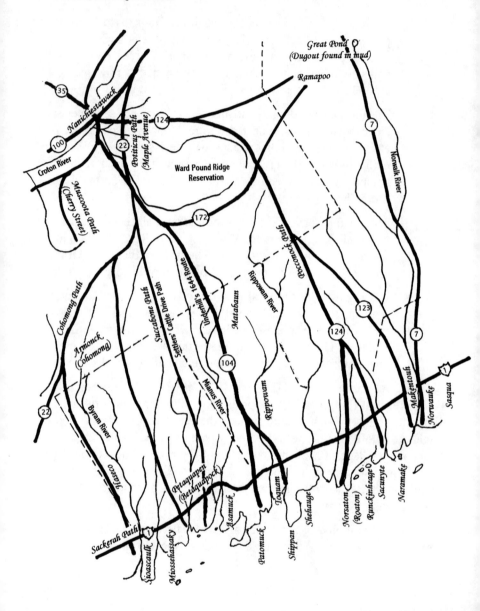

Figure 13

Some 17th Century Wiechquaeskeck Footpaths and Camps

CHAPTER 6

DOGS, CANOES, DEER, CORN, FISH AND PALISADES

Native American Dogs, Dugout Canoes, White-Tailed Deer, Indian Corn (Maize), Seafood, and Palisaded Forts were all prominent in Eastern Woodlands Indian life. They were central to the Wiechquaeskeck world in the early 17th century. They all give fine illustrations of the prehistoric *diffusion* of ideas and methods.

The Native Americans were always open to new ideas. The diffusion of these new ideas was steady, and came from every direction. Along the great river highways, and the coasts, there was a slow but steady *transfer of technology* that extended from Central America to Maine. For example, maize horticulture moved by diffusion in about a millennium from Mexico to the Northeast *(17)*.

There were some major differences among the different areas in the northeast. For example, in the 16th century, northern New England Indians had birchbark canoes. Massachusetts Natives had both birchbark and dugout canoes. The Lenape used only dugout canoes, although they had seen birchbark canoes come down the Hudson River. There were simply not usable Paper Birch trees in the Delaware area. Another example is that some conical teepees were built in northern New England, in addition to their round bark and rush wigwams. Most of the northern teepees were covered with large animal hides. This is because there were still many larger animals, such as bison and moose, there. A few of the skins of those animals made a reasonably watertight teepee covering with very few sewn seams. The advantage of the teepee is that it could be taken down, moved, and re-erected more readily than could the wigwam. Its poles were not dug into the ground, but it was held down by putting rocks on the outside edge. (On the Great Plains, one can still see circles of stones that were used over a century ago to hold down teepees.) The larger game had been mostly killed off in southern New England by the 17th century, however. That is one reason that they built the wigwams with bark and rush mat coverings. When the Dutch first explored both the Hudson and Connecticut Rivers, they recorded seeing both birchbark canoes and conical teepees in their travels, but not among the Wiechquaeskeck.

European Observers of Wiechquaeskeck Life

There is a variety of information about Wiechquaeskeck life from several educated observers who wrote letters, reports, and descriptions about their travels. The question obviously arises as to whether those written observations accurately portrayed Native life in the 17th century. For each writer, we have to consider their reasons for writing, as their motivations varied greatly. Some were simply recording their thoughts. On the other hand, some of the Dutch letters were written to impress the authorities in Amsterdam in order to influence their decisions. We can expect such observations to be slanted favorably to Dutch ideas. The explorers, Verrazano and Hudson, however, were trying to impress with their geographical discoveries, and had no reason to color their descriptions of the Indians in their log books. In the order of the list used in this book for 17th century references *(e.g. deLaet)*, some of the various European observers, who wrote descriptions, were:

Johan de Laet *(deLaet)* wrote **New World** in 1625, 1630, 1633 and 1640. The translation was edited in 1909 by J. Franklin Jameson in **Narratives of New Netherland 1609-1664**. DeLaet described Hudson's exploration and wrote about "The Nature of the Land and Manners of the Folk on the Great River of Mountains" *(River Montagne, later Hudson River)*. He was writing officially to "Their High Mightinesses" in the West India Company and put things in the best light from the viewpoint of the settlers to get support, and proper consideration of their needs.

Isaack de Rasieres *(deRasieres)* wrote a letter, probably in 1628, to the director of the West India Company, Samuel Blommaert, in Amsterdam, concerning "the situation of New Netherland and its neighbors." DeRasieres was the chief commercial agent of the West India Company and was involved in business and trading. He was hoping for good relations with the Natives. As secretary of New Netherlands, he can be considered an authority. His letter was first found in Holland and translated in 1847 by John Romeyn Brodhead, who had been sent by New York State to Europe to search the archives for materials dealing with the colonial history of the state. It was also edited by Jameson.

David Pietersz de Vries *(deVries)* wrote **Korte Historiael Ende Journaels Aenteyckeninge, 1633 to 1643**. The translation was also edited by Jameson. DeVries was sent out by the West India Company to report on the progress of New Netherland. Thus, he wrote favorably about the Dutch administration in New Netherland, while other writers were complaining about them. He was not interested in the plight of the Natives. He observed many Native activities and wrote well, in detail, however, and his writings are useful.

J. Franklin Jameson wrote **Journal of New Netherland**, which is part of **Narratives of New Netherland, 1609-1644**. These were translations from New Netherland writings that were edtied by Jameson, and published in 1909. There have been further translations and publications of the some of the same letters. The Journal has many details about the 1640's and discusses the causes of the New Netherland War with the Wiechquaeskeck. The many narratives vary greatly as to whether they were factual or were striving to influence opinion.

John Josselyn *(Josselyn)* wrote **Two Voyages to New England**, about trips he made with private funding in 1638 to 1639 and in 1663 to 1671. He was a rich Englishman with a fascination for geography, anthropology, and natural history. He was probably a fairly unbiased scientific observer. He gave many original details of Native life that are worth including because he was describing other Algonquian peoples in the Northeast, with lifestyles and technologies that were similar to those of the Wiechquaeskeck.

Adriaen van der Donck *(vanderDonck)* was probably the most accurate of the Dutch reporters about Indian life and natural history. He was sent to America in 1641 by Van Rennselaer. Unfortunately, he argued often with the local authorities. He was close to the land and friendly with the Indians. He had a large patroonship, 24,000 acres, in what is now the Bronx and Westchester County, and he lived among the Wiechquaeskeck. His title, Jonkheer, meaning gentlemen, is the root of the name of the city of Yonkers. Van der Donck wrote **A Description of the New Netherlands** when he was later detained in Amsterdam and forbidden to go back to the Bronx. It was published in 1655. It was the first book written by an established resident of what is now New York. First published in English in 1841, a translation was published by Syracuse University Press in 1968.

Hendrick (Henry) Hudson *(vanMeteren)* in 1609 explored the Mauritius River, also called the River of Mountains, and later called the Hudson River. He was English, but had been hired and sent by the Dutch East India Company to seek a northeastern passage to China. After he started in a yacht, The Half Moon, he changed his projected course and sailed to the Mauritius River area. He encountered both friendly and unfriendly Natives in the Hudson valley. He described visits to Wiechquaeskeck villages, and was probably accurate. He wrote facts in a log book, as he saw them. His log was transcribed by Emanuel van Meteren *(vanMeteren)* and published in Jameson's translation. Van Meteren was also quoted by Johan de Laet *(deLaet)*.

Giovanni da Verrazano *(Verrazano)* sailed from 1524 to 1528 for merchants in Lyons, France, to see what territory there was north of Spain's huge claims in the Americas. This was the first recorded visit of Europeans to the New York area, and is therefore important as an early description. Verrazano was amazed by what he observed around Manhattan Island and Rhode Island. He reported in glowing terms. He received an amazing welcome from the Native Americans in the outer New York harbor. Some of the Wiechquaeskeck had probably joined the Manhattan and the Canarsie gathered on the shore and dressed in feathered finery to look at the strange apparition. Others paddled their canoes around Verrazano's ship. His ship's log would have been an accurate report, as he observed the Indians. It was edited by Lawrence C. Wroth, and reprinted by Yale University Press in 1970.

Nicolaes van Wassenaer *(vanWassenaer)* wrote **Historich Verhael** concerning the years 1624 to 1630 in New Netherland. He was evidently writing an official history of New Netherland for the Lords States General of the West India Company in Amsterdam. He also calls them the "Right Honorable Directors of the Chartered West India Company in the United Netherlands." He seems to have been a fair observer, but we have no idea how he slanted his ideas to Company thinking. The translation was edited by Jameson in 1909.

Roger Williams *(Williams)* was the founder of the Colony of Rhode Island because of his zeal for religious liberty. He believed in the separation of church and state, and he was banished from the Massachusetts Bay Colony in 1636. He walked to Narragansett Bay and purchased the Providence area from the Natives. His comments must be included because he was an intelligent observer who spent much time actually living and traveling with the Indians. They were the Narrangansett, who were Algonquian-speaking Eastern Woodland Indians, very similar to the Wiechquaeskeck. There would have been some interaction, trade, and technology transfer between them. Williams insisted that "king's patents," or land grants, in America were invalid and that only direct purchase from the Indians gave a just title to the land. This led to land transfer agreements such as those described in Chapter 8. Williams wrote **A Key into the Language of America**, in which he enriches his Algonquian word definitions with "observations" (Obs.). These give us many insights into northeastern Native life at the time.

A. THE NATIVE AMERICAN DOG

Native American Dogs had a true **symbiotic relationship** to the Indians. They lived together and were dependent on each other. Biologists define symbiosis as the intimate living together of two organisms of different species for mutual benefit. It was a matter of basic existence in prehistoric times. Man and dog needed each other. From the Wiechquaeskeck's viewpoint, this relationship had clear advantages:

- Dogs were friendly and enjoyable companions.

- Dogs were excellent guards and allowed the Indians to sleep at night in their village or on the trail. They would protect from large prowling animals or even poisonous snakes. They would sound an alarm if enemies were approaching stealthily.

- The dogs watched over babies and young children, sometimes pulling them from danger, or barking if there was trouble.

- There were a great many large and small herbivorous animals around, such as deer and rabbits, which could devastate the unfenced Indian gardens. The dogs would try to drive them away, and sometimes get a meal in the process.

- There were also mice, voles, and related species which could dig and bite into the fiber storage baskets full of corn and squash. The dogs competed with the Indians in catching and devouring these animals.

- Dogs were useful in hunting. They are shown in a 17th century picture helping to chase deer into pounds *(Fig. 18)*.

- A good fat dog was considered a great delicacy, and was eaten at special festive occasions or when an important visitor was invited to dine *(deLaet: 49)*.

- The process of preparing game and fish for cooking in Indian camps produced piles of scraps and offal which were always a health problem. The dogs enjoyed cleaning up such scraps.

- Dogs were pleasant to have in a wigwam on a cold night.

The dogs had equal, and almost identical, advantages. This Indian-Dog symbiotic relationship had far more favorable factors for both participants than do most text-book examples of other symbiotic living examples among animals. There was possibly one disadvantage to this relationship, that the Indians accepted. Roger Williams *(Williams: 56)* said:

> In middle of Summer, because of the abundance of Fleas, which the dust of the house breeds, they will flie and remove on a sudden from one part of their field to a fresh place.

Early Reports of Native American Dogs

The English and Dutch writings of the 17th century have only a few reports on Indian dogs among the Wiechquaeskeck. This may be because the English and Dutch had dogs in their houses as well, and they were considered an ordinary part of living, and not worthy of mention. The early narrators were interested in describing Indian activities that were different from the European norm. Johan de Laet *(deLaet: 49)* quoted from "Hendrick Hudson's" journal about the Hudson River in 1609:

> I sailed to the shore in one of their canoes, with an old man, who
> was the chief of a tribe . . . On our coming near the house, two mats
> were spread out to sit upon, and immediately some food was served
> in well made red wooden bowls; two men were also despatched with
> bows and arrows in quest of game, who soon after brought in a pair
> of pigeons, which they had just shot. They likewise killed at once a
> fat dog, and skinned it in great haste, with shells which they get out
> of the water.

William Bradford *(Bradford: 73)* wrote about Captain Standish, with his crew in a large shallop exploring the coast from Cape Cod to Plymouth in 1620:

> . . . when they had marched about the space of a mile by the seaside,
> they espied five or six persons with a dog coming towards them,
> who were savages; but they fled from them and ran up into the
> woods . . .

Adriaen Van der Donck wrote in detail about many wild birds, animals, and fish in 1656, but only once did he mention a dog. He said *(vanderDonck: 89)*, in describing a Feast:

> They eat lustily on such occasions, and everyone devours as much
> food as would serve each of them for three days, as nothing may be
> left at their frolics; what is not eaten by them or by their dogs must
> be carried back.

There were few pictures of Indian Dogs painted at the time. There is one painting of a famous Mohawk chief with a dog. He was Thayendanega (Joseph Brant), who had fought with the British in the Revolutionary War. It was painted in the mid 1800s, not painted from life. The dog is medium sized and nondescript in the picture.

The Story of the Native American Dog

There were dogs living with the Native Americans all across the continent in the 17th Century. They do not appear to have been a single breed. The dogs of Canada and the West, which probably arrived on the continent later than those in the East, were more of a dark coyote or small wolf type. The dogs of eastern United States were possibly a single breed of a pariah type, but were certainly not the same size and shape everywhere. Figure 14, **The Native American Dog**, shows a Carolina dog, typical of those now being bred in South Carolina from a strain that was recovered from the wilds. That breed is probably close to the dogs

A Native American (Carolina) Dog

http://www.carolinadogs.org/photo.html

Tara, an old Native American Dog in Colorado

Figure 14

The Native American Dog

of the Wiechquaeskeck. For information about these dogs, contact the Carolina Dog Association. The current contact (2001) is: Jane Gunnell, Box 278, Ridge Spring, SC 29129. Information can also be obtained on the Web at http://www.carolinadogs.org. The other dog pictured in Figure 14 is Tara, an old Native American Dog who lived near Berthoud, Colorado. Her strain was of unknown purity, but she had many of the behavioral characteristics of Native American dogs, such as digging a nest beside large rocks and curling around into it. There are many similar dogs throughout the West. The purity of their strain can now be tested genetically.

The Native dogs in the southeast, now called Carolina dogs, or "yaller" dogs, looked like modern Nordic dogs. There were also the Kentucky Shell Heap Dogs and the Basketmaker Dogs that were similar. In the northwest, the dogs were darker, the color of Alsatians. Many of them were smaller, reported to be like mixed terriers in appearance. The Dutch said that the Wiechquaeskeck dogs were small, and the local Natives were amazed at the sight of the large Dutch dogs. Of course, all Native American dogs had long curved tails, as the idea of cropping tails is European.

The eastern Native American dogs are believed to be decendants of domesticated canines that came with the early Asian peoples across a land bridge to America 12,000 to 15,000 years ago. The forming of the great Laurentide Ice Shield had lowered the level of the oceans, and the continents were joined. Various peoples had fanned out from their early settlements in Southwest Asia, where they had probably domesticated a wild canid at least 15,000 years ago. Some of these people populated America with their dogs. These dogs that arrived early were not related to the native wolves and coyotes in North America, although many have inter-bred with them over the years. This has been established with modern gene analysis *(47)*.

Lehr Brisbin and Thomas S. Risch *(47)* say that the first primitive dogs to accompany humans across the Bering Land Bridge into North America entered a continent already inhabited by other species of **Canis:** the Gray Wolf (*C. lupus*), the Coyote (*C. latrans*), and the Red Wolf (*C. rufus*). Eventually, there were hybridizations with those and also with the many imported European species of dogs. It is unlikely that more than a few, if any, remnants of the original primitive dog type still exist in a genetically pure state.

The Carolina Dog Association *(47)* believes that today we still have a window to the past, however, with the pariah dogs that have long lived in the woods and swamps of the South. These "yaller" dogs have a sharp pointed muzzle, erect pointed ears, and a fox-like appearance. They are generally reddish-yellow to ginger with pale undersides, and they have a brushy fish-hook tail. Molecular genetic studies have shown that they are related to the Australian Dingo *(Canis lupus dingo)* and the New Guinea Singing Dog *(Canis hallstromi)*. The American primitive dogs are now registered as Carolina Dogs. They are considered a separate breed from any of the modern domestic breeds of dog. They have several unique traits, and the pattern for estrus cycles for females is quite different from that of the domestic strains. It is adapted to the expectation of a short life and to having many pups when young.

The Carolina Dog Association *(47)* has changed the breed name to **Native American Dog**, to reflect that the breed probably represents all the dogs that had a strong human-dog bond with Native Americans over the millenia, at least in the East. They are attempting to preserve the Carolina Dog against being killed off or intermixed with the stronger, untamable Coyote, which is rapidly and steadily moving into their area. They feel that the breed is truly a National Treasure.

It seems probable that the large number of feral dogs that inhabited remote areas of the southestern United States originally came from the forced removal of many of the tribes of Cherokee Indians in 1838 to Oklahoma. Many dogs just moved then into the woods and swamps.

The Native American Dog was undoubtedly common, and was enjoyed as a friend, among the Wiechquaskeck. Archaeologists have discovered buried bones of dogs in the New York area, with the dogs placed in a formal, curled, burial position, indicating affection and regard for their dogs. Formal canine burials were frequent in New York State, and were common throughout America *(ARCH2)*. Ernest Wiegand found three dog burials at the Indian Field Site in Greenwich *(51)*.

B. THE DUGOUT CANOE

The technology of the Wiechquaeskeck dugout canoe is of particular interest because it matches native dugout canoe technologies around the world. There are European pictures drawn of Native American dugout canoes from Connecticut to Ohio, and to the Carolinas, that show features that are like those of the Wiechquaeskeck dugout canoes. Everywhere, dugouts were made in similar ways, using adze-like tools and fire. This is much like the modern concept of having standard boat shapes, but they had no mail-order catalogs and no World Wide Web. They simply had tribe-to-tribe diffusion of ideas.

The Eastern Woodland Indians south of central Connecticut did not have the Paper Birch trees of the North to make the fabled Indian birchbark canoes. They also did not have the huge red cedars of the Northwest to make dramatic and graceful dugouts. They had some good straight trees, however, that were big enough. A variety of trees were used, such as pine, tulip, oak, and chestnut *(Williams: 38)*. The most reliable wood for the Wiechquaeskeck to make sturdy, useful, buoyant canoes was the tulip-tree *(Liriodendron tulipifera)* of the magnolia family. The tulip trees grew straight with smooth grain in western Connecticut, with no branches making knots for forty feet up the trunk. (In those days, there were many tulip trees of larger diameter than there are now. Most of the large tulip trees were cut down to make flooring and interior wood for the settlers.) The white pine *(Pinus alba)* was also used because it had a large straight trunk. If it was among other trees, most of its lower branches would also have dropped off, leaving the sap wood knot-free. It could be burned out readily because of its pitch content, and it was soft, so it could be cut easily with stone tools.

From such trees, the Wiechquaeskeck made dugout canoes of all sizes. A few have even been partially preserved to modern times, deep in the anaerobic mud at the bottom of lakes and in the soil of Manhattan. We know what they looked like. There are also 17th century drawings and descriptions of them among other Algonquians.

The first European to report on the Native canoes was Verrazano in 1524. Writing about sailing into New York harbor, he said *(Verrazano: 136):*

> We saw many of their little boats made out of a single tree, twenty
> feet long and four feet wide, which are put together without stone,
> iron, or any other kind of metal. . . . They use the fourth element
> [fire] and burn the wood as much as necessary to hollow out the
> boat: they do the same for the stern and the prow so that when it
> sails it can plow through the waves of the sea.

Note that Verrazanno said that the canoes were up to four feet wide
and had pointed prows. Many "reproduction" canoes, carved today, are
much too thick and narrow, and have stubby bows. Boats like that would
only have been made for near-shore fishing. Verrazano had entered New
York Harbor in a sloop *(Fig. 7)*, leaving his large ship in the bay. He
wrote of the excitement of the people on land "which we found densely
populated". Some of them would have been Wiechquaeskeck, "dressed
in bird feathers of various colors and they came towards us joyfully,
uttering loud cries of wonderment." He continued *(Verrazano: 137)*:

> About 30 of their small boats ran to and fro across the lake with
> innumerable people aboard who were crossing from one side to
> another to see us.

Note that their canoes cut readily through the water, so they must
have had a shaped bow. Later, Verrazano sailed to Rhode Island and
reported about the Narragansett *(Verrazano: 139)*:

> They use . . . stone instead of iron for cutting trees, and make their
> little boats with a single log of wood, hollowed out with admirable
> skill; there is ample room in them for fourteen to fifteen men; they
> operate a short oar, broad at the end, with only the strength of their
> arms, and they go to sea without any danger, and as swiftly as they
> please.

The Shape of a Dugout Canoe

Figure 15, **The Native American Dugout Canoe**, shows three
different canoe shapes. The top one is drawn from a dugout canoe
unearthed in Manhattan in the 20th century, the second is from a 17th
century woodcut, and the third is from a 17th century map.

One of the best preserved dugout canoes, that shows the original
Wiechquaeskeck design and bow shape, in Figure 15, was pictured in the
American Museum Guide Leaflet No. 41, **Indians of Manhattan Island
and Vicinity** *(45)*. In 1906, New York Edison workmen made an
excavation eight feet deep at the corner of Cherry and Oliver streets, and

Wiechquaeskeck Dugout Canoe
Excavated in Manhattan, 1906
Preserved at the American Museum of Natural History

Fishing and Working Dugout Canoe
For use close to shore and on lakes
(see Figures 17 and 22)

*Navis ex arboris trunco
igne excavata.*

Pequot "Beaked" Dugout Canoe
"Boat from a tree trunk dug out by fire"
From Willem Blaeu's Map of 1635
Described by Capt. John Mason *(Mason: x)*

Figure 15
The Native American Dugout Canoe

they came across an old Indian canoe. The workmen cut it up into three pieces to get on with their work, and only one piece was saved. The part saved is about 7 feet long, 3 feet wide, and 14 inches deep. Note that it is wide and shallow, and thus seaworthy. It tapers to a rounded prow which is fairly sharp, somewhat like the western Indian canoes. The whole was hewn from a solid log of white pine, over twenty feet long. They believed it had been buried for at least a hundred years.

This remnant of a dugout canoe shows that the Weichquaeskeck and Manhattan were quite advanced in ship design. The lines are graceful, the sides are thin, and the canoe would have cut well through the water. It is obvious that they used their adzes with great dexterity. This particular canoe was probably made in the late 18th century with a European steel adze. Earlier, the Indians had only stone adze-like tools and could cut away only wood that had been selectively burned. Steel adzes, therefore, soon became popular trade items when the Europeans arrived. An adze is similar to an axe, except that the blade is set at right angles to the handle and curves inward towards it. A shipwright, swinging the adze down, almost between his feet, can make a very smooth surface on the wood. The Wiechquaeskeck were evidently experts. These were not awkward log boats, as commonly seen in displays, but were smoothly designed vessels to ride in, and slice through, the waves.

They made dugout canoes of various sizes. Some were about 8 feet long, suitable for a few people on an inland lake or stream. Others were around 20 feet long and 3 feet wide, the size and buoyancy of many small power-boats today. They would hold 6 to 8 people in any water. Still others were around 30 feet long and over 4 feet wide. They would have been used for travel on the ocean or for fighting. Roger Williams said *(Williams: 98)*:

> Some of them will not carry above three or foure: but some of them twenty, thirty, forty men.

It is hard to imagine the larger sizes that were carved from a log, but John Mason describes Pequots returning from a raid on Wethersfield *(Mason: x)*:

> They came down the River of Connecticut . . . in three Canoes with about one hundred Men, which River of necessity they must pass: We espying them, concluded they had been acting some Mischief against us, made a Shot at them with a piece of Ordnance, which

beat off the Beak Head of one of their Canoes, wherein our two Captives were: it was at a very great distance: They then hastened, drew their Canoes over a narrow Beach with all speed and so got away.

Mason was writing about the mouth of the Connecticut River, which is wide and has many sandbars. Notice that the Indians were in large canoes that held about 35 men each, yet they were able to run against a sandbar, jump out, and pull it over the bar, then jump back in and paddle away out of danger. They could not do this if the canoe was narrow or a hulking log. They could only do this if the canoe was broad, well-balanced, and hollowed out with relatively thin sides, reducing its weight. Evidently the canoes were beautifully made, with smooth lines.

Some of the prows of the dugout canoes pictured on the early 17th century maps are of particular interest because various shaped prows are shown, and some had the "Beak Heads" *(Figs. 5, 15)*. The prows were clearly integrally carved from the trunk of the tree as the canoe was being shaped. The canoes could then be equally well paddled in either direction with the paddlers simply turning around.

On most dugout canoes, the prows were fairly short. These were intended to "plow through the waves," as Verrazano noted. They would break a wave so that it sprayed to either side and not into the canoe. On some of the larger dugout canoes, however, the prows are pictured as quite long, possibly four feet or more, and pointed straight or slightly down with a knob at the end. Clearly, these prows were not just "wave cutters," but were made for marine warfare. Smooth water cutting is done by the shape of the front of the canoe prow *(Fig. 15)*. It is probable that this elongated prow design was peculiar to the Pequot *(Sect. 3, The Pequot)*.

The long, heavy bowsprits, or rams, on each end of those large canoes were probably the "Beak Heads" that Mason described. They were clearly shown on the early maps *(Figs. 5, 15, 19)*. It appears from the pictures that one of the prows or bowsprits was pointed slightly down and had a large knob or "beak" on it. It is speculative, but the only reasonable design explanation for that would be so the canoe could be paddled fast, broadside into an enemy canoe. The beak would then go over the enemy's gunwale and hold it. These were large prows, and men could easily run across them with war clubs and tomahawks and board their enemy's canoe. The straighter heavy bowsprit could have been simply a ram, used to hit the enemy's canoe and turn it over, or to hit the men inside it. The momentum of a rapidly-paddled thirty-foot canoe would have been tremendous. Battles on the open water then would have been a process of maneuvering to strike the opponent amidships, while having some archers pouring arrows at the enemy. These are only engineering conjectures, made from the apparent design and from Mason's notes.

A description of such a battle, written by Roger Williams, has already been noted *(Chap. 3)*. The Pequot had the best fleet and were the most skilful at handling their large military dugouts. They won that battle, and they became the undisputed rulers of Long Island and of the Connecticut shore down to New Haven. It is very likely that they occasionally penetrated to Wiechquaeskeck territory. Thus, we have a picture of very large dugouts, beautifully formed, that could be paddled on open water about 180 miles, carrying warriors ready to fight.

We have no way of knowing whether the Pequot were the only Native tribe with these effective naval ships, or whether the Munsee-speaking Delawares built them also. They are shown on the 1635 map drawn by Willem Janszoon Blaeu *(Fig. 44)*, and on the first painting of Manhattan that is known *(Fig. 5)*, where the canoes are obviously copied from Blaeu. Those pictures were drawn in the Netherlands, and interesting illustrations may have been juxtaposed. For instance, the smaller one-man canoes shown in Figure 5 are not a Munsee design. They have the shape of an Abenaki (Maine) birch-bark canoe, with an interesting raised gunwale beside the paddler that shows features of northern kayaks. It is unlikely that the Munsee had any small canoes of that shape, since they did not have adequate birch bark. This could mean that the mapmakers in The Hague simply saw sketches or examples of Indian canoes of unusual shapes, and they dropped them onto the map without knowing where they correctly belonged.

We do know that the Munsee-speakers made fine, large, seaworthy canoes of an advanced design, from the dugout unearthed in Manhattan *(Fig. 15)*. This canoe did not have a "beak," but had graceful lines. We do not know whether any of the Delaware bands built large canoes with rams or whether they simply withdrew to their forts when the Pequots came raiding. It is entirely possible that the Pequots ruled only eastern Connecticut down to New Haven, and Long Island down to about Port Jefferson. They could have visited New Amsterdam harbor as traders in their "beaked" canoes, however.

Native American canoes were not all like the graceful Wiechquaeskeck canoes or the powerful "beaked" canoes of the Pequot. Many were much more easily and simply built with stubby ends *(Fig. 17)*. These would be quite useful for work on ponds or close to shore. They would be good for floating out to fish, gather clams, or tend nets. They would not have been very good for open water on the Sound or for shooting rapids, as Williams described. Since they were easier to build than graceful canoes, and could do a decent job, many of them were probably constructed. They have become the design of choice for amateurs making dugouts today. No one could have gone from Stamford to Manhattan through Hell's Gate in one, however.

The construction and building of the dugout canoe is a likely candidate for the diffusion of ideas around the world. The building of such boats was ingenious, and not obvious. Yet, dugouts were found on every continent by the Middle Ages, wherever suitable trees grew. In the entry, *Ship*, in the Encyclopaedia Britannica, there is a dugout canoe pictured on the Congo River that is comparable in design to some of the Wiechquaeskeck canoes, though not as well made. Similar dugouts were used throughout the Americas. The coastal Native Americans along the Pacific Northwest had much finer dugouts, because the Western Red Cedar *(Thuja plicata)* was ideally suited to shaping canoes up to 60 feet long and 8 feet wide. The eastern trees could not match that, but could be made into seaworthy dugouts.

Daniel Gookin wrote many descriptions of the Indians of New England. About the dugout canoe, he said *(Gookin: 12)*:

> For their water passage, travels, and fishing, they make boats, or canoes, of great trees, either pine or chestnut, made hollow and artificially; which they do by burning them; and after with tools, scraping, smoothing, shaping them. Of these they make greater or lesser. Some I have seen will carry twenty persons, being forty or fifty feet in length, and as broad as the tree will bear.

Adriaen Van der Donck described the various trees in the land of the Wiechquaeskeck *(vanderDonck: 23)*, and noted about the Tulip tree:

> white-wood trees, which grow very large - the Indians frequently make their canoes of this wood, hence we name it **Canoe-wood**: we use it for flooring because it is bright and free of knots.

George Rockwell, in **The History of Ridgefield, Connecticut** *(40)*, says that a large canoe, twenty feet long, was found in Great Pond in Ridgefield in 1875. It had lain in the mud for at least 100 years, and the bow had rotted off. Since there was no bow left on either end, it would seem reasonable that the original canoe had a graceful and thinly carved bow. A heavy stubby bow would not have been the first part to rot. If it had not been deep in the mud, the whole canoe would have long since rotted away. Some muds are anaerobic, meaning that they have no air and rot does not occur. Unfortunately, this canoe was left to lie on a Connecticut field for people to see, and it has since rotted on dry land.

It is interesting to speculate about how the Wiechquaeskeck got the Ridgefield canoe to Great Pond. It is at the upper limits of the Norwalk River, which is certainly not navigable today. Clearly, the river ran deeper and broader then *(Sect. 2A)*. In three hundred years the ground water level from the melting ice has dropped considerably.

The Making of a Dugout Canoe

Every fall, the Wiechquaeskeck burned the underbrush and small trees to maintain their farming land and to keep their nearby forests open for hunting. Sometimes, they purposely set wild fires to drive deer and other game to a killing point. These fires would have had little effect on taller trees, as the fire would have only singed their bark. Thus, we can picture small groves and some large trees in park-like scenes near the coast, with many corn fields and scattered communities. Within a short distance inland, where there was less soil and more rocks, the forests would often have been denser and continuous. Considering the relatively small population density, there was an adequate number of good tall tulip trees and pine trees, close to the water, with which to make dugouts.

The Wiechquaeskeck could cut down a tree up to six inches in diameter with their stone axes, but they used fire to cut larger trees. They lit a fire around the base of a tree in a controlled burn. They probably had some woven baskets of water standing by to keep the fire burning the way they intended. After a period of burning, they would hack away at the charcoal and weakened wood with their stone axes, until it fell.

The present-day Wampanoag, at their Museum in Mashpee, Cape Cod, have pictured on a mural how they believe the Native Americans controlled the burning of the trees that they felled with fire. They have drawn a picture of a tree with a fat collar of clay and branches, to hold the fire, about six or eight feet above the ground. Figure 16, **Felling a Tree by Burning the Base,** was sketched from this mural. They could have thrown water periodically onto the clay collar and to keep the felling fire from running up the tree and torching it. This seems to portray an ingenious and reasonable explanation.

Once the tree was felled, the Indians cut it into the desired length, again by burning. It was probably mounted horizontally in a fixed position for hollowing and shaping. This process is shown in Figure 17, **Making a Dugout Canoe.** This English drawing was probably first sketched on site, with the artist traveling with an early explorer. The picture shows the log mounted on bars held up by very heavy forked sticks. There is a written reference to the Indian use of cross bars on forked sticks, at least for cooking. Mourt's Relation *(Mourt: 28)* describes the inside of a wigwam from which the Indians had recently fled:

> In the midst of them were four little trunches [*knobbed or forked stakes]* knocked into the ground, and small sticks laid over, on which they hung their pots, and what they had to seethe. *[simmer]*

It would seem reasonable that the Natives would also have mounted the logs on rocks, which would have held them firmly with a minimum of lifting.

They obviously understood the construction of a support as pictured in Figure 17. They were remarkable artisans, as they could burn, scrape, and hollow out a large log into a smooth canoe shape with sides of even thickness. Modern Indians have found that an individual can make a ten-foot dugout in about eight days. These generally do not have well-shaped bows, however. Obviously, a number of people would have worked together on a larger canoe.

Roger Williams made three interesting observations about the dugout canoe *(Williams: 98):*

> Obs. Mishoon, an Indian Boat, or Canow made of Pine or Oake, or Chestnut-tree: I have seene a Native goe into the woods with his hatchet carrying onely a Basket of Corne with him, and stones to strike fire when he had felled his tree (being a Chestnut) he made

Figure 16

Felling a Tree by Burning the Base

A protective collar of clay, seaweed and sticks was put on the trunk

Adapted from a mural at the Mashpee Wampanoag Indian Museum,
Cape Cod, Massachusetts

Figure 17

Making a Dougout Canoe

This is one of a series of views of Algonquian Indians in Virginia, near the Indian town of Pomicoog. They were in a report to Sir Walter Raleigh, who had sent an expedition there in 1584. Engraved by Theodor deBry in his *Grand Voyages*, 1590. Reproduced from the Collections of the Library of Congress, USZ62-52443, 904181.

him a little House or shed of the bark of it, he puts fire and followes the burning of it with fire, in the midst in many places. . . :he boyles and hath the Brook by him, and sometimes angles for a little fish: but so hee continues burning and hewing until he hath within ten or twelve dayes (lying there at his work alone) finished, and (getting handes,) lanched his Boate; with which afterward hee ventures out to fish in the Ocean.

Obs. Their owne reason hath taught them, to pull off a Coat or two and set it up on a small pole, with which they will saile before a wind ten, or twenty mile &c.

It is interesting that the Indians had learned to put up a sail, even if they could only sail "before they wind" because they had no keels or sail trimming methods. It helps explain how the Abenaki very quickly learned to sail European shallops, open boats about 25 feet long, after they were allowed to trade for them. Williams also said:

Obs. It is wonderfull to see how they will venture in those Canoes, and how (being oft overset as I have myselfe been with them) they will swim a mile, yea two or more safe to Land; I have been necessitated to pass Waters diverse times with them, it hath pleased God to make them many times the instruments of my preservation; and when sometimes in great danger I have questioned safety, they have said to me: Feare not, if we be overset I will carry you safe to Land.

There was always the problem of the rotting of Wiechquaeskeck dugout canoes. Connecticut soil is acidic, which favors the bacteria that cause wood to rot when a boat is lying on the shore. A dugout that stayed in salt water would also have rotting problems from teredoes and other shipworms. The Indians learned that they could preserve a dugout for a longer period if they sank it in the mud of a fresh-water lake in the winter. They would take their canoe to a lake with a mud bottom, fill it with large stones, and sink it into the mud for the winter. In the spring, they would dive down the ten or fifteen feet and remove the stones, floating the canoe. This preservation method has been the source of the very few canoes that have been found in lake bottoms in New England, including the canoe that was found in Great Pond. That canoe was either a Wiechquaeskeck or a Tankiteke canoe that had been sunk to the bottom of Great Pond for preservation. The owners may have left the area, or died.

C. THE WHITE-TAILED DEER

The **white-tailed deer** was a supermarket of food and merchandise for the Algonquian Indians. It was a main source of protein, and it supplied a wide array of clothing and household goods. It has been estimated by the Wildlife Management Institute *(22)* that the average yearly per-hunter kill was 10 to 14 whitetails.

The Wiechquaeskeck would use every bit of a whitetail. They would hang a deer up to a tree by its hind legs *(Fig. 19)*, skin it, then carefully dissect it. Some of the uses to which they put the whitetail *(22)* were:

- Deerhide clothing - including leggings, shawls, dresses, breechclouts, moccasins, sashes, shirts, robes, skirts, headwear and mittens. Deerskin was their common fabric.

- Whitetail hide was used to make rugs or blankets, storage bags, pipe pouches, wrist guards, shield covers, quivers, straps, and the ball for a lacrosse game. Thongs, cordage, and bowstrings were made by placing a knife point in the center of a deer-skin and cutting in a spiral pattern outward. The skin thongs were then moistened, twisted, and dried.

- After the hides were carefully removed, using their stone knives, stone scrapers were used to gather the fat on the hide for cooking, usually mixing it with corn meal. The longer hair was taken off with sharp scrapers, then plaited into decorative cords and bands. The leg sinews of the deer were pulled out during the butchering and treated to maintain their flexibility. They made strong cords, and, if long enough, fine bow strings.

- The meat was carved from the bones with their stone tools. Some of it was roasted, some pieces went into the corn meal porridge, and some was dried as pemmican. Pemmican was lean meat, dried, pounded fine, and mixed with melted fat, for eating on the trail.

- The internal organs were sorted. Some were stewed, stomachs were used as bags, and scraps were fed to the dogs. The entrails were also used as cordage.

- They had found that the brains made an excellent tanning agent. The deer's hide would be stretched between poles, the deer's brains would be rubbed all over it, and left to do the tanning. The messy job of tanning whitetail skins was part of the women's responsibilities.

- The antlers were used as gardening tools, with horn pieces lashed to a pole. Parts were used as handles to hold sharp stone tools. Sharpened pieces were used as the heads of war clubs. Smaller pieces were cut into fish hooks for large fish, or for lobster spears. They were also used for decorations, both hanging in the wigwam or worn. Sometimes, they wore antlers on their head with a deer skin, as camouflage when hunting. Occasionally, they were used as a dramatic headdress. We have learned of the many uses of the antlers from archaeological studies and from old pictures.

- Young men would fasten the tail, or "flag" of the whitetail in a headband as an upright adornment, or roach. Women used them to make a brush.

- Whitetail bones were of great utility to the Indians. The large bones were cracked open for the marrow. Many peoples, very early in the history of the human race, had discovered that marrow was a special food. Also, from the cracking open of the bones, they got sharp pieces that could be used as needles of all sizes, tools to engrave pottery, fishhooks, and projectile points for small game.

- Leg bones were used as digging sticks. Scapulas (shoulder blades) were used as hoes. They were also used as a noisemaker. Women and children would beat on a wide scapula bone with another bone to help drive deer into pounds (Fig. 18). Also, the scapula was pierced, attached to a buckskin thong, then twirled as a "bull roar" to send signals.

- They found that the various glands of animals could be ascribed medicinal properties, whether they worked or not. A famous export in early America, in the Wiechquaeskeck area, was the castor gland of the beaver

(Castor), which was used as a perfume ingredient. Deer had large glands, and some were good for musky perfumes also.

- They had learned that boiled horn and hooves made an excellent glue. (Similar glues were also widely used by Europeans making furniture up to the 1940s, when better synthetic glues began to be developed.)

- The two hooves on each foot and the dewclaws were carveable, and they were made into ceremonial rattles or decorative pieces.

This utilization list could be extended. No other animal provided the Wiechquaeskeck with such a larder and treasure house. It was not surprising that when they moved back into the woods for the deer hunt in the fall, whole families would go along for the great seasonal harvest. Only the elderly, and the women with babies, would stay behind in their coastal villages.

Early Reports about Deer and the Indians

Jacob Frederick Stam, one of the earliest European reporters, wrote in 1635 *(Stam)* that they had:

> Coats of deer skins, otters, beaver, racoon & bear . . . dressed and converted into good leather with the hair on. . . . If anyone comes into their house they will spread a mat & skins & let him lye.

Thomas Morton writes from the same sources as Jacob Stam, with some different wording. He says in **New English Canaan** *(Morton: 20):*

> . . . and Coates of Deares skinnes . . . which they have dressed and converted into good lether with the haire on for their coverings and in this manner they lye as warme as they desire in the night . . . Nay if any one, that shall come into their houses . . . they will spreade a matt for him . . . and lay a roule of skinnes for a boulster, and let him lye.

Edward Johnson, writing in the year 1633 *(Johnson: 56),* says what the settlers did when they found the cleared Indian land:

> . . . they inclose Corne fields, the Lord having mitigated their labours by the Indians frequent fiering of the woods, (that they may not be hindered in hunting Venson, and Beares in the Winter

season which makes them thin of Timber in many places, like our Parkes in England.

Adriaen van der Donck wrote many details about the Wiechquaeskeck region *(VanderDonck: 17)*. Some of his comments were:

Here our attention is arrested in the beautiful landscape around us. . . . here also the huntsman is animated when he views the enchanting prospects presented to the eyes; on the hills, at the brooks and in the valleys, where the game abounds and where the deer are feeding, or gamboling or resting in the shades in full view.

Buffaloes are also tolerably plenty . . . Their meat is . . . more desirable than the flesh of the deer . . . The deer are incredibly numerous in the country. Although the Indians throughout the year and every year (but mostly in the fall) kill many thousands, and the wolves, after the fawns are cast, and while they are young, also destroy many, still the land abounds with them everywhere, and their numbers appear to remain undiminished. We seldom pass through the fields without seeing deer more or less, and we frequently see them in flocks. The meat digests easily and is good food. Venison is so easily obtained that a good buck cashes for five guilders, and often for much less. *(ibid.: 45)*

There are also white bucks and does, and others of a black colour in the country. The Indians aver that the haunts of the white deer are much frequented by the common deer. *(ibid.: 46)*

Van der Donck also describes large moose and elk further back in the interior of the country not far from the Wiechquaeskeck area. He said *(vanderDonck: 63)*: "Wolves are numerous in the country, but these are not so large and ravenous as the Netherlands wolves are." He also said:

The autumns . . . the woods are now burnt over . . . This is also the Indian hunting season, wherein such great numbers of deer are killed, that a person who is uninformed of the vast extent of the country, would imagine that all these animals would be destroyed in a short time. *[but]* . . no diminution of the deer is observable. The Indians also affirm, that before the arrival of the Christians, and before the small pox broke out amongst them, they were ten times as numerous as they now are . . . then . . . many more deer were killed than there now are, without any perceptible decrease in their numbers. *(ibid.: 64)*

Their Methods of Hunting Deer

The Eastern Woodland Indians are traditionally identified with stalking the whitetail. They did stalk deer, but stalking required more time and energy than most Indians could afford. More effective methods were necessary for the well-being of the hunter and his tribe. Communal hunting methods, which resulted in kills of large numbers of deer on a single occasion, far outweighed lone hunting in importance to tribal subsistence *(22)*. Hunting, for the Indians, was a difficult necessary activity, and not a sport.

Deer were hunted year-round with arrows and traps, but the communal hunting for the Wiechqueaskeck was in the fall, when the deer were in their prime, and were gathered in herds. Summer farming and fishing were over, and the leaves were off the trees, and dry. One of their most successful hunting methods was the **fire drive** *(Johnson: 55)*. Not only was the autumn fire drive productive, but it cleared the vines and vegetation in an area and prepared it for farming the next year *(22)*. In such a drive, the better hunters would wait with their arrows and spears at the natural escape end of the burn. Other hunters, women, and children would go the far side of the woods and set fire to it. They would also run around and make a noise. The animals would flee before the fire, then be killed when they emerged from the woods.

The Wiechquaeskeck hunted deer by several methods, including arrows, spears, snares, pursuing them when swimming across lakes, setting fire to woods, and using large entrapments, or pounds. One of the earliest records of their ingenuity was written about Pilgrim experiences in 1620 in *Mourt's Relation (Mourt: 23):*

> As we wandered we came to a tree, where a young sprit *[sapling]* was bowed down over a bow, and some acorns strewed underneath. Stephen Hopkins said it had been to catch some deer. So as we were looking at it, William Bradford being in the rear, when he came looked also upon it, and as he went about, it gave a sudden jerk up, and he was immediately caught by the leg. It was a very pretty device, made with a rope of their own making and having a noose as artificially *[artfully]* made as any roper in England can make, and as like ours as can be, which we brought away with us.

Rogers Williams actually went on hunts with the Narrangansett, and describes what he saw *(Williams: 141)*. (We can assume that the Wiechquaeskeck hunted similarly to the Narragansett):

The Natives hunt two wayes: First, when they pursue their game (especially Deere . .) I say, they pursue in twentie, fortie, fiftie yea, two or three hundred in a company, (as I have seene) when they drive the woods before them. Secondly, they hunt by Traps of severall sorts . . . in spring time and Summer . . . they goe ten or twentie together, and sometimes more, and withall, if it be not too farre, wives and children also, where they build up little hunting houses of Barks and Rushes (comparable to their dwelling houses) and so each man takes his bounds of two, three, or foure miles, where he sets thirty, forty or fiftie Traps, and baits his Traps with that food the Deere loves, and once in two days he walkes his round to view his Traps.

Their hunting methods and the entrapment of deer by the use of palisade enclosures are described by two observers. These are illustrated in Figure 18, **Deer Hunting.** Adriaen van der Donck writes *(vanderDonck: 96)*:

To hunting and fishing the Indians are all extravagantly inclined, and they have their particular seasons for these engagements. . . Near the seashores and rivers . . . they hunt deer, where many are killed. Those are mostly caught in snares, they also shoot them with arrows and guns. The Indians sometimes unite in companies of from one to two hundred when they have a rare sport. On those occasions they drive over a large district of land and kill much game. They also make extensive fikes *(pounds or enclosures)* with palisades, which are narrow at their terminating angles, wherein they drive multitudes of animals and take great numbers. At a word, they are expert hunters for every kind of game, and know how to practice the best methods to ensure success. . . . There are some persons who imagine that the animals of the country will be destroyed in time, but this is unnecessary anxiety.

David de Vries describes their deer hunting methods, *(deVries: 220),* and the use of a deer pound, which he calls a *fuyk.* (Actually, a Dutch fuyk is a form of net, large at the entrance and terminating in a snare. It is an apt name for a deer pound.):

There are great quantities of harts and hinds, which the savages shoot with their bows and arrows, or make a general hunt of, a hundred more or less joining in the hunt. They stand a hundred paces more or less from each other, and holding flat thigh-bones in the hand, beat them with a stick, and so drive the creatures before them to the river. As they approach the river, they close nearer to each other, and whatever is between any two of them, is at the mercy of their bows and arrows, or must take to the river. When the animals swim into the river, the savages lie in their canoes with

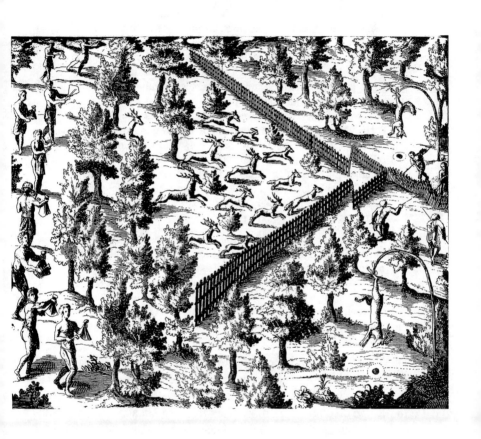

Figure 18

Deer Hunting

This picture of deer hunting using a pound *(fuyk)* and snares is an engraving from *Les Voyages du Sieur de Champlain* by Samuel de Champlain (Paris, 1613) F1030.1.C446.R3. From the Collections of the Library of Congress, Rare Book and Special Collections Division, , USZ62-116707.

lassos, which they throw around their necks, and tighten, whereupon the deer lie down and float with the rump upwards, as they canot draw breath. At the north, they drive them into a fuyk, which they make of palisades split out of trees, and eight or nine feet high, and set close to each other, for a distance of fourteen or fifteen hundred paces on both sides, coming together like a fuyk, as is shown in the plates *[Fig. 18]:* the opening is one or two thousand paces wide. When the animal is within the palisades, the savages begin to become nearer to each other, and pursue it with great ardor, as they regard deer-hunting the noblest hunting. At the end of the fuyk it is so narrow that it is only five feet wide, like a large door, and it is there covered with the boughs of trees, into which the deer or animal runs, closely pursued by the savages, who make a noise as if they were wolves, by which many deer are devoured, and of which they are in great fear. This causes then to run into the mouth of the fuyk with great force, whither the Indians pursue them furiously with bows and arrows, and from whence they cannot escape; they are then easily caught. They also catch them with snares, as may be seen in the plate.

There are elks, chiefly in the mountains; also hares, but they are not larger than the rabbits in Holland; foxes in abundance, multitudes of wolves, wild cats, squirrels - black as pitch, and gray, also flying squirrels - beavers in great numbers, minks, otter, pole-cats, bears, and many kinds of fur-bearing animals, which I cannot name or think of. The savages understand the preparing of deer-skins, of which they make shoes and stockings, after their fashion, for the winter.

The Wiechquaeskeck maintained a large deer pound in what is now Ward Pound Ridge Reservation in Westchester County, New York. It was in a sharp valley on the southeastern side of the Reservation in the Pound Ridge area about six miles from Bedford Village. The palisades were erected along the steep hills. They were so sturdy that they were still used by the settlers for penning cattle in the eighteenth century.

David de Vries said that the *fuyk* was "at the north" from New Amsterdam. There were many dozens of Indian deer pounds scattered throughout Westchester and southwestern Connecticut. We only know the location of a few of the deer pounds today. The one in Ward Pound Ridge Reservation was well known because it was still being used after the settlers arrived. Just south of it, there is a Pound Ridge in New Canaan, which must have been the location of another one. In Greenwich, there is a "Double Pound Ridge" off Round Hill Road, between it and Buckfield Lane. That means that there were two locations with steep rock walls that facilitated the building of the palisades to entrap the deer. In Greenwich, there is also a "Pound Ridge Brook" east of Lake Avenue, near Lower Cross Road beside Lynche's Ridge. The Wiechquaeskeck needed deer, and we can assume that they built many deer pounds where the local topography allowed them to erect a palisaded funnel.

Preparing the Deer Skins

The Indian men did most of the deer stalking, hunting, and killing, as only they handled the bows and arrows. They also carried the deer back to the camps where they hung the deer up by its hind legs. Figure 19, **Butchering Deer,** is a facsimile of the corner of a map in the Library of Congress. It was published by "the Office of the Chief of Engineers U.S. Army 1876." It says the map was printed in 1635, which would indicate a copy of a Blaeu map. The figure shows hunters, and some deer hanging for butchering. in the background. A woman is skinning a deer in the foreground. Another man has a tied bundle, probably of beaver skins, wrapped in a deer hide for shipping. There is also a fine drawing of a "beaked" canoe, showing that the beak was integral, and that the canoe had thin sides. The figure shows hunters, and some deer hanging ready for butchering. in the background. The deer shown are small to medium in size; and many, after gutting, could be carried by a single man *(Fig. 27)*.

If the skin was to be used for clothing, the deer hair was removed when the deer was hanging up. It was scraped off with sharpened clam shells. Later, the hair was woven into decorative cords. If the skin was to be used for blankets, the hair was not removed.

Fresh deer meat did not keep well. It had to be eaten during the hunt or soon afterwards, or dried into pemmican for the winter. Internal organs were eaten the day the animal was killed. The women had to sort through the organs to get the parts that were delicacies, and those useful for cords and containers.

The women also did the tanning of the deer skins. After the hair was removed on one side, all the fat had to be scraped off the other side and kept for either cooking or painting. The hide was stretched on crude wooden frames, using thongs, for the tanning. Tanning is a chemical process to make the leather soft, supple, and resistant to decay.

Figure 19
Butchering Deer

An illumination on an early map, *Novi Belgii quod nunc Novi Jorck vocatur Novae Angliae & Partis Virginiae*, drawn by Arnoldus Montanus, probably from the Willem Janszoon Blaeu map of 1635. It was published by the Chief of Engineers, U.S. Army, in 1876. From the Collections of the Library of Congress, Geography and Maps Division.

Europeans had found the most effective natural tanning agents to be in the barks and roots of willow trees, and certain salts. Some Native Americans used boiled bark to make colors, and found they had more effective tanning materials at the same time. We do not know if the Wiechquaeskeck had discovered the European method of using willow bark, but it is likely they had. It is fairly certain that they used deer brains for tanning.

Deer brains, when boiled, were a very effective tanning agent, although somewhat messy. The liquid mixture would have been hand rubbed onto the stretched hide. After a period of time, it had to be cleaned off. More than one application would have been necessary. They knew that the resulting soft warm skin was well worth the effort.

The Wildlife Management Institute Research

The Wildlife Management Institute is a private scientific and educational organization based in Washington, DC. Its objective is to help advance restoration and proper management of North America's natural resources. It published a major research study entitled **White-Tailed Deer: Ecology and Management** *(22)*. Some of the information in the Historical Retrospection section of the book applies directly to the Wiechquaeskeck. They point out, however, that there were tremendous cultural and economic differences among aboriginal groups within the vast range of the white-tailed deer. A few of their findings that are applicable to the Wiechquaeskeck have been noted.

When Europeans reached the "New World," the whitetail's greatest abundance occurred in the open lands along the eastern seabord. They preferred the forest edges, upland glades, and riverine woodlands. Each year, the Natives intentionally fired thousands of square miles in the range of the whitetails. This prompted vegetation attractive to the deer, and thus helped to sustain the deer population. The first colonists to settle in Maryland in 1634 included Roman Catholic priest Father Andrew White, who observed whitetails so plentiful "that they are rather an annoyance than an advantage."

Recent analytical studies of deer populations in the Contact Period have arrived at estimates of about 8 to 11 per square mile *(22)*. This is only an average for large areas of the country. That would have been a low estimate for western Connecticut and Westchester County, which were ideal for deer subsistence, with plentiful grazing and water.

Deer were a source of meat for the Wiechquaeskeck in the winter, together with beaver, black bear, bison, and occasionally moose and elk, when they were available. In the summer, the Wiechquaeskeck had unlimited supplies of fish, other seafood, ducks, and geese for their protein. Great flocks of passenger pigeons came through their area also, and were easily harvested. In an archaeological study in West Virginia, it was determined that there the whitetail accounted for 89.2 percent of all animal food (22). It would have been a somewhat lower percentage for the Wiechquaeskeck, who ate considerable seafood.

D. INDIAN CORN (MAIZE)

Corn (maize), beans, squash, pumpkins and probably sunflower seeds, were staple foods of the Wiechquaeskeck. Their economy was partly agricultural in the 16th and 17th centuries. They relied heavily on the fruits of their gardens, and their women did most of the work in the fields.

There are stories about the Pilgrims facing hard winters in 1620 and 1621, with little food. They had insufficient English grain seeds for planting, and their imported strains were marginally useful at first. Many Pilgrims died. The colony may well have been wiped out, if they had not found stores of Native corn, beans, and squash, left by the Indians who had died in their wigwams, or had fled before the plagues of smallpox. Even on the first reconnaisance by Standish, before the Plymouth Rock landing, the Pilgrims had already found Indian stores of corn and beans in large woven baskets in the ground. The Pilgrims used the Native supplies as seed corn in 1621. The Wiechquaeskeck worked with the same horticultural methods as did the Wampanoag of Plymouth.

Early Reports of Native Horticulture

The earliest reports of Wiechquaeskeck horticulture are in the writings of Samuel Purchase, who was on Henry Hudson's ship when it anchored several times near Westchester (Purchas: 592-595). He described the Wiechquaeskeck coming to the ship with "green Tabacco," and said that,

"They have great store of Maiz or Indian Wheate," and that they brought "Beanes and Pompions" (pumpkins). One small boat that was sent out from the ship reported that, "The Lands were as pleasant with Grasse and Flowers, and goodly Trees, as ever they had seene, and very sweet smells came from them."

William Bradford wrote about Standish looking for a site for the Pilgrims to settle in 1620 *(Bradford 2: 73):*

> . . . marched to this supposed river, and by the way found a pond *[Pond Village, Truro]* of clear, fresh water, and shortly after a good quantity of clear ground where the Indians had formerly set corn . . . further they saw new stubble where corn had been set the same year. . . and heaps of new sand paddled with hands. Which, they digging up, found in them divers fair Indian baskets filled with corn, and some in ears, fair and good, of divers colours, which seemed to them a very goodly sight . . . took with them part of the corn and buried up the rest. And so, like the men from Eshcol who carried with them of the fruits of the land and showed their brethren . . . they were marvelously glad and their hearts encouraged.

"The men from Eschol" (Numbers 13: 23-26) were Joshua and his men who spied out the land of Israel for Moses. They brought back to the wandering Israelites a large bunch of grapes, some pomegranates, and figs to show how fruitful the land was.

> Also there was found more of their corn and of their beans of various colours; the corn and beans they brought away, purposing to give them full satisfaction when they should meet with any of them as about six months afterwards they did, to their good content. . . here they got seed to plant them corn the next year, or else they might have starved. *(Bradford2: 74)*

The only contemporary authority for the "Landing of the Pilgrims on Plymouth Rock" on Monday, December 21, 1620 describes the reconnaisance party sailing in a shallop from Cape Cod *(Bradford 2: 79):* "On Monday they sounded the harbour and found it fit for shipping, and marched into the land and found divers cornfields and little running brooks, a place fit for situation."

Mourt's Relation, A Journal of the Pilgrims at Plymouth gives a description very similar to Bradford's. It said *(Mourt: 21):*

> . . . found much plain ground, about fifty acres, fit for the plow, and some signs where the Indians had formerly planted their corn. . . found new stubble of which they had gotten corn this year. . . dig-

ged further and found a fine great new basket full of very fair corn of this year, with some thirty-six goodly ears of corn, some yellow, and some red, and others mixed with blue, which was a very goodly sight. The basket was round, and narrow at the top; it held about three or four bushels, which was as much as two of us could lift up from the ground, and was very handsomely and cunningly made.

Note that Mourt says "about fifty acres" of cleared ground. That was a sizable area for agriculture. In Greenwich, if an observer had described the Wiechquaeskeck corn growing on Strickland Plains (Cos Cob) the estimate would very likely also have been fifty acres. The same estimate would also have applied to the Stamford cornfields near Westcott Cove.

Both writers indicate that some of the land had been planted that year and some had lain fallow. It is possible that the Indians had discovered the advantages of crop rotation, leaving some land fallow each year. On the other hand, the Wampanoag in that area had been hit hard by smallpox, and it may have been that land was fallow because fewer people were planting.

The Native baskets that held the corn in holes in the ground, or in the wigwams, were well made. They wove wide strips of ash or elm, or coiled strips of fibers, that were sometimes close enough together to hold liquid. A four-bushel basket would be about thirty inches in diameter and twenty inches high with a narrow neck, to more easily close with a lid.

Roger Williams gave us several descriptions of Native agriculture applicable to the Wiechquaeskeck. He tells about the corn meal they took when traveling *(Williams: 5)*:

Nokehik, Parch'd meal, which is a readie very wholesome food, which they eate with a little water, hot or cold; I have travelled with neere 200 of them at once, neere 100 miles through the woods, every man carrying a little Basket of this at his back, and sometimes in a hollow Leather Gridle about his middle, sufficient for a man for three or four daies.

With this readie provision, and their Bow and Arrowes, they are ready for War, and travel at an houres warning. With a spoonfull of this meale, and a spoonfull of Water from the Brooke, have I made many a good dinner and supper.

Williams also makes an observation about the planting of the corn: *(Williams: 92)*:

Obs. The Women set or plant, weede, and hill, and gather and barne all the corne and Fruits of the Field: yet sometimes the man himselfe, (out of either love to his Wife, or care for his Children, or being an old man) will help the Woman which (by the custome of the Countrey) they are not bound to. *[see Fig. 20, Cultivating Corn with a Stone Hoe]*

When a field is to be broken up, they have a very loving sociable speedy way to dispatch it. All the neighbours men and Women forty, fifty, a hundred, &c. joyne, and come in to helpe freely. With friendly joyning they breake up their fields, build their Forts, hunt the woods, stop and kill fish in the Rivers, it being true with them as in all the World in the Affaires of Earth or Heaven: by concord little things grow great, by discord the greatest come to nothing.

Roger Williams traveled and ate with the Narrangansett for weeks at a time, and he describes many foods. *(Williams: 90ff)*:

Obs. The Indians have an Art of drying their chestnuts, and so to preserve them in their barnes for a daintie all the yeare.

These Akornes also they drie, and in case of want of Corne, by much boyling they make a good dish of them.

Of these Wallnuts they make an excellent Oyle good for many uses, but especially for their anoynting of their heads.

This *[Strawberry]* is the wonder of all the Fruits growing naturally in these parts: it is of itself Excellent. . . The Indians bruise them in a Morter, and mixe them with meale and make Strawberry bread.

. . . these Currants dried by the Natives, and so preserved all the yeare, which they beat to powder, and mingle it with their parcht meale, and make a delicious dish.

Obs. There be divers sorts of this Corne, and of the colours.

The Indian women to this day (notwithstanding our Howes) doe use their naturall Howes of shells and Wood.

Askutasquash, their Vine apple - Which the English from them call Squashes about the bignesse of Apples of severall colours, a sweet, light, wholesome, refreshing.

Henry David Thoreau made a study of early Native American use of wild fruits and seeds. His book, **Wild Fruits** *(48)*, was recently reprinted. He found records of widespread Algonquian use of all types of blueberries *(Vaccinium),* huckleberries *(Andromeda),* and other berries He quotes Champlain, Josselyn, Williams, Wood, and others. He said that one version of the United Brethren Narratives *(Heckewelder)* reported, "strawberries grow so large and in such abundance, that whole plains are covered with them as with a fine scarlet cloth."

He noted that Roger Williams *(Williams)* said:

> In some parts, where the natives have planted, I have many times seen as many [strawberries] as would fill a good ship…The Indians bruise them in a moartar, and mix then with [corn] meal, and make strawberry bread.

He also quoted Champlain, writing in 1609:

> The natives make a kind of bread of pounded corn sifted and mixed with mashed beans which have been boiled – and sometimes they put dried blueberries and raspberries into it.

Thoreau said that this was probably the first account of huckleberry cake, which later became a favorite of the Pilgrims.

The Indian Use of Fertilizer

Fertilizers were in general use throughout the world in the 17th century, but little was understood about how they worked. The Pilgrims were given a practical lesson in the use of fertilizers by Squanto, an Indian in the New World who had learned English. He was evidently more advanced than they were in the process. The sandy soils of Massachusetts were poor for farming unless fertilizers were used. The Native Americans had figured this out. They had learned about the fertilizing capabilities of both fish scraps and wood ashes simply by observation. The chemicals in these products, nitrogen, phosphorus, and potassium are the main ingredients in most of our fertilizers today.

The first information about Indian fertilizers that we have is the story of Squanto at Plymouth. William Bradford *(Bradford1: 114)* wrote about Squanto, "a native of this place, who had been in England & could speake better English than" the friendly Samoset. The Natives arrived in Plymouth about March, 1621 with "their great Sachem, called Massasoyt," and "made a peace of friendship." The Pilgrims had gone through a hard winter, and "many lay sick & weake," so they were pleased to get help from the Indians. Then, in April *(Bradford1: 121)*:

> Afterwards they . . . began to plant ther corne, in which servise Squanto stood them in great stead, showing them both ye maner how to set it, and after how to dress & tend it. Also he tould them excepte they gott fish & set with it (in these old grounds) it would

come to nothing, and he showed then yt in ye middle of Aprill . . .
and taught them how to take it.

Edward Johnson also writes in New England in 1636 *(Johnson: 83)*:

> But the Lord is pleased to provide them with a great store of Fish in
> the spring time, and especially alewives about the bignesse of a
> Herring, many thousands of these, they used to put under their
> Indian Corne, which they plant in Hills five foote asunder, and
> assuredly when the Lorde created this Corne, hee had a speciall eye
> to supply these his peoples wants with it, for ordinarily five or six
> graines doth produce six hundred.

It is reasonable to think that the Wiechquaeskeck also knew about the
advantages of putting a fish under each mound of corn seed, just as did
their fellow Algonquians, the Wampanoag. Early colonists used fish
products and seaweed in their gardens throughout New England. They
had used seaweed in England. (It is interesting that, if you go to a florist
today, you will find many bottles of liquid fish fertilizer that are highly
recommended.) Fish make good fertilizer, and the Wiechquaeskeck were
observant.

Fertilizers are defined as materials that increase the productivity of
plants. Samuel Aldrich *(1)* points out that, even with attempts at growing
plants, fertilizers can mean the difference between plenty and starvation.
The Woodland Indians had reasonable growing weather, soil, and plenty
of water. Their garden plots were on rough ground; and the soil was
acid, so fertilizers were important to their success. Aldrich notes that, in
many countries, farmers keep moving to new land rather than fertilizing
the used land. The Algonquian-speaking tribes seem to have learned how
to keep their lands fertile. Their major villages stayed in place for many
years.

The size of Indian shell middens, or piles of shells, is one indication as
to how long coastal camping and agricultural sites were used. Shells
were of particular importance in Connecticut, because the soil is generally
acidic, from the underlying siliceous rock, and needs the calcium from
shells to make it sweet for farming. There is little doubt that this became
obvious to the Natives. They knew that shells were beneficial, simply
because of observation over the centuries. We do not know how often
the Wiechquaeskeck moved their summer farming and fishing camps,
although some of the shell middens were of large size in Norwalk
(ARCH10), indicating that they were used for a great many years. An
agricultural area with fish, ashes, and shells available could have been

continuously farmed for generations. Whether they knew what was happening or not, they profited from the presence of the shells. Road building and construction have destroyed most of the Native shell heaps, or middens, in southwestern Connecticut, even in the Norwalk wetlands.

We can assume that the Wiechquaeskeck learned something about crop rotation and the use of fertilizers, as did other tribes in America, by the diffusion process. The Meso-Americans (Mexico and Central America) had developed quite efficient agriculture to support their large cities. Everyone in the ancient world seemed to have learned that the growing of legumes (such as beans) and the use of ashes are both beneficial to the soil.

The Wiechquaeskeck must also have learned, again by observation, that manure and ashes were good fertilizers. This fact is obvious to farmers. Manure is a supplier of nitrogen. Fish supplied both nitrogen and phosphorus. They would also have found that plants grew better where ashes had been strewn. Scientists know that ashes contain the necessary element, potassium, which gets its name from "pot ashes" or the ashes from cooking fires. The Wiechquaeskeck cleared their lands by burning the trees and underbrush. The ashes from the burning provided the needed potassium. Each year they would burn away the weeds, vines, and shrubs that had grown, putting even more fertilizer on the soil.

The Wiechquaeskeck had also learned, again probably by diffusion from Mexico, that it is helpful to plant beans in the same mound as the corn. This was not just to give a good stake for the beans to climb on. The roots of beans "fix" nitrogen from the air and make available another necessary element for plant growth. The Indians did not know the technical details. They just knew that the process worked.

Adraien van der Donck *(vanderDonck: 71)* described this procedure:

> They have a peculiar mode of planting them, which our people have learned to practice:- when the Turkish wheat *[Indian corn]* or, as it is called, maize, is half a foot above the ground, they plant the beans around it, and let them grow together. The coarse stalk serves as a bean-prop, and the beans run upon it. They increase together and thrive extremely well, and thus two crops are gathered at the same time.

Van der Donck probably did not understand about the nitrogen-fixing ability of the beans, but he saw that the whole process worked very well. It is technically called "intercropping," and it served the Indians because the hills of corn with several other vegetables, such as beans, squash, and pumpkins made the cultivation easier for women using their heavy stone hoes.

Early Reports of Wiechquaeskeck Horticulture

Thus the Wiechquaeskeck were advanced in their horticulture, for the 17th century. They tilled large plots, and hilled the corn and beans together. They hoed and weeded regularly. They used fish, wood ashes, manure, shells, and organic materials as fertilizer in their gardens. This gave them well-balanced fertilization, and nutritious vegetables. The results would have been irregular for them, but almost as good as we can get from the bags of granular fertilizer that we purchase today. With their women working hard at hilling the corn, hoeing, and weeding, their corn grew high with good ears. They stored their produce in tight baskets buried in sandy soil for the winter.

Figure 27, **The Wiechquaeskeck Village at Indian Field, Greenwich**, includes a corn field near a camp, with small huts in which children and old men would sit, and drive away crows and blackbirds. This field is specifically mentioned in the Feb.1, 1686 land transfer of the Horseneck Plantation (Greenwich), because the remaining 30 acres of "planting land" could support the dwindling band. A corn and bean field was an integral part of a Wiechquaeskeck camp. The Indian Field camp was about 30 acres, and the nearby Petaquapen planting fields were probably well over 50 acres, scattered all the way to Betuckquapock (North Mianus).

Figure 20, **Cultivating Corn with a Stone Hoe**, is an artist's conception of a Native woman at work in her band's fields. The drawing is by Monte Crews and Kenneth Phillips and is part of Dorothy Cross' portfolio, **The Indians of New Jersey**, which depicts the Lenape Indians of the 17th century (Courtesy of New Jersey State Museum). The woman is young, with her papoose strapped in a basket and hung on a tree branch, but she is aging fast with the incessant work. She is using a stone hoe *(compare with Fig. 41)* that is hafted with leather thongs to a branch handle. The corn is planted on hills in reasonably straight rows, depending on the rocks and stumps.

Figure 20

Cultivating Corn with a Stone Hoe

Original drawings by Monte Crews and Kenneth Phillips from "The Indians of New Jersey PORTFOLIO OF PRINTS." Courtesy of the New Jersey State Museum, Trenton, NJ.

The efficient corn farming methods of the Wiechquaeskeck impressed the early Dutch settlers. Isaack de Rasieres wrote in 1628 *(deRasieres: 103)*:

> . . . savages . . . support themselves by planting maize.
>
> At the end of March they begin to break up the earth with mattocks . . . They make heaps like molehills, each about two and a half feet from the others, which they sow or plant in April with maize, in each heap five or six grains; in the middle of May, when the maize is the height of a finger or more, they plant in each heap three or four Turkish beans, which they grow up with and against the maize, which serves for props, for the maize grows on stalks similar to the sugar cane. It is a grain to which much labor must be given, with weeding and earthing-up, or it does not thrive; and to this the women must attend to very closely. The men would not once look at it, for it would compromise their dignity too much unless they are very old and cannot follow the chase. Those stalks which are low and bear no ears, they pluck up in August, and suck out the sap, which is as sweet as if it were sugar cane. When they wish to make use of the grain for bread or porridge, which they call Sappaen, they first boil it then beat it flat upon a stone; then they put it into a wooden mortar, which they know how to hollow out by fire, and then they have a stone pestle . . . with which they pound it small, and sift it through a small basket . . . of the rushes.

De Rasieres described how the Native women cooked the corn *(deRasieres: 107)*:

> The finest meal they mix with lukewarm water, and knead it into dough, then they make round flat little cakes of it, of the thickness of an inch or a little more, which they bury in hot ashes, and so bake into bread; and when they are baked they have some clean fresh water by them in which they wash them when hot, one after another, and it is good bread, but heavy. The coarsest meal they boil into a porridge . . . and it is good eating . . . very soon digested. The grain being dried, they put it into baskets woven of rushes or wild hemp, and bury it in the earth, where they let it lie, and go with their husbands and their children in October to hunt deer, leaving at home with their maize the old people who cannot follow; in December they return home, and the flesh which they have not been able to eat while fresh, they smoke on the way, and bring it back with them. They come home as fat as moles.

Thoreau, about 1860 *(48:44-52)*, glowingly described the Indian use of "whortleberries" in Indian cooking. With whortleberries, he included several varieties of blueberries *(Vaccinium)* and huckleberries

(Gaylussacia). He noted that the berry bushes in the area are "sort of minature forest surviving under the great forest," and became very prolific when the forest was cleared by burning. The berries were heavily used by all Algonquian people. He quoted Champlain, from 1615, who observed that the Indians collected and dried them for winter use. "They made a kind of bread of pounded corn sifted and mixed with mashed beans which have been boiled – and sometimes put dried blueberries and raspberries into it." This sounds just like the tasty huckleberry cake that the Pilgrims learned to make 100 years later. Thoreau noted that Roger Williams described a similar recipe in 1643.

Johan de Laet, in 1633 *(deLaet: 54)*, was impressed with the nature of the climate and soil in New Netherland. He wrote:

> . . . when cultivated with the labor and industry of man, maize or Indian corn, for example, yields a prolific return. So with various kinds of puls, especially beans, which have an admirable variety of colours; pumpkins of the finest species, melons and similar fruits of a useful character; so that nothing is wanting but human industry.

(De Laet did not mention that most of the "human industry" among the Natives for horticulture came from the Indian women!) De Laet also quoted "Hendrick Hudson," saying that: "Their food is Turkish wheat *[maize]* which they cook by baking, and it is excellent eating."

Pulse, from the Latin *puls*, is often reported by the colonists. It refers to either the edible seeds of leguminous plants, or to the porridge (Indian *sapaen*) made from them. These "pulse" plants with seed pods include peas, beans, lentils, etc.

Van der Donck *(vanderDonck: 68)* describes the successful vegetables grown by the Dutch settlers, and adds:

> The natives have another species of (pumpkin) peculiar to themselves, called by our people *quaasiens,* a name derived from the aborigines, as the plant was not known to us before our intercourse with them. It is a delightful fruit, as well as to the eye because of its fine variety of colours, as to the mouth for its agreeable taste. . . when it is planted in the middle of April, the fruit is fit for eating by the first of June. . . They gather the squashes and immediately place them on the fire . . . The natives make great account of this vegetable. It grows rapidly, is easily cooked, and digests well in the stomach, and its flavour and nutritive properties are respectable.

Roger Williams *(Williams: 93)* described the same plant as:

> *Askutasquash*, their vine-apples, which the English from them call
> *squashes*; about the bigness of apples, of several colours, a sweet,
> light, wholesome refreshing

Samuel Purchas *(Purchas: 592)* recorded the voyage of Henry Hudson. He described a mixed reception from the Wiechquaeskeck and Manhattan Indians, sometimes friendly and sometimes fighting, and was impressed with the bounty of the country. He said:

> They have great store of Maiz or Indian Wheate, whereof they make
> good Bread. The country is full of great and tall Oakes...and some
> Currants... The people came aboard us, and brought Tobacco and
> Indian Wheat, to exchange for Knives and Bread...and brought us
> ears of Indian Corne, and Pompions [pumpkins] and Tabacco;
> which wee bought for trifles.

Van der Donck also describes the melons growing large and very abundantly, up to seventeen pounds in weight, growing in newly cleared woodland, and the water citron (watermelon), with very sweet juice, "the size of a man's head." He said, "it melts when it enters the mouth, and nothing is left but the seeds." He said that it was "a fruit that we have not in the Netherlands." It is unlikely, however, that these watermelons were native plants in America. The Natives grew a great variety of small squash and pumpkins. The melons and "water citron" were probably brought from the Mediterranean by Portuguese traders. They were then grown by the settlers rather than by the Indians, but the Wiechquaeskeck could have traded very early for some of them. They were another indication of the international aspect of the port of New Amsterdam (New York) early in the 17th century.

The Story of Indian Corn in the Northeast

Indian corn (maize), beans, and squash were not native to northeastern America. They had been brought from southwestern America and Meso-America (central Mexico to Nicaragua in pre-Columbian times) *(15, 18, 25, 36)*, over many centuries, by the process of diffusion. It is interesting that the tribal memory of the Wiechquaeskeck included something about this history. Van der Donck *(vanderDonck: 4)* said:

> ... the Indians ... say that their corn and beans were received from
> the southern Indians, who received their seed from a people who

> resided still farther south . . . The maize may have been among the
> Indians in the warm climate long ago.

> . . . our Indians say that they did eat roots and the bark of trees in-
> stead of bread, before the introduction of Indian corn or maize.

Oral histories can go back many hundreds of years, as three generations of people living into their eighties can span 200 years in storytelling. It is the old folks who tell the stories. Since the Indians were strong on oral history to keep their tribe's beliefs intact, they could have had good tribal memories for many hundreds of years.

The first time that Europeans learned about Indian corn is described in the writings of Father Hernandez about 1570 *(36: 78)*. Spain was getting a vast amount of silver and gold from the New World, and Philip II sent out a naturalist, Fr. Hernandez, to discover and record its "various natural productions." The subsequent importations to Europe of potatoes, corn, beans, squash, and other vegetables, had a much more beneficial effect on Europe's economies that did the soon-wasted silver and gold. Fr. Hernandez celebrated the many ways maize was prepared. He derived the word from the Haytian word *mahiz.*

Prescott *(35: 78 Mexico, 802 Peru)* found references to ubiquitous maize production and other advanced agriculture throughout the Caribbean, in Mesoamerica, and down the Andes as far as Chile. In Mexico, everyone cultivated the soil except high nobles and soldiers. He describes the advanced Native farming methods throughout the area that the Spaniards conquered. Throughout Mexico, there were carefully prepared plots and planned farming. It is obvious that some of the methods also diffused northwards to southwestern America.

There has been considerable academic study of Indian corn (maize). Dr. Walton Galinat wrote several papers *(15, 16, 17, 18)* about the evolution of sweet corn in America, through his investigations into the ancient gene pools of maize, and its evolution through human selection of seeds. He noted that the breeding of uniform, high yielding food crops as a part of the "green revolution" has become essential to feed our rapidly expanding human populations. The Native Americans had their own "green revolution," although it took many hundreds of years.

One process of further improving varities is to examine the genetic variation carried by the original varieties to insure continued progress in breeding. The modern Dent corn, in the Corn Belt, that is now a major factor in feeding the world, came from interbreeding the Maiz de Ocho, or Northern Flint corn, grown by the Wiechquaeskeck and other northeastern tribes, with the multi-rowed Southern Dent (gourd seed) corn that diffused in ancient times along a different route across southern America, and was grown by the southeastern Native Americans *(15: 355)*.

Galinat *(15: 355)* said that the spread of corn took about 700 years or from 700 AD in the Southwest to 1400 AD in New England. "The increase in food production associated with the introduction of Maiz de Ocho into the Southwest apparently triggered a sort of prehistoric population explosion and an expansion out into a new land where corn would grow."

In discussing the evolution of sweet corn as a vegetable crop, Galinat *(16: 7)* noted that the first variety to become established in New England, called **Papoon**, was introduced into the region about Plymouth, Massachusetts by the Iroquois Indians of the Susquehanna River basin. There were several varieties, however. Papoon had eight rows, and its ears were short. The core of Papoon was red and the kernels were white or pale. Other varieties in the northeast had longer ears, more rows, and multiple colors. Some Iroquois corn was all black *(16: 11)*. Evidently the hard flint corns grew best in the northeast. The softer flour corns had grown well on the Plains, but when stored in baskets in the ground, they tended to mold and rot during the wet fall weather of the northeast.

Galinat said *(17: 117)* that "the origin and diffusion of maize *(Zea mays)*. . . is of interest . . . because of its association with the growth and spread of those prehistoric cultures in which this cereal played a prime role." At about 1000 AD, the first sedentary horticultural complexes appear, apparently full blown, in the Central Plains, extending as far north as northern Nebraska. In earliest historical times, there was "a nearly solid Caddoan-speaking block extending from Texas into South Dakota." The history of maize diffusion is complex, but when it entered an area, "it may have triggered a population expansion." "The introduction of Maiz de Ocho into what is now the United States probably did more to change the way of life of more of its people in a short time that did any other single prehistoric innovation." *(17: 136)*.

A chart of the distribution of Maiz de Ocho in prehistoric and historic times *(17: Plate XXII)* illustrates that it swept up from Mexico, spread across the Great Plains, down the St. Lawrence River, and up the Ohio

River to cover the Northeast. Maize became ubiquitous in this area.

Walton Galinat summed up his lifetime of studying maize in 1994 *(18)*, while speaking of its origin:

> Ten thousand years ago, the unreliability and limitation of wild food together with increases in human populations probably stimulated a decision to gradually try farming along with hunting and gathering . . . to supplement the wild food supply.

> . . . an accidental fire may have set the stage when it burned trees and brush and, thereby, opened the land to sunshine and to growth by annuals . . .

> Fire could serve as a management practice to bring forth the growth of food plants

> Thus there came to be a co-evolution between crops and culture. Increases in the productivity of the food crop allowed more time and energy to settle doen, to improve health with better nutrition and medication and to build a more complex society . . .

Johannessen and Hastorf's book, **Corn and Culture in the Prehistoric New World** *(25)*, covers a conference in 1993 that summarized much of what had then been learned about maize. It noted:

> . . . the role of maize in prehistory, as it was passed from hand to hand from Mexico to as far as Chile and the boreal forests of North America, diversifying into hundreds of shapes, colors, and forms, and becoming a unifying motif in human cultures ranging from the Andean empires to the farming villages of the Missouri River.

We may add, "and to the tilled lands of the Wiechquaeskeck."

Maize *(Zea mays)* originated in Meso-America and the Caribbean about 5000 BC. It started with a small seed head, but it already had great variability when it was diffused towards the northeast. About 1000 BC, it began to appear in Arizona and New Mexico. It soon moved up to Utah and Colorado. It has been easy to trace in the West because it has been preserved in the dry climate and sparse vegetation. For example, in Lizard Cave, New Mexico (on the Philmont Scout Ranch), there are big piles of small cobs lying on the cave floor. They are about two to five inches long, with the grain earlier eaten by animals (Kenneth Buckland, private communication, 1940). These were primitive corns of a type not grown in the northeast in later centuries, but were in the *Zea mays* family.

By 1,000 AD, many Plains Indian populations had agricultural economies dominated by maize *(25)*. Little has changed in the next

1,000 years! Corn is still dominant in the Midwest.

Corn, beans, and squash thus took many centuries to diffuse from MesoAmerica to Wiechquaeskeck territory. It was slow, but it was continuous over the years, because the vegetables were healthful and could be stored over the winter. Knowledge of vegetables was good news to all Native Americans. For theWiechquaeskeck, it allowed a shift from a foraging to a farming economy, while still gathering meat.

Corn, beans and squash were first consumed in New England about 1000 AD. They became widespread within two hundred years. (Jeffrey C.M. Bendremer and Robert E. Dewar *(25: 371)*. Some of the crops grown in New England were corn *(Zea mays)*, beans *(Phaseolus vulgaris)*, squash *(Cucurbita sp.)*, and sunflower seeds *(Helianthus annuus)*. Historical observers also mentioned gourds *(Lagenaria siceraria)*, pumpkin *(Cucurbito pepo)*, and tobacco *(Nicotiana sp.)*. These gave the Wiechquaeskeck an excellent diet (except for the tobacco!) when combined with the seafood, meat, nuts, and a variety of plant foods that they collected in the wild.

By the time of first European contact in the 16th century, maize cultivation was distributed throughout eastern North America from mid-Florida to Quebec. It had become the staple food of Native Americans, always combined with beans and squash *(12)*. Fish and other seafood were the staple proteins for the Wiechquaeskeck in the summer. Deer and other animals were consumed in the fall and winter. The combination was excellent. It is interesting that, wherever maize was the staple food of the Indians in all of America, the women did most of the horticultural work. *(12: Map 8)*.

The maize in Connecticut was an eight-rowed Northern Flint corn with several ears on multi-stemmed plants. Figure 21, **Eight-rowed Indian Corn, or Maize**, shows the Indian corn plant as it probably looked in the 17th century in Connecticut. The drawing of the corn plant on the left is the earliest known picture of Indian corn. It was published in a 1542 book on botany by Leonard Fuchs. The illustration on the right is of an ear of a modern "ornamental Indian Corn," of a type that is widely sold today. The multi colors and irregular rows, from 8 to 10, are probably close to their appearance three centuries ago, as they were described by Winthrop.

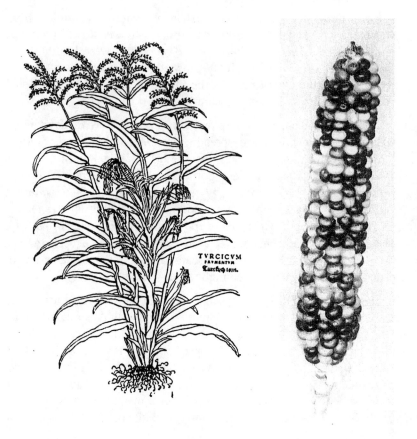

TVRCICVM
FRVMENTVM
Turckich korn.

Figure 21

Eight-rowed Indian Corn, or Maize

This drawing of the corn plant is the earliest known picture of Indian corn, or maize. It was published in the 1542 edition of *De historia stirpium*, a book on botany by Leonard Fuchs. The picture is from the collection of Paul Weatherwax, Department of Botany, Indiana State University.

The picture of the ear of corn is of a modern "ornamental Indian corn." The several colors and the irregular rows, from 8 to 10, are probably close to their appearance four centuries ago.

Governor John Winthrop of Massachusetts said that the stalks were six to eight feet tall and bore ears eight to nine inches in length. (There is no archaeological evidence of that size.) Winthrop also noted that the kernel colorings were ". . . yellow, white, red, blue, olive, greenish, black, speckled, striped, etc."

The early Dutch observers of the Wiechquaeskeck were duly impressed. They found large areas under cultivation, with little hills of corn growing with beans and squash entwined around them. All of the coastal areas of the Wiechquaeskeck and along the Hudson River were under reasonably intensive cultivation. This includes most of the Bronx. The European settlers here had a relatively easy time starting their farms because of the intensive Indian farming efforts that had preceded them. The lands were cleared, and much had been tilled before the settlers arrived. Many of the Indian lands lay fallow, however, and most of the wigwams were empty because of the earlier plagues that had decimated the population.

It is likely that the Wiechquaeskeck stored their maize for the winter in woven baskets in holes in the ground, similar to those described in Massachusetts *(Bradford: 74)*. Near South Windsor, Connecticut, Bendremer *(25)* found some maize pits that were quite massive, with volumes over 4.5 cubic meters. They had been lined with baskets of Big Blue Stem, the common "prairie grass" across eastern America. That grass was evidently the most mold-resistant of the available grasses and reeds. Since the acid Connecticut soil rapidly destroys all fibrous material, however, we can only assume that the Wiechquaeskeck used similar maize pits. A small amount of maize has been found in archaeological digs in Indian Field in Greenwich and in the Rowayton section of Norwalk *(52)*.

E. FISH, FISHING, AND SEAFOOD

In the early 17th century, Long Island Sound, the Hudson River, and the lakes and small rivers emptying into them, abounded with fish. The lakes and rivers were larger than they are today. They flowed more strongly because the water from the melting of the great ice sheets was still sponged into the land. Where today we see a swamp and a shallow brook, the Wiechquaeskeck saw a pristine, deep lake and a bubbling stream, teeming with trout and salmon in the Fall. Where today we see thousands of bunker, sometimes chased into bays by bluefish, they saw millions of bunker and thousands of bluefish. It was a fisherman's paradise, and the Wiechquaeskeck made the most of it. They were great swimmers, and completely at home in and on the water *(Williams: 99)*.

The Abundance of Fish

It was the plentiful fish off the New England and Canadian coasts that had first attracted thousands of Europeans to sail across the Atlantic. In 1498, John Cabot had caught cod on the Grand Banks of Newfoundland simply by lowering a weighted basket over the side *(32: 180)*. The mass of cod in the water actually slowed down the passage of ships *(32: 203)*.

Before the end of the 16th century, many hundreds of European fishing boats were going ashore to dry their catch of cod, in order to take more home. These people soon also found a huge source of furs; and the fur-trading business started with the Native Americans. This was a century before the settlers arrived at Plymouth. Europeans first came to the Wiechquaeskeck area searching for fish and furs.

We have many records of the multitudinous fish off New England around Cape Cod, which received its name very early. We can also be sure that there were also great schools of fish in Long Island Sound. There are many Lenape stories of shad filling the Delaware River. They called them "south fish," because they annually came north up that river. They also migrated north up the Hudson River and the rivers of Connecticut, so the Wiechquaeskeck knew shad well.

Van der Donck *(vanderDonck: 54)* says in "Of the Fishes:"

> All the waters of the New Netherlands are rich with fishes. Sturgeons are plenty in the rivers . . . Salmon are plenty in some rivers, and the striped bass are plenty in all the rivers and bays of the sea. . . The drums are a tolerably good fish . . . they caught many shad . . . There are also carp, snook, forrels, trout, suckers, thickheads, flounders, eels, palings, brickens, and lampreys.

He also describes large sun-fish, "so tame that many are caught with the hand," and the many codfish, plus: "shellfish, week-fish, herrings, mackerel, roah, hallibut, scoll, and sheeps-heads", and also: "black-fish, porpoises, herring-hogs, sharks, turtles, and whales."

The naturalist, John Josselyn *(Josselyn)*, made two voyages to New England to describe its natural history. On his second trip, he amassed a list of over a hundred species of fish in the Atlantic and on the American shore. There was a vast amount of seafood available to the Wiechquaeskeck when they set up their summer wigwams along the coast of Connecticut.

Indian Methods of Fishing

The Europeans were amazed at the efficient methods of fishing that were practiced by all the Woodland Indians on the east coast from Virginia to Maine. They had effective nets, traps, spears, and hooks, using only wood, natural fibers, stone, and bone. On shore, their camps were set for cleaning, cooking, drying, and smoking the catch. Many of these camp sites are marked today by middens, which are heaps of oyster and clam shells and household garbage. (The fish bones have long since decayed.) The Natives worked cooperatively on their seafood harvest.

Figure 22, **"The manner of their fishing"** was drawn by John White from observing some Algonquian-speaking tribes in Virginia. There would have been some differences in Connecticut, but we can assume that the Wiechquaeskeck used similar fishing methods. We do know that they used spears, both straight and forked. We know that the Wiechquaeskeck made fish traps, which may not have been of the design in Figure 22, but may have had funnels, such as shown in Figure 27. The interesting fish in the foreground in Figure 22 may, or may not, have come as far north as the Wiechquaeskeck.

They knew when to expect the great runs of salmon, herring, eel, and shad each year. Isaack de Rasieres *(deRasieres: 105)* talks about the shad run in 1628 on the Hudson River in April, May, and June:

> They follow the course of these (fish), which they catch with a dragnet they themselves knit very neatly, of the wild hemp, from which the women and old men spin the thread.

David de Vries *(deVries: 222)* also describes the shad run:

> It is caught in large quantities and dried by the savages, for at this time the squaws are engaged in sowing their maize, and cultivating the land, and the men go a-fishing in order to assist their wives a little by their draughts of fish. Sometimes they catch them with

Figure 22

"The Manner of their Fishing"

Reproduction of a watercolor drawing by John White, in Paul Hope Hulton, *The American Drawings of John White, 1577-1590 . . .*, vol. 2, plate 42. From the Collections of the Library of Congress, Rare Book and Special Collections Division, USZ62-576, 915413/CO.

seines from seventy to eighty fathoms *[over 400 feet]* in length, which they braid themselves, and on which, in place of lead, they hang stones, and instead of the corks which we put on them to float them, they fasten small sticks of an ell *[45 inches]* in length, round and sharp at the end. Over the purse, they have a figure made of wood, resembling the Devil, and when the fish swim into the net and come to the purse, so that the figure begins to move, they then begin to cry out and call upon the Mannatoe, that is, the Devil, to give them many fish. They catch great quantities of this fish; which they also catch in little set-nets, six or seven fathoms long *[40 feet]*, knit single like a herring-net. They set them on sticks into the river, one, and one and a half, fathoms deep. With these they catch many of this fish. In the fresh waters are pike, perch, roach and trout.

Thomas Hariot *(Hariot)* wrote from the Roanoke Colony in Virginia in 1585-86 that the Indian people:

> . . . have likewise a notable way to catche fishe in their Rivers. For whear as they lacke both yron and steele, they fasten unto their Reedes or longe Rodds, the hollowe tayle of a certain fishe like to a sea crabbe *[horseshoe crab]* in steede of a poynte, wehr by nighte or day they sticke fishes, and take them opp into their boates *(Fig. 16)*.

Roger Williams *(Williams: 102)* makes several observations about Woodland Indian fishing:

> *[Sturgeon]* Obs: Divers part of the Countrey abound with this Fish; yet the Natives for the goodnesse and greatnesse of it, much prize it, and will neither furnish the English with so many, nor so cheape, that any great trade is likely to be made of it . . . The Natives venture one or two in a Canow, and with a harping Iron, or such like Instrument, sticke this fish, and so hale it into their Canow; sometimes they take them by their nets, which they make strong of Hemp.

> Ashop, their nets. Which they set thwart some little River or Cove wherein they kill Basse (at the fall of the water) with their arrows, or sharp sticks, especially if headed with iron, gotten from the English, &c.

> Basse. The Indians (and the English too) make a dainty dish of the Uppaquontup, or head of this Fish; and very well they may, the braines and fat of it being very much, and sweet as marrow.

> Breame. Obs: Of this Fishe there is an abundance, which the Natives drie in the Sunne and smoake.

> Whales. Which in some places are often cast up; I have seene some of them, but not above sixtie feet long. The Natives cut them out in severall parcells, and give and send farre and neere for an acceptable present, or dish.
>
> Lines. The Natives take exceeding great paines in their fishing, especially in watching their seasons by night, so frequently they lay their naked bodies many a cold night on the cold shoare about a fire of two or three sticks, and oft in the night search their Nets, and sometimes go in and stay longer in frozen water.

John Josselyn *(Josselyn 1: 100)*, on his second voyage to New England in the 1660s, wrote:

> Bark which breaks out into flame & holds it over the side of his Canow, the Sturgeon seeing this glaring light mounts to the Surface of the water where he is slain. . . the Alewives they take with Nets like a pursenet put upon a round hoop'd stick with a handle in fresh ponds where they come to spawn. . . The Bass and Blew-fish they take in harbours, and at the mouth of barr'd Rivers, being in their Canows, striking them with a fisgig, a kind of dart or staff, to the lower end whereof they fasten a sharp jagged bone . . . with a string fastened to it . . . in dark evenings when they are upon the fishing ground near a Bar of Sand . . . the Indian lights a piece of dry Birch- and taken with a fisgig . . . Salmons and Lampres are catch'd at the falls of Rivers.

These writings describe a remarkable variety of the Indian means of fishing. They are well summarized in Figure 22.

Lobsters, Oysters and Clams

A mark of ancient Native American habitation on all the coasts of North America is often a large heap of old oyster and clam shells mixed with sediments and detritus. Many an archeologist has dug through such shell middens and extracted gems of artifacts that have helped to interpret the lost culture. They were the "kitchen middens," where not only the shellfish remains were thrown, but also all the broken household items and considerable garbage.

There are only a few shell middens left in Wiechquaeskeck and Tankiteke territory *(Sect. 13A)*. The largest remaining midden is in Norwalk *(ARCH10)*. One of the most prolific for interpretation was the Manakaway site in Greenwich *(ARCH1)*.

The Woodland Indians caught many lobsters, but their chitinous carapaces did not last through the centuries. The calcium and magnesium carbonates of clam and oyster shells can last almost indefinitely, if they are not subjected to acid waters. That is one reason the Indians made wampum from clam shells. Not only could they be worked readily, but also they endured with a polish over many generations. The lobster chitin, however, is an organic material, a horny polysaccharide. It is readily broken down chemically over the years.

An unusual report about lobsters was written by Jacob Frederick Stam *(STAM)* in Massachusetts in 1637: "The Bear is a tyrant at a Lobster and at low water will go down to the rocks & grope after them with great diligence." This gives us a picture of one aspect of life in a coastal New England Indian camp. Black bears came down to the water to feed, close to the small wigwams, and would be undeterred by humans. Mountain lions would do the same. This is not surprising, because many bears and cougars move down to the beaches today, close to houses, in the Northwest and Alaska, as they search for dead fish and large clams. Some foraging bears also still come close to humans in New England.

Stam also said that, in addition to a number of different fish, the Natives ate "lobsters, oysters, mussels, clams . . . cockles and scallops." Their seafood cuisine was varied.

John Josselyn, Colonial Traveler, *(Josselyn: 100)* described the seafood of the Massachusetts Woodland Indians in great detail. About lobsters, he said:

> The Lobsters they take in large Bays when it is low water, the wind still, going out in their Birchen-Canows with a staff two or three yards long, made small and sharpen'd at one end, and nick'd with deep nicks to take hold. When they spye the Lobster crawling upon the Sand in two fathom water, more or less, they stick him towards the head and bring him up. I have known thirty Lobsters taken by an Indian lad in an hour and a half . . Clams they dig out of the Clambanks upon the flats and in creeks when it is low water, where they are bedded sometimes a yard deep one upon another, the beds a quarter of a mile in length, and less.

The Wiechquaeskeck did not have Birch-Canoes, but probably fished the same way in their dugouts.

One of van der Donck's *(vanderDonck: 55)* interesting comments is:

> Lobsters are plenty in many places. Some of those are very large,

being from five to six feet in length; others again are from a foot to a foot and a half long, which are the best for the table. There are also crabs.

Van der Donck goes on to describe oysters that "are very plenty," and "I have seen many in the shell a foot long." "Some . . . are fit to be eaten raw," and they "are proper for roasting and stewing." Van der Donck was a reasonably accurate observer, and there is no reason to suspect that he was exaggerating about the size of the lobsters and clams. His observations were made along Wiechquaeskeck shores.

Two of Roger Williams *(Williams: 103)* observations about clams were:

> Obs. This is a sweet kind of shellfish, which all Indians generally over the Countrey, Winter and Summer delight in; and at low water the women dig for them: this fish, and the naturall liquors of it, they boile, and it makes their broth and their Nasaump (which is a kind of thickened broth) and their bread seasonable and savoury, in stead of Salt:

> Obs. This . . . a little thick shellfish which the Indians wade deepe and dive for, and after they have eaten the meat there (in those which are good) they breake out of the shell, about halfe an inch of the blacke part of it, of which they make their Suckauhock *[purple wampum]*, or black money, which is to them precious.

Clearly the Wiechquaeskeck had a varied and flavorful seafood cuisine. They added fish and shellfish to their *sapaen,* or boiled corn dishes, and to their breads. They also added a wide variety of meats and herbs. Roger Williams, after living with Woodland Indians for months at a time, made many favorable remarks about the food. Figure 23, **"The broyling of their fish over the flame of fier,"** was painted by John White in Virginia. It shows that they used reasonable broiling methods on their fires and did not normally eat the fish raw. They do not appear to have "cleaned" their fish, however. The broiling of the whole fish would have helped in the cleanliness and smell around their camps.

Figure 24, **Gathering and Smoking Shellfish for Winter Use**, *i*s an excellent artist's interpretation of their summer activities along the shore (Courtesy of New Jersey State Museum). This picture was drawn to show the New Jersey shore Lenape people, who would have been the same people as those in the southwestern Connecticut summer camps. The men have brought the oysters and clams ashore in their dugouts. They carry them in woven baskets. One woman is cracking the shellfish

The broyling of their fish ouer the flame of fier.

Figure 23

"The broiling of their fish over the flame of fier."

Reproduction of a watercolor drawing by John White (1577-1590). From the Collections of the Library of Congress, Rare Book and Special Collections Division, USZ62-581

Figure 24

Gathering and Smoking Shellfish for Winter Use

Original drawings by Monte Crews from the "Indians of New Jersey Portfolio of Prints," Courtesy of the New Jersey State Museum, Trenton, New Jersey.

open, while another is stringing them on fiber strips. The shellfish were then hung over a smoky campfire to dry for winter storage. Early explorers saw thousands of such smoking fires along both shores of Long Island Sound.

F. VILLAGES, PALISADES AND PALISADOES

The Wiechquaeskeck had only stone implements and fire to fell trees, split timbers, and erect habitations, but they did a remarkable job of creating strong and useful structures. Trees up to six inches in diameter could be felled by stone axes without fire. To fell heavier timber, they lit a fire around its base. This is described in Sect. 6-B, **The Dugout Canoe** *(see Figs. 16 and 17).* With their stone celts, they could also split tree trunks into heavy planks.

They had a variety of cutting tools, depending upon the stones that they had to work with. The most common was the "celt" *(Fig. 41).* It was a tapered stone about four to eight inches long with a wide cutting edge. The tapered end was fit snugly onto a haft and lashed with leather thongs. It was not swung like an adze, but was struck by a club or another stone. They could shape logs for structures with the celt.

In the Late Woodland Period, the Indians learned to polish the stones, making more effective tools. They first pecked the stones into shape, then sharpened them by rubbing with an abrasive stone. The Native word *"coscobuque"* means whetstone or grinding stone. It is probably the origin of the place name "Cos Cob," in Greenwich. There may have been useable, quartz, abrasive stones on Diamond Hill in Cos Cob. Usually, whereever archaeologists find celts, they find whetstones. Whetstones were constantly used by the Indians to sharpen their stone tools and projectile points.

When trading started with the Europeans, celts were replaced with the iron cleaving tools called "frows" or "throws," which are essentially steel wedges with a handle, that can be used for splitting logs. Since the Wiechquaeskeck had few beaver to trade, however, and their number was depleted rapidly by disease, it is doubtful that they were able to trade for many of the more efficient European steel tools.

Axes were grooved at the back *(Fig. 41)*, so that the haft could be bound on more tightly with leather thongs. If they were lucky, they found a stone that could be ground down on the face to provide a thinner cutting surface. Designs varied greatly, depending on the stone available. Some axes were rough chipped while others were ground down. Some smaller stones were hafted simply with leather thongs, making a hatchet-like tool. This could be used to cut small trees, or as a tomahawk.

Their woodworking tools were primitive, but, with a lot of cooperative work, they were able to construct strong shelters and palisades that served their purposes. The palisades did not stand against gunpowder, but they stood well against marauding Indian enemies who also only had stone weapons.

There was no standard design for a village or for a palisade. Native Americans did not make drawings of designs and exchange them. They got ideas for construction through visiting between tribes, then built according to their immediate needs and available materials. There are old pictures of "Indian villages" that look neatly made with a row of vertical logs to make the palisades, but those villages did not have Connecticut's uneven rocky soil to contend with. Some accounts describe vertical log palisades that were built by the Native Americans in preContact times in eastern Connecticut, Massachusetts, and parts of northern New York. Some of the designs on the maps were obviously drawn in Europe by artists who had not been in America, however.

A good example of the palisades that were built by the Wiechquaeskeck is shown in Figure 25, **Betuckquapock, a Wiechquaeskeck Palisado, Greenwich**, which is Bryan Buckland's rendition of the fort that was in North Mianus, Greenwich. It was on the flat site of what is now the old community building. Bryan Buckland drew it from van der Donck's description of a fort in the Wiechquaeskeck area *(vanderDonck: 81)*, and Champlain's 1609 drawing of a fort in New York *(Fig. 26)*. This palisado was situated at the end of an inlet at high tide and at the foot of the most direct trail from the coast to Nanichiestawack. It also sat astride the main east-west **Sackerah Path** along the shore line *(Fig. 11)*. It may have had a few wigwams inside, but there was not room for a full village. It was a defensive fort, held by young men when an alarm went out. The defensive walls were logs and piled brush. There was an opening at the back that led to the path to Nanichiestawack.

Figure 25

Betuckquapock, a Wiechquaeskeck Palisado, Greenwich

(North Mianus)

Illustration by Bryan K. Buckland

Details of the palisado were taken from Samuel de Champlain's Drawing of an Iroquoian Fort *(Fig. 26)*, and from Adriaen van der Donck *(vanderDonck: 81)*, who described the construction of Wiechquaeskeck palisadoes. The site was sketeched at North Mianus, Connecticut.

Drawn on site in America in 1609, Figure 26, **Champlain's Drawing of an Iroquoian Fort,** shows that many of the forts in New York and Quebec were made in the Wiechquaeskeck style of piled brush palisades. Van der Donck, who was very familiar with the area in the 17th century, described the Wiechquaeskeck forts, and noted that it was the Dutch settlers who "set up post and rail, or palisado fences." In the Wiechquaeskeck area, there were very few places, possibly near marshes, where it would have been possible to erect a palisade of logs set three or more feet into the ground for any great distance.

Champlain's drawing in Figure 26 depicts his Algonquian Huron allies attacking an Onondaga palisadoe in 1609. It is the best picture we have from that time of what the Native palisadoes, or defensive forts, looked like, and it very closely fits van der Donck's descriptions. Champlain drew another picture of a very large palisaded village where Quebec City is now, and the construction was a similar pile of brush and logs. It truly looked like a "castle." Champlain's report of his time in Quebec is considered to be reasonably accurate.

Van der Donck noted that the Wiechquaeskeck palisades were very rough structures of piled logs, trees and brush. Obviously, the Indians in the 16th century built a great variety of palisades from whatever materials were at hand. The Wiechquaeskeck had their own style in their glacier-scoured land, where the soil was thin.

The Wiechquaeskeck sometimes built "longhouses" in their villages. These were possibly even as large as the famous Iroquois longhouses. They were of appreciable size, and were efficient shelters for large numbers of people, with shared cooking and heating fires. SomeWiech-quaeskeck villages that were palisaded by brush piles were impressive enough to be called "castles" by the Dutch.

Van der Donck *(vanderDonck: 79)* gives a first-hand description of the larger Wiechquaeskeck village houses, located near his plantation in The Bronx:

> Sometimes they build their houses above a hundred feet long; but never more than twenty feet wide. When they build a house, they place long, slender hickory saplings in the ground, having the bark stripped off, in a straight line of two rows, as far asunder as they intend the breadth of the house to be, and continuing the rows asfar as it is intended the length shall be. Those sapling poles are bent over towards each other in the form of an arch, and secured together,

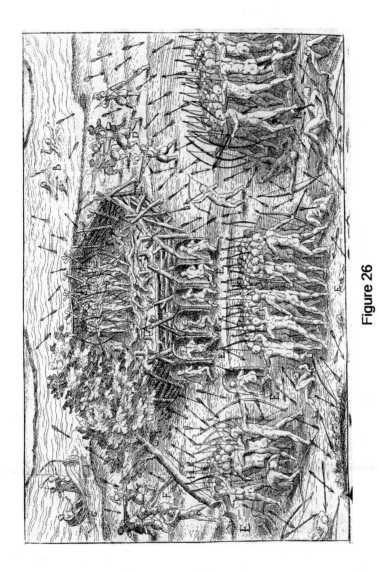

Figure 26

Champlain's Drawing of an Iroquoian Fort

This drawing depicts Champlain's attack on an Iroquoian fort near the present site of Fort Ticonderoga, New York, in 1609. Champlain and his men had joined a war party of Algonquins and Hurons from Quebec. Reproduced from the Collections of the Library of Congress, USZ62-077107, 915413/CO.

having the appearance of a garden arbour. The sapling poles are then crossed with split poles in the form of lathing, which are well fastened to the upright work. The lathings are heaviest near the ground. A space of about a foot wide is left open in the crown of the arch. For covering they use the bark of ash, chestnut, and other trees, which they peel off in pieces about six feet long, and as broad as they can. They cover their houses, laying the smooth side inwards, leaving an open space of about a foot wide in the crown to let out the smoke. They lap the side edges and ends over each other, having regard to the shrinking of the bark, securing the covering with withes to the lathings. A crack or rent they shut up, and in this manner they make their houses proof against wind and rain. They have one door in the center of the house. . . Durability is a primary object in their houses. In short, their houses are tight and tolerably warm, though they know nothing of chambers, halls and closetings. They kindle and keep their fires in the middle of their houses, from one end to the other, and the opening in the crown of the roof lets out the smoke. From sixteen to eighteen families frequently dwell in one house, according to its size. The fire being kept in the middle, the people lay on each side thereof, and each family has its own place. If they have a place for a pot or kettle, with a few small articles and a place to sleep, then they have room enough; and in this manner, a hundred, and frequently many more, dwell together in one house. Such is the construction of an Indian dwelling in every place, unless they are out on fishing or hunting excursions, and then they erect temporary huts or shanties.

Several of the Dutch writers refer to the Wiechquaeskeck "castles." That was their best term for either a village surrounded by brush palisades, or for a smaller palisado, or fort. Betuckquapock *(Fig. 25)* would clearly have looked like a little castle to Dutch observers from their boats. In flatter lands in America, the palisades around villages were evidently sometimes a straighter, more regular shape. Among the stony Wiechquaeskeck hills, the palisadoes would have fitted into the land, with logs, earth, and brush holding them together. In the flatter area of the Bronx, Van der Donck saw palisadoes large enough for twenty or thirty houses *(vanderDonck: 81)*:

We have measured their houses, and found some of them to be a hundred and eighty yards long, and as narrow as before stated. In those places, they crowd an astonishing number of persons, and it is surprising to see them out in open day.

The "one hundred and eighty yards" was probably exaggerated in the translation from the Old Dutch, but there is no doubt that the central village houses of the Wiechquaeskeck were very long. When Capt. John Underhill attacked Nanichiestawack *(Jameson: 282-284)*, he described the village (which did not have palisades) as being houses "set up in three rows, street fashion, each row eighty paces long.," which meant over 200 feet long. The way they were set on fire by the Dutch indicates that these were single, long houses, not separated wigwams. There were from 500 to 700 people in the three Nanichiestawack long houses *(Chap. 9)*.

The Wiechquaeskeck palisades were thus not made of twelve-foot posts dug into the ground. Native Americans could possibly do that in the soft lowlands of Virginia and Maryland, but not in the shallow irregular earth of Connecticut, with its underlying ledge rock. Van der Donck *(vanderDonck: 80)* describes a Wiechquaeskeck palisade:

> In their villages and their castles they always build strong, firm works, adapted to the places. For the erection of these castles, or strongholds, they usually select a situation on the side of a steep high hill, near a stream or river, which is difficult of access, except from the water, and inaccessible on every other side, with a level plain on the crown of the hill, which they enclose with a strong stockade work in a singular manner. First, they lay along the ground large logs of wood, and frequently smaller logs upon the lower logs, which serve for the foundation of the work. Then they place strong oak palisades in the ground on both sides of the foundation, the upper ends of which cross each other, and are joined together. In the upper cross of the palisades they then place the bodies of trees, which makes the work strong and firm. Thus they secure themselves against the sudden invasion of their enemies. But they have no knowledge of adding flankings and curtains to their fortifications. Those belong not to their system. Near their plantations they also frequently erect small works, to secure their wives and children against the sudden irruption of the small marauding parties of their enemies.

These palisadoes *(Fig. 25)* had been built to defend against other Indian tribes with primitive weapons. They proved useless against guns fired through the jumble of branches or into the rear openings. They soon abandoned their use against the Europeans. After the Wiechquaeskeck left, the settlers used the logs of the palisadoes to build barns and fences.

Still speaking of the Bronx area near his plantation, Van der Donck continued *(vanderDonck: 81)*:

> Besides their strongholds, they have villages and towns which are enclosed. Those usually have woodland on one side, and corn lands on the other sides. They also frequently have villages near the water sides, at fishing places, where they plant some vegetables; but they leave those places every year on the approach of winter, and retire to their strong places, or into the thick woods, where they are protected from the winds, where fuel is plenty, and where there is game and venison. Thus they subsist by hunting and fishing throughout the year.

These are the best descriptions we have of the Wiechquaeskeck palisadoes, or forts, and palisaded villages, but there were no two the same in Wiechquaeskeck territory. There is little archaeological evidence of the size of these palisades and villages because they were constructed of wood, which has long since been removed or rotted. The settlers would have taken any usable logs for their own construction and burned the rest to make room for planting. The rotted remains of posts set in the ground for wigwams are frequently found on archaeological digs as brown, cylindrical tubes of soil. Thus, archaeologists have often found and identified the posts of round wigwams and smaller houses. It is difficult to find the remains of the very large houses, however, as there has been too much digging and construction in the past four centuries throughout the Wiechquaeskeck territory.

The villages were fit to the land and to the requirements for protection. The very long houses with palisades would only have been those in the Bronx, where the land was flat and fertile, and where there was a high population density before the plagues. The village of "Weichquaesgeck", on the Hudson River at Dobbs Ferry, was evidently a fairly large palisaded town with large corn fields nearby. The village of Nanichiestawack was smaller and not palisaded, probably because it depended on its remoteness among the hills for protection. It had large longhouses, however.

In the Greenwich area, Betuckquapock was a strong palisado *(Fig. 25)*, but it could not hold many houses, certainly not a longhouse, because of the limited space on the site. The soil at Betuckquapock was shallow, meaning that the palisaded structure, large enough to be put on a map, was simply piled brush and logs, as in the illustration. There were related long-houses scattered down to Strickland Plains in Cos Cob, which the Dutch destroyed in 1634. They have been called "Petaquapen", but that is the same Algonquian word as Betuckquapock. Together with houses in the small valley and substantial corn fields on Strickland Plains, the whole combination would have made a single settlement area. It could easily have supported the young men in the several palisadoes. The palisadoes had evidently worked against the Pequot, but were easily destroyed by the Dutch and English. They are shown on the Dutch maps at the entrance to the Mianus River. This was the area where the famous Mayn Mayanos *(Chap. 3, Fig. 9)* was the leader. Before the plagues hit, this widespread village was both powerful and fruitful with many people, extensive corn fields, large oyster beds, and a shallow bay for fish traps. Above Betuckquapock were forests with deer and other game, and a path to Naniechiestawack, the tribe's central village. The "town planners" had done well.

In the Stamford area, the Shippan Indians around Westcott Cove undoubtedly had some forts nearby, as they had large corn fields, many fish traps, and were spread out. They were also exposed to the Sound, the highway of the raiding Pequots. We can assume that there were summer Indian villages on every bay along the Fairfield County coast, such as Stamford Harbor, Holly Pond, Scotts Cove, etc. Archaeological digs have shown that there were many villages and palisades along the Norwalk River also *(Fig 37)*.

As has been noted, the northeastern forts were not neatly palisaded like the drawings of the forts in Virginia. The drawings of palisades that Europeans put on some of the early maps of the Northeast clearly came from early reports from the South. The difference is that the southern forts were built on deep soil that had never been scoured by a glacier. The Indians could dig down the necessary three feet for the posts, which is still amazing, considering the poor tools that they had. Many of the northern forts were built on rocky ground and shallow soil. There was no way that the northern Natives, with primitive implements, could erect tall picketed palisades except in occasional deep soft soil or in marshlands. In the Norwalk area, the largest aggregation of Natives lived at Wilson Point in a village called Naramake *(38)*. In the early records, there are entries alluding to the Indian fort on the east bank of the Norwalk river close to where there were large shell middens. It is possible that a vertically-palisaded fort was built in the marsh by the Norwalke Indians, as it is pictured in the mural in the Norwalk Historical Museum, because the soil there was deep and soft. This was the summer village of the

Norwalke people, and the palisade was for coastal defence. In the winter, many of the tribe would have moved up the Norwalk River to live in hunting camps more protected from the weather, and from incursions from the sea.

Wassenaer gives another description of palisadoes, in which there is a tree in the center *(Wassenauer: 80):*

> When they wage war against each other, they fortify their tribe or nation with palisades, serving them for a fort, and sally out the one against the other. They have a tree in the center, on which they place sentinels to observe the enemy and discharge arrows. None are exempt in war . . . but the women who carry their husbands' arrows and food.

In the **Journal of New Netherlands** *(Jameson),* there is an account of the the abortive Dutch attack on the Wiechquaeskeck near the Mianus River in 1644 *(Chap. 9).* It appears to be exaggerated, as it says:

> The old Indian captured above having promised to lead us to Wetquescheck, which consisted of three castles, sixty-five men were dispatched under Baxter and Pieter Cock, who found them empty, though thirty Indians could have stood against two hundred soldiers since the castles were constructed of plank five inches thick, nine feet high, and braced around with thick balk full of port holes. Our people burnt two, reserving the third for a retreat. Marching eight or nine leagues further, they discovered nothing but some huts which they could not surprize as they were discovered. They came back having killed only one or two Indians, taken some women and children prisoners and burnt much corn.

This account does not match other descriptions of the "castles," which were the palisado forts scattered around the mouth of the Mianus River to protect the Wiechquaeskeck heartland from marauding Pequots. Since they are shown on an early Dutch map, however, they were substantial.

In this account, we see the "parched earth" policy of the Dutch towards the dwindling Wiechquaeskeck, and it says that the Indian forts contained "planks" or split logs. It is possible that, in the preceding years, the Wiechquaeskeck had traded beaver pelts for the steel wedges, mauls, and throes that could be used for splitting logs. It is more likely, however, that the forts had been built before the Wiechquaeskeck traded with the Dutch, and they had used stone wedges and stone celts for the job. Forts had been built well before the Europeans came to settle the area. Evidence of them has not been uncovered in this area by archaeological excavations, because they were all dismantled, but they are amply described in the reports written at the time.

Campsites and Wigwams

The Wiechquaeskeck crowded into their longhouses, central villages, and palisado forts when they gathered for important occasions, winter lodging, war training, and celebrations. Much of the time, however, they scattered to farming, fishing, and hunting camps where there were few longhouses. There they lived mostly in wigwams, dome-shaped wooden structures that held a few people or a whole family. A wigwam could be built by two or more people. Wigwams were of similar construction throughout the Algonquian world of the east, but varied greatly in size and shape and in their internal arrangements. They were as randomly built as our houses are today. Their villages were also diverse, and simply fit the available space and purposes. Campsites were built for specific fishing, hunting, or farming needs.

A campsite could have been established, for example, near a palisado at Westcott Cove in Stamford where there was flat land, a clear stream nearby, a beach to launch the dugout canoes, oyster beds, and a good area for fish traps. There were many acres of cleared, tillable land for their cornfields. The natural resources were the important factor. The proximity to a palisado for protection was not really necessary, because they offered limited safety. If war canoes were seen approaching, there may have been time for the women and children to flee into the woods.

There were campsites scattered higher along the Mianus, Rippowam, Five Mile, and Norwalk Rivers, for winter shelter and hunting *(52)*, as well as on every other river in the area. When most of the Natives moved to winter quarters, some old folks and young mothers would have stayed behind because of the effort involved in moving. The Dutch raiding party of 1643 found this out at Petaquapen *(Sect. 9)*.

Figure 27, **The Wiechquaeskeck Village at Indian Field, Greenwich**, is Bryan Buckland's concept of what the Indian Field village may have looked like before the European settlers arrived. There have been archaeological digs in that area *(ARCH3, 52)*, so we know that it was occupied as a summer fishing camp, and it was used later by the remnant Wiechquaeskeck after the1686 purchase of the Horseneck Plantation (Greenwich) *(Sect. 8)*. The picture shows some wigwams,

Figure 27

The Wiechquaeskeck Village at Indian Field, Greenwich

Illustration by Bryan K. Buckland

This is an artist's conception of Indian Field, Greenwich. It was noted in the early land transfer documents, which mentioned the corn fields and fish traps. The picture is based on archeological studies by Robert Suggs in 1956 *(ARCH1)*, and Bernard Powell in 1958 *(ARCH3)*.

and people in various occupations, including a hunter who has just returned successfully. A few Indians in dugout canoes are tending a fish trap. To the left is a corn field with a hut for those who stay there to drive away the crows and blackbirds. Dugouts are pulled up in the bay.

Bernard Powell *(ARCH3)* dug extensively at Indian Field in 1958. Ernest Wiegand has conducted several recent digs there *(52)*. He even found some formal dog burials. Wiegand *(ARCH14)* has also found evidence that one of the sheltered winter camping and hunting sites of the coastal Stamford Indians was on the Rippowam River where Stillwater and Long Ridge Roads meet.

The Wiechquaeskeck had no set patterns for campsites, and no council discussions about zoning and planning for their houses. They simply built what was the most useful to them, in locations where they wanted to be at the time. When they learned from other tribes about better patterns of habitation construction, toolmaking, and agriculture, they often adopted the new ideas, and profited from them.

The wigwam was a fine example of an optimum pattern. It could be built of materials at hand by a few people. It was efficient, comfortable, and provided good shelter. The wigwam was not completely portable, like the famous Indian teepee of the North and West, but it filled the same function just as well. The rush mats and sheets of bark covering the wigwam were sometimes carried from site to site. They did not build teepees, because they required large sheets of leather from large animals, such as elk, moose or buffalo, which were not abundant in the lower Hudson valley.

Wigwams required only trees and rushes or bark to construct, and there were plenty of those available. A tree was often killed by the removal of its bark, to prepare it to make a dugout canoe. The whole tree was thus effectively used for the canoe, palisades, wigwams, and fuel. Trees were a marvelous resource, and there were many near the Connecticut coast.

Figure 28, **Reproduction of a Wigwam, Ward Pound Ridge Reservation**, is a photo of a wigwam built in recent years at the Trailside Museum in the Ward Pound Ridge Reservation in Westchester County. It has been covered with thick sheets of bark. Wigwams close to the shore, where there are many reeds, were often covered with woven reed mats, and they were more flexible and portable.

Figure 28
Reproduction of a Wigwam, Ward Pound Ridge Reservation

This reproduction of a bark-covered wigwam was made with all natural materials near the Trailside Museum, Ward Pound Ridge Reservation, Westchester County, New York. Bark was probably the most common covering material used inland. Wigwams along the shore were often covered with woven rush mats.

The best descriptions of wigwams came from the English in New England. The Dutch were so enthralled by the great "castles" they saw that they wrote little about the lowly wigwam dwellings. Jacob Frederick Stam *(STAM)* wrote in New England in 1637:

> . . . to build their houses . . . they gather poles in the woods and put the great end in the ground . . . in the form of a circle, and bending the tops in the form of an arch . . . bind them together with bark of Walnut trees, which is wondrous tuffe. . . . cover with matts, some made of reeds and sedges . . . Mattes could be rolled up or let down . . . Severall dores according to the wind.. . . *[they]* laye on planks 12 inches to 18 inches above ground . . . on rayles born by forks. *[and to heat the wigwam at night, they]* Fell a tree . . . burn both sides at end . . . shorter and shorter. . . burns night and day.

Mourt's Relation *(Mourt: 28)* says:

> The houses were made with long young sapling trees, bended and both ends stuck into the ground. They were made round, like unto an arbor, and covered down to the ground with thick and well wrought mats, and the door was not over a yard high, made of a mat to open. The chimney was a wide open hole in the top, for which they had a mat to cover it closed when they pleased. One might stand and go upright in them. In the midst of them were four little trunches. *[stakes]* knocked into the ground, and small sticks laid over, on which they hung their pots, and what they had to seethe. *[simmer, boil]* Round about the fire they lay on mats, which are their beds. The houses were double matted, for as they were matted without, so were they within, with newer and fairer mats. In the houses we found wooden bowls, trays and dishes, earthen pots, handbaskets made of crabshells wrought together, also an English pail or bucket . . . There was also baskets of sundry sorts, bigger and some lesser, finer and some coarser; some were curiously wrought with black and white in pretty works, and sundry other of their household stuff. We found also two or three deer's heads, one whereof had been newly killed, for it was still fresh. There was also a company of deer's feet stuck up in the houses, harts' horns, and eagles' claws, and sundry such like things there was, also two or three baskets filled with parched acorns, pieces of fish, and a piece of broiled herring. We found also a little silk grass, and a little tobacco seed, with some other seeds which we knew not. Without was sundry bundles of flags, and sedge, bulrushes, and other things.

When Verrazano sailed up the coast in 1524, he wrote delightedly about the Narrangansett Indians and his reception in the Rhode Island area *(Verrazano: 139)*. He mentioned their wigwams:

> When we went farther inland we saw their houses, which are circular in shape, about 13 to 15 paces across, made of bent saplings; they are arranged without any architectural pattern, and are covered with cleverly worked mats of straw which protect them from wind and rain. There is no doubt that if they had the skilled workmen we have, they would erect great buildings. . . They move these houses from one place to another according to the richness of the site and the season. They need only carry the straw mats, so they have new houses made in no time at all. In each house there lives a father with a very large family, for in some we saw 25 to 30 people.

The early settlers and English visitors to New England wrote about wigwams because they were often invited to stay in them. Some of the earliest settlers lived in deserted wigwams until they could build or buy a house. John Josselyn, on his natural history expedition to New England about 1630 *(Josselyn: 91)* wrote:

> Their houses which they call Wigwams, are built with Poles pitcht into the ground of a round form for most part, sometimes square, they bind down the tops of their poles, leaving a hole for smoak to go out at, the rest they cover with the bark of Trees, and line the inside of their Wigwams with mats made of Rushes painted with several colours, one good post they set up in the middle that reaches to the hole in the top with a staff across before it at a convenient height, they knock in a pin on which they hang their Kettle, beneath that they set up a broad stone for a back which keepeth the post from burning; round by the walls they spread their mats and skins where the men sleep, whilst their women dress their victuals, they have commonly two doors, one opening to the South, the other to the North, and according as the wind sits, they close up one door with bark and hang a Dears skin or the like before the other. Towns they have none, being always removing from one place to another for conveniency of food, sometimes to those places where one sort of fish is most plentiful, other whiles where others are. I have seen half a hundred of their Wigwams together in a piece of ground and they shew prettily, within a day or two, or a week, they have been all dispersed.

Daniel Gookin also described wigwams at length, noting their different coverings and sizes *(Gookin: 9)*.

Verrazano's comment, incidentally, about "skilled workmen erecting great buildings" shows foresight because, in the 20th century, Mohawks became famous in New York City for their ability to work fearlessly at the top of great skyscrapers during construction.

Sweathouses

David de Vries, while in Wiechquaeskeck territory, described another kind of house, the sweathouse. This is interesting, because today many Native Americans have revived this ancient practice. On private lands and sacred sites, they have built hundreds of sweathouses that are very similar in their construction and use to the Wiechquaeskeck sweathouses, all across America. The only real difference in construction is that, in 1642, the Indians sometimes used clay to seal the steam in. Today, they are more apt to use canvas or plastic sheets *(personal observation)*. De Vries wrote *(deVries: 217):*

> Wickquasgeck Indians. . . Their pride is to paint their faces strangely with red or black lead. . . When they wish to cleanse themselves of their foulness, they go in the autumn, when it begins to grow cold, and make, away off, near a running brook, a small oven, large enough for three or four men to lie in it. In making it, they first take twigs of trees, and then cover them tight with clay, so that smoke cannot escape. This being done, they take a parcel of stones, which they heat in a fire, and then put in the oven, and when they think that it is sufficiently hot, they take the stones out again, and go and lie in it, men and women, boys and girls, and come out so perspiring, that every hair has a drop of sweat on it. In this state they plunge into the cold water; saying that it is healthy, but I let its healthfulness pass; they then become entirely clean, and more attractive than before.

John Josselyn *(Josselyn: 94)* wrote about the European-introduced plagues that were destroying the Native Americans. He discussed one of their attempted cures, using sweathouses. This cure had probably worked well for minor diseases before, but could not cure smallpox:

> . . . they use their own remedies, which is sweating, etc.. Their manner is when they have plague or small pox amongst them to cover their Wigwams with Bark so close that no Air can enter in, lining them . . . within, and making a great fire they remain there in a stewing heat till they are in a top sweat, and then run out into the Sea or River, and presently after they come into their Hutts again they either recover or give up the Ghost. . .

The ancient sweathouse practices of Scandinavia and northern Asia may have been transferred by diffusion over the whole world. The practices are similar everywhere. They may have developed independently on the different continents, of course.

Animals drawn on the Willem Blaeu Map of 1635

CHAPTER 7

WHAT EUROPEANS SAW IN WOODLANDS VILLAGES

There are no known pictures of Wiechquaeskeck from the 17th century, but there are two portraits of old Delaware leaders that were painted in 1735 *(Figs. 29 and 30)*. The Wiechquaeskeck were part of the well-known Delaware, or Lenape, people. These are the only likenesses that exist of the famous Lenape tribe. Their use of neck pouches, necklaces, and tattoos was probably typical

The two left portraits in Figures 29 and 30, **Lappiwinsa, a Delaware Chief,** and **Tishcohan, a Delaware Chief** were painted from life about 1735, just before their signing of the infamous "Walking Purchase" of southeastern Pennsylvania *(see Kraft's description, 27:102)*. These portraits were painted by Gustavus Hesselius, a Swedish artist, for the two sons of William Penn. They are in the Collection of The Historical Society of Pennsylvania (HSP). (Accession Nos. 1834.3 and 1834.1) The two right portraits in Figures 29 and 30 are copies of Hesselius' paintings that were made around 1845 to illustrate a book, McKenny and Hall's **History of the Indian Tribes of North America (1836-1844).** The artist who drew the copies, a century later, anglicized them considerably.

Both the chiefs were old when they were the portraits were painted, and their names had probably been changed to reflect their current status. The name **Lappawinsa** (also spelled :Lappawinsoe), according to Heckewelder, meant "he is gone away gathering corn, nuts, or any thing eatable." The name **Tishcohan** (also spelled Tasucamin, Teshakomen, and Tishekunk), and means, according to Heckewelder, "he who never blackens himself."

Lappawinsa was a chief among those of the Forks of the Delaware, at Easton, Pennsylvania. This was the northern point of the "Walking Purchase." It was not far from Wiechquaeskeck lands.

These men pictured have heavy, woollen, European, blue cloth wrapped around their bodies and thrown over their shoulders. It was called "Duffels cloth," because it was made in the town of Duffel, near Antwerp, then in "The Netherlands." (It is now in Belgium.) Duffel's cloth was a popular trade item throughout the 17th century. In the earlier years of the century, the Natives would have been using woven fiber sashes and animal skins in the same way. The thick, woolen Duffel's cloth was quickly very desirable to them.

Both chiefs wore muskrat skins for tobacco pouches, suspended by leather thongs. Tishcohan has a Dutch clay pipe in his tobacco pouch, and the skin is decorated with wampum beads in patterns. Lappawinsa is wearing a bead necklace, which appears to be made of small trade beads. He also has tattoos on his forehead and cheek.

Henry Hudson's Descriptions in 1609

Samuel Purchas (*Purchas: 592-595*) wrote about what Henry Hudson saw near Manhattan and Westchester in 1609. These were the Wiechquaeskeck. On one trip ashore:

> … our Masters Mate went on land with an old Savage, a Governor of the Countrey, who carried him to his house and made him good cheere.

> They goe in Deere skins loose, well dressed. They have yellow Copper. They desire Cloathes, and are very civill.

> This day many of the people came aboard [*the Half Moon*], some in Mantles of Feathers, and some in Skinnes of divers sorts of good Furres. Some women also came to us with Hempe. They had red Copper Tabacco pipes, and other things made of Copper they did weare about their neckes.

> …two great Canoes came aboard full of man; the one with their Bowes and Arrowes, and the other in shew of buying of Knives to betray us; but we perceived their intent.

Verrazano's Descriptions in 1524

Verrazano sailed up the coast in 1524 and reported on the Native Americans. He sailed into New York Harbor. Some of his reports about what he saw included (*Verrazano: 134-139*):

> They go completely naked except around the loins they wear skins of small animals like martens, with a narrow belt of grass around the body, to which they tie various tails of other animals which hang down to the knees; the rest of the body is bare, and so is the head. Some of

Painted around 1845 from the
originals for a book illustration

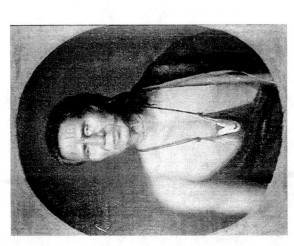

Painted from life in 1735
By Gustavus Hesselius

Figure 29
Lappawinsa, a Delaware Chief
(also Lappawinsoe)
Name meant, "He is gone away gathering corn, nuts, or anything eatable"

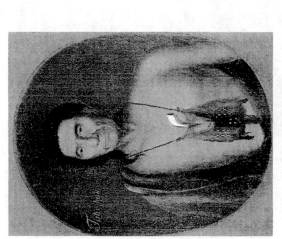

Painted from life in 1735
By Gustavus Hesselius

Painted around 1845 from the
originals for a book illustration

Figure 30
Tischcohan, a Delaware Chief
(also Tasucamin, Teshakomen, Tishekunk)
Name meant, "He who never blackens himself"

them wear garlands of birds feathers. They are dark in color...with thick black hair, not very long, tied behind the head like a small tail. They have broad chests, strong arms...and are well composed.

The old man had on his naked body a stag skin, skillfully worked like damask with varius embroideries; the head was bare, the hair tied back with various bands, and around the neck hung a wide chain decorated with many different-colored stones.

Their women are just as shapely and beautiful; very gracious, of attractive manner and pleasant appearance...they go nude except for a stag skin embroidered like the men's, and some wear rich lynx skins on their arms; their bare heads are decorated with various ornaments made of braids of their own hair which hang down over their breasts on either side...both men and women had various trinkets hanging from their ears...they had many sheets of worked copper...

Adriaen van der Donck in Westchester in 1640-50

Adriaen van der Donck, the "jonkheer" (a young noble) who was the eponym for the town of Yonkers *(Sect. 6)*, was probably the best observer of life in Wiechquaeskeck villages. He was friendly with the Wiechquaeskeck who lived around his large plantation in the Bronx, and he frequently visited them in their wigwams. He was one of the few voices of moderation in dealing with the Natives during the Governor Kieft period. His description of New Netherland *(vanderDonck)* is well translated and readily available.

One of the sections of Van der Donck's book is, "of the manners and peculiar customs of the Natives of the New Netherlands." This is a selection from his writings *(vanderDonck: 71-76):*

Of their Bodily Form and Appearance

Their appearance and bodily form, as well of the men as of the women, are well proportioned, and equal in height to the Netherlanders, varying little from the common size. Their limbs are properly formed, and they are sprightly and active. They can run very fast for a long time, and they can carry heavy packs.

. . . to heavy slavish labour the men have a particular aversion, and they manage their affairs accordingly, so that they need not labour much . . . The men and women commonly have broad shoulders and slender waists. Their hair, before old age, is jet black, sleek and uncurled . . . on other parts of the body they have little or no hair, and if any appear on their chins they pluck it out by the roots.

The men and women all have fine brown eyes and snow-white teeth . . .
The colour of their skin is not so white as ours.

Their women are well favored and fascinating. Several of our
Netherlanders were connected with them before our women came over,
and remain firm in their attachments. Their faces and countenances are
as various as they are in Holland.

[we] hold different names to distinguish different nations. . . . They
were called Wild Men (Wilden).

Of the Food and Subsistence of the Indians

In eating and drinking the Indians are not excessive, even in their feast
days. . . Their common drink is water from a living spring. . . .
Sometimes in the season of grapes, when they have fresh meat or fish, .
. . they will press out the juice of the grapes and drink it new. They
never make wine or beer *(vanderDonck: 74)*.

Drunken men are called fools. When they associate much with our
people, and can obtain liquor, they will drink to excess. . . nor have
they any diseases or infirmities that are caused by drunkeness.

Their common food is meat, and fish of every kind, according to the
seasons . . . They have no pride, or particular methods, in preparing
their food. Their fish or meat they usually boil in water. . . Seldom do
they warm up or boil any food, unless it be small pieces of meat or fish,
when they travel or are hunting.

For bread they use maize . . . which the women pound fine into meal . . .
of which they bake cakes . . . Their common food is *pap* or *mush* . . .
they seldom pass a day without it. . . . We seldom visit an Indian lodge
at any time of the day, without seeing their *sapaen* preparing, or seeing
them eat the same. . . . Without sapaen they do not eat a satisfactory
meal . . . they frequently boil fish or meat with it . . . when they have the
articles dried hard and pounded fine. . . . They also use many dry beans,
which they consider dainties. *[Sect. 6-D]*.

They observe no stated time for their meals . . . but they suppose it best
to eat when they are hungry. . . . They have no excessive eaters or
gluttons among them.

On extraordinary occasions, when they wish to entertain any person,
then they prepare beavers' tails, bass heads, with parched corn meal, or
very fat meat stewed with shelled chestnuts bruised.

Of the Clothing and Ornaments Worn . . .

Their clothing usually is of one fashion, and they are not proud of their
dress, except some of their young persons . . . Their women are more

inclined to dress, and to wear ornamental trinkets *[vanderDonck: 79]*.

The males until they are twelve . . . run nearly naked in summer. . . . The females, when they are able to run about, wear a little covering. They are all accustomed to wearing a leather girdle, which is usually ornamented with pieces of whales' fins, whale-bones or wampum.

When the men can procure duffels cloth, then they wear a piece of the same . . . which they gird around their waists, and draw up with a fold to cover their nakedness, with a flap of each end hanging down front and rear.

The women also wear a cloth around their bodies, fastened by a girdle, which extends down below their knees, and is as much as an undercoat. . . they wear a dressed deer-skin coat, girt around the waist. The lower border of this skirt they ornament with great art, and nestle the same with strips, which are tastefully decorated with wampum . . . frequently worth from one to three hundred guilders. . . . The men and women usually wear a plaid of duffels cloth . . . over the right shoulder, drawn in the form of a knot around the body, with the ends extending down below the knees. This plaid serves them for a covering by day and a blanket by night.

The men usually go bare-headed, and the women with their hair bound behind, in a club of about a hand long, in the form of a beaver's tail; over which they draw a square cap, which is frequently ornamented with wampum. When they desire to appear fine, they draw a head-band around the forehead, which is also ornamented with wampum &c. . . . Their headdress forms a handsome and lively appearance. Around their necks they wear various ornaments, which are also decorated with wampum. . . . They wear beautiful girdles, ornamented with their favorite wampum, and costly ornaments in their ears. Their young women and their courtiers, when they desire to appear superfine, also paint a few black stripes on their faces . . . The men paint themselves uniformly, particularly their faces, with various colours . . . Some of them wear a band about their heads, manufactured and braided of scarlet deer-hair, interwoven with soft, shining red hair. . . . They however seldom decorate themselves in this manner, unless they have a young female in view. Otherwise they are naturally filthy and negligent in their dress. . . . In winter . . . The men, to defend themselves against the cold, grease themselves with bear and raccoon fat. They also wear clothing made of weasel, bear, deer, and buffalo skins, &c.

Of Their Feast Days and Particular Assemblies

Feasts and great assemblages are not common among the Indians, yet they occur sometimes, and on special occasions, as on the subjects of

> peace, war, alliances, treaties . . . or in relation to the fruitfulness of the
> seasons, or to celebrate some successful occurrence by frolicking and
> dancing . . . on all important matters all the chiefs and persons of any
> distinction in the nation assemble in their councils, when each of them
> express their opinions freely *[vanderDonck: 88]*.
>
> They kindle large fires and dance around and over the same, lengthwise
> and across, they roll, tumble overhead, and bend themselves, and
> continue their violent exercises until the sweat pours out . . . When they
> have stuffed themselves like cattle and can scarcely move, then the old
> and middle-aged conclude with smoking, and the young with a
> *kintecaw,* singing and dancing, which frequently is continued until
> morning.

Van der Donck wrote about the Wiechquaeskeck trying "to enchant and charm the devil and to carry out witchcraft" *(vanderDonck: 88)*. What he said is interesting, but he probably knew little about what they were really thinking. Other writers, in both New Netherland and Massachusetts, were similarly intrigued, but did not know what was going on. They observed from their background as nominal Christians and reported the Indian ceremonies in many different ways. Most of the Native Americans evidently believed that there was a spiritual Power above them. They lived with Nature, and how else could they explain what was happening around them? They went through ceremonies with great emotional and physical impact. Often the young people spent the rest of the night "singing and dancing . . . until morning." The thoughts of the Wiechquaeskeck are impossible to discern from European observations.

Another quote from van der Donck may be of interest because most Americans have always been preoccupied with "Indian wars" and fighting *(vanderDonck: 99)*:

Of Their Wars and Weapons

> The principal command and authority among the Indians is developed
> in war. . . . They are artful in their measures, furious in their attacks,
> and unmerciful victors. When their plans are hazardous, then they are
> conducted covertly and privately by night. . . . when they are surrounded
> and cannot escape, they fight obstinately . . . The victors accept of no
> ransom, nor are their captives certain of their lives until they are given
> over to persons who have previously lost connections by blood in war.
> They seldom destroy women and children, unless it be in their first fury
> . . . The women they treat as they do their own, and the children they
> bring up as their own to strengthen the nation.

Their weapons formerly were bows and arrows, with a war-club hung to the arm and a square shield which covered the body up to the shoulders. Their faces they disfigure . . . they bind bands or snake-skins around the head, and place a fox's or wolf's tail perpendicularly upon the head, and walk as proud as peacocks. At present many of them use firearms, which they prize highly, and learn to use dexterously . . . At present they also use small axes (tomahawks) instead of their war-clubs, and thus they march onward.

David deVries *(deVries: 223-224)* made some comments about Native warfare between tribes, "At the North I saw savages who were going to war, their weapons were bows and arrows...a shield of leather...buffalo skin." On Feb. 22, 1643, he wrote, "Mayekender *(Mahican)* savages, who came from Fort Orange and wanted to levy a contribution upon the savages of Wiechquasgeck and Tapean."

Nicholas van Wassenaer *(vanWassenaer: 80)* wrote, "When they wage war against each other, they fortify their tribe with palisades...None are exempt in war."

John Josselyn *(Josselyn 1:103)* observed, "Their Wars are with Neighboring Tribes but the Mowhawks are enemies to all other Indians" and "Their weapons are Bowes & Arrows."

Roger Williams' Observations in New England

There are many descriptions of Wampanoag (who were also Algonquian) village life in the writings of the Puritans and early English travelers. They have been published widely. A problem with those descriptions, however, is that the Puritans had arrived at the peak of one of the several devastating smallpox epidemics. All they could see were scattered groups of Natives and many deserted wigwams.

We have some fine details of Narragansett village life, however, in the writings of Roger Williams. He went to live in what is now Rhode Island and spent much time with the Natives in their villages. He even went on marches through the "wilderness" with them, once for a two-month period. His writings are of interest because the Narrangansetts were also Algonquian-speaking Woodland Indians, and they once controlled much of Long Island, so would have had contact with the Wiechquaeskeck. Some of Roger Williams' observations about Native life, recorded in his book, **A Key Into the Language of America** *(Williams)*, are:

They generally all take *Tobacco*, and it is commonly the only plant which men labour in, the women managing all the rest, they say they take *Tobacco* for two causes; first, against the rheume, which causeth the toothake, which they are impatient of: secondly, to revive and refresh them, they drinking nothing but water *[Williams: 35]*.

If any stranger come in, they presently give him to eat of what they have, many a time, and at all times of the night (as I have fallen in travel upon their houses) when nothing hath been ready, have themselves and their wives, risen to prepare me some refreshing.

Obs. Insteed of shelves, they have several baskets, wherein they put all their householdstuff, they have some great bags or sacks made of Hempe, which will hold five or sixe bushels *[Williams: 50]*.

... bewailing is very solemne amongst them morning and evening, and sometimes in the night they bewail their lost husbands, wives, children, brethren, or sisters &c *[Williams: 54]*.

... for generally all men throughout the Countrey have a Tobacco-bag with a pipe in it *[see Fig. 30]* hanging at their back; sometimes they make such great pipes of wood and stone, that they are too feet long, with man or beasts carved, so big or massie, that a man may be hurt mortally by one of them, but these commonly come from the *Mauquauwwogs [Mohawks]*, or the men eaters ...

[removing a wigwam] They are quicke, in a half day, yea, sometimes a few houres warning to be gone and the house up elsewhere, especially, if they have stakes readie pitcht for their Mats. .... The men make the pole or stakes, but the women make and set up, take downe, order and carry the *Mats* and householdstuffe.

Obs. I have heard of many English lost, and have oft been lost my selfe and others have often been found, and succoured by the Indians *[Williams: 58]*.

Birds

Obs. Of this sort *[Blackbirds]* there be millions, which are great devourers of the *Indian* corne as soon as it appears out of the ground. . . .Against the Birds the *Indians* are very careful, both to set their corne deep enough that it may have a strong root so not so apt to be pluckt up. . . . as also they put up little watch-houses in the middle of their fields, *[see Fig. 27]* in which they, or their biggest children lodge, and early in the Morning prevent the Birds, &c *[Williams: 85]*.

Obs. These Birds *[Crows]*, although they do also some hurt, yet scarce will one *Native* amongst an hundred will kil them, because they have a tradition, that the Crow brought them at first an *Indian* Graine of Corne in one Eare and an *Indian* or *French* bean in another, from the Great

God *Kautanantouwits* field in the Southwest from whence they hold came all their Corne and beanes.

Obs. These *[Cormorants]* they take in the night time, where they are asleepe on rocks, off at Sea, and bring in at break of day great store of them.

Obs. *[They lay nets]* on shore, and catch many fowle upon the plains, and feeding under oaks upon akrons, as Geese, Turkies, Cranes, and others, &c.

Obs. *[Passenger Pigeons]* these Fowle breed abundantly, and by reason of their delicate Food, especially in Strawberrie time when they pick up whole large fields . . . they are a delicate fowle. And because of their abundance, and the facility of killing them, they are and may be plentifully fed on *[Wlliams: 87]*.

Wushowunan, the Hawke. Which the Indians keep tame about their houses to keepe the little Birds from their Corne.

John Josselyn in New England

Josselyn, an English tourist, described plants, natural history, medicines, and treatments in his **New England Rarities Discovered** (*Josselyn2*). He concludes with an interesting description of an Indian "SQUA...trick'd up in all her bravery." He wrote:

The Men are somewhat Horse Fac'd, and generally...with Beards: but the Women many of them have very good Features...all of them black Eyed, having even short Teeth, and very white; their Hair black, thick and long, broad Breasted; handsome streight Bodies, and slender...and saving here and their one, of a modest deportment.

Their garments are a pair of Sleeves of Deer, or Moose skin drest, and drawn with lines of several Colours into Asiatick Works, with Buskins of the same, a short Mantle of Trading Cloth, either Blew or Red, fastened with a knot under the chin, and girt about the middle with a Zone, wrought with white and blew Beads into pretty Works; of these Beads they have Bracelets for their Neck and Arms, and Links to hang in their Ears, and a fair Table curiously made up with Beads likewise, to wear before their Breast; their Hair they Combe backward, and tye it up short with a Border, about two handfuls broad, wrought in Words as the other with their Beads.

CHAPTER 8

THE FIRST FAIRFIELD COUNTY REAL ESTATE BOOM

The Land Rush After the Pequot War

The English authorities in New England and the Dutch authorities in New Netherland did not coordinate their relationships with the Wiechquaeskeck in the late 1630's. While the Dutch were having skirmishes with the Wiechquaeskeck, the Raritan and the Tappan, among others, the English saw an opportunity to move settlers closer to New Netherland. In fact, the English, fresh from defeating the Pequot, made a decision to move settlers in rapidly, partly to prevent the Dutch from moving eastward from their area. The pawns were the Housatonic, Paugussett, Tankiteke and Wiechquaeskeck. The prize was what would become southwestern Connecticut. Thus, there was a land rush by English settlers to Fairfield County starting about 1638. The Wiechquaeskeck already had enough problems with diseases and the Dutch. The few remaining did not understand what was happening as new people started arriving, first overland from Hartford, and then by boat from the East.

The surge of settlers had all begun in 1620 at Plymouth, Massachusetts, when the first successful colony in New England slowly, and at great loss, sustained itself. The Pilgrims lived peacefully with the Wampanoag. The word got back to England, by 1625, that this was a "new Land of Canaan, flowing with milk and honey." The Great Migration started. From 1628 to 1643, at least 21,000 settlers sailed from England to the Massachusetts Bay Colony area. After the first fleets arrived, fewer and fewer of the immigrants were really "Puritans." They simply were groups of people from English towns who saw a great opportunity for themselves and their families.

With this rush of immigrants, the good lands in eastern Massachusetts were quickly taken, and the new settlers had to move elsewhere. Some groups moved southwest to Connecticut towards the Dutch-controlled area. These were the immigrants who intruded on the Wiechquaeskeck.

This was quite different from how the Dutch settlers had moved into New Netherland. The Dutch had come primarily as a trading company, looking for furs and timber, and anything that they could extract from the land. They developed a good deal of farming, mainly to sustain the colony. Most of the farms were under "patroons," with important individuals controlling great acreages. The English colonists, on the other hand, were all looking for freedom and their own farms.

By 1635, English settlers and traders began to move overland into the Connecticut River valley. Settlements were established at Hartford, Windsor, Wethersfield, and Saybrook. That area became the Connecticut Colony.

The westward-moving colonists were soon clashing with Native Americans as they searched for more land. The Great Migration was at its peak, but only the bravest ventured down the coast to the Connecticut Colony, as it meant passing the powerful Narraganset and Pequot tribes. The Pequots were actively attacking the new settlers along the Connecticut River, killing and taking prisoners *(Mason: iv, x, 2, 4)*. A strong Pequot force attacked the Wethersfield plantation. The Pequot War of 1636 to 1638 then changed the whole picture. In 1637, a Boston force made a devastating attack against the main Pequot village at Mystik *(Mason: 1-10)*. After the destruction of the Pequot's Mystik village, the English pursued some escaping Pequot as far down the coast as Southport, where they killed or captured them in the Great Swamp fight, very close to the Wiechquaeskeck. Many settlers had already reached western Fairfield County by then, and were in the middle of that fighting.

With the end of the Pequot War, Fairfield County suddenly became attractive to the English colonists. Until King Philip's War of the 1670's, a generation later, no concerted Native effort was left to block the settlers' movements. Because the plagues of smallpox had decimated the coastal Native Americans in southwestern Connecticut, there were thousands of acres of arable land that the Indians had previously burned over for hunting, and had prepared for agriculture. There were hundreds of plots of land that the Indians had tilled to grow corn, beans, and squash, and much of it was now deserted. In the early days, there was even good seed corn and seed beans left behind in their buried storage baskets, as the Natives died or fled. Many fertile farming lands of the Native American villages in southwestern Connecticut thus lay fallow. Fairfield County was prime development area, and the land-hungry settlers, who kept pouring over the Atlantic from England, were ready to "plant" new settlements there.

The United Colonies agreed quickly to move cooperatively into southwestern Connecticut to accomodate the flood of new immigrants who had read about **The Good News from New England** by Edward Johnson, and other similar books. The leaders were also eager to block Dutch settlers who were probing east from New Amsterdam. This movement westward on the Connecticut coast continued for about a hundred years. By the mid-1700s, all the arable land had been acquired by immigrants. The most active real estate boom in southwestern Connecticut was in the first six years of this influx. It was complicated near Greenwich and Stamford, however, by an uprising in Westchester of the remaining young Wiechquaeskeck *(Chap. 9).*

The Land Companies Come to Western Connecticut

By 1639, there were three competing land companies pressing the Wiechquaeskeck and Tankiteke remnants for deals on prime land. They were the Connecticut Colony around Hartford (Wethersfield), the New Haven Colony (Quinnipiac), and the Massachusetts Bay Colony at Boston.

Individual English and Dutch settlers had already moved into this very desirable land, and time was of the essence. Companies were formed and their land agents moved in with trade goods, ready to write "legal" deeds, according to English Common Law, with the Wiechquaeskeck and Tankiteke. Several individuals had already made their own deals with local sagamores, but those agreements do not seem to have been recorded by any later Town Clerk, except for the cryptic "Keofferam hath sould all his Right in ye above sd Parkes unto Jeffere Ferris" appended to the July 8, 1640 land transfer in Greenwich.

Jeffrey Ferris is one of the few we know about who beat the land companies to western Connecticut by at least a year, but there must have been several others. One of them would have been the famous Dutchman, Labden. There is an oral story about him being chased by young Wiechquaeskeck raiders and leaping off "Laddin's Rock" in Old Greenwich to his death. In this oft-repeated tale, Labden had left his wife and 16-year-old daughter in their cabin to hold the door as he rode off. Labden's wifeand daughter were scalped.

Jeffrey Ferris had come to America about 1635 and was made a freeman in Boston. (Ferris family records, The Historical Society of the Town of Greenwich) He removed to Wethersfield, Connecticut, where he bought four acres of land and built a house. He lived there four years, but on February 6, 1639, he was called before the General Court *(Trumbull)*. He was fined 20 shillings for "damages land upon his swine in regard his fence is found to be insufficient, and his Cowes were proved to be in Westcoatts Corne." That was too much for him to accept, so he took his family, goods, and animals, trekked to the Old Greenwich area, and bought land from Keofferam, probably in 1639. His land apparently stretched from Greenwich Cove to the Innis Arden Golf Course area. The same story of farmers' animals eating the corn and vegetables of other farmers, and the crops of the neighboring Indians, was repeated time and again. Good fencing was unknown. This problem was to be one of the causes of Kieft's War with the lower Hudson Lenape, which included the Wiechquaeskeck *(Chap. 9)*.

The Wiechquaeskeck and the Tankiteke had little idea about the power that lay behind the friendly land agents, and about how they were losing their future. They were in trouble with diseases and with Dutch hostility. They were were willing to sell their land for any gifts that would help them live. The sakimas (sachems) and sagamores who signed these agreements were the few older leaders who were still in the area. They probably looked very much like Lappawinsa and Tishcohan, pictured in Figures 29 and 30.

The first land agent to make a big deal was **Captain Daniel Patrick**. He was an impressive man who spoke some Algonquian. He had been a hero after the Pequot War, but was forced out of Boston because of his behavior with married women. He came with trade goods from wealthy friends in Boston. On April 20, 1640, he made a deal with sachem **Mahachemo**, shown in Figure 31. He purchased the land between the Norwalk River and the Five Mile River from the Indians of "**Norwake and Makentouh**," now western Norwalk and Rowayton. He used up many of his trade goods in this purchase, which left him short when he made a deal in Greenwich three months later, in July.

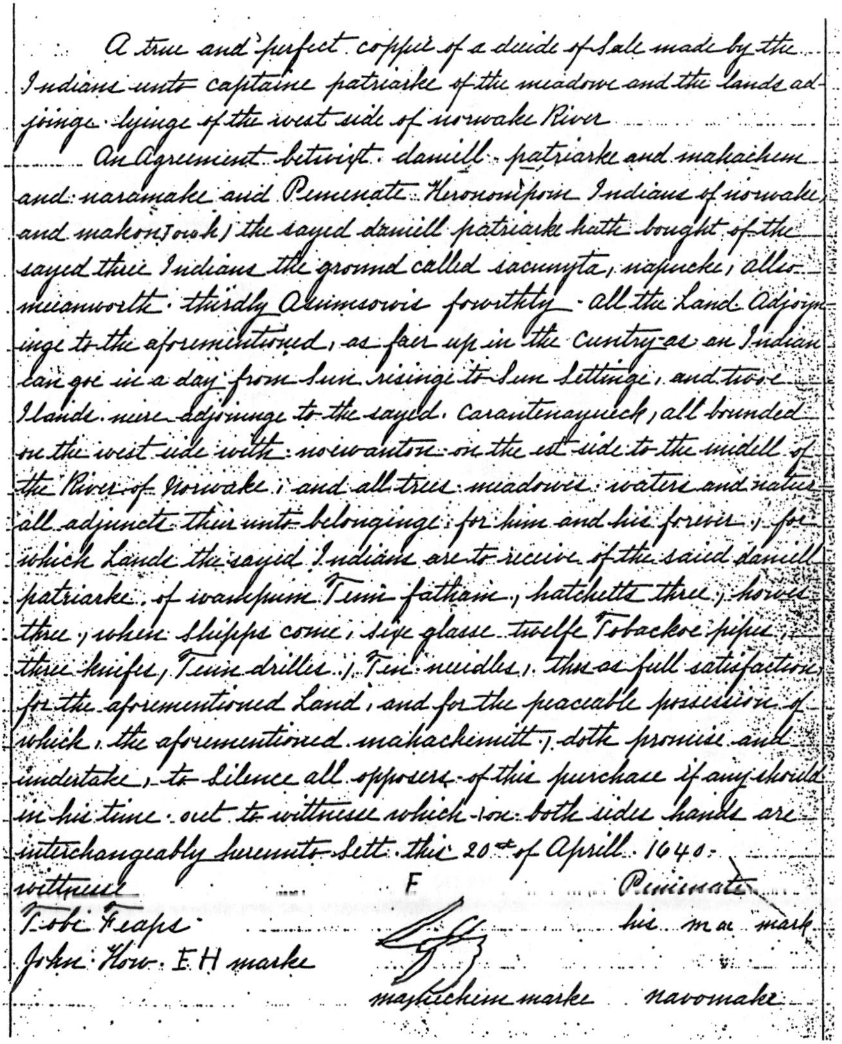

A true and perfect coppie of a deede of sale made by the Indians unto capitaine patriarke of the meadowe and the lands adjoinge lyinge of the west side of norwake River

An Agreement betwixt daniell patriarke and mahachem and naramake and Pemenate Heronompone Indians of norwake and makonjouske; the sayed daniell patriarke hath bought of the sayed three Indians the ground called sacunyta, nasucke, allso micanworth thirdly Ocumsowie fowrthly. all the Land Adjoyinge to the aforementioned, as farr up in the cuntry as an Indian can goe in a day from Sun risinge to Sun settinge, and two Ilande neere adjoinnge to the sayed, Carantenayueck, all bounded on the west side with noiwanton on the est side to the middell of the River of Norwake; and all trees meadowe waters and natne all adjuncte them unto belonginge; for him and his forevir; for which Lande the sayed Indians are to receive of the sayed daniell patriarke of ioaskpum Tenn fathame, hatchette three, howe three; when shippes come, sixe glasse twelfe Tobackoe pipe, three knifes, Tenn drilles; Tenn needles, this as full satisfaction for the aforementioned Land, and for the peaceable possession of which, the aforementioned mahachemitt, doth promise and undertake, to silence all opposers of this purchace if any should in his time out to wittnese which one both sides hande are intrchangeably hereunto sett this 20th of Aprill. 1640.

wittnese

Tobe Feaps

John How EH marke

F

mastchim marke

Pemenate
his m a mark

navomake

Figure 31

The Norwake and Makontouh sell West Norwalk
April 20, 1640

Norwalk Town Land Records

The second land deal was made by **Captain Nathaniel Turner** for the New Haven Colony at Quinnipiac. He dealt with "**Ponus, Sagamore of Toquams, and Wascussue, Sagamore of Shippan.**" On July 1, 1640, he signed a land transfer agreement for most of the present lands of Stamford and Darien east of the Five Mile River and stretching back into Pound Ridge and Bedford, shown in Figure 32. It was one thing to buy the land and another to settle it, however. Evidently Stamford was settled by people from the Wethersfield Men's Plantation rather than by Turner's people from New Haven. The New Haven settlers had only just arrived there and were not ready to move again, while the Wethersfield settlers were already feeling crowded by new neighbors. Stamford still remained a rigid Puritan town under the General Court of New Haven. This caused later arguments with the nearby Greenwich settlers, who were less religious.

Daniel Patrick moved quickly in 1640. He leapfrogged Stamford, which had just been sold to New Haven. He went to stay with Jeffrey Ferris in Greenwich (now the Old Greenwich area), who had already bought some land there from Sagamore Keofferam, in 1639. Angel and Robert Heusted, Andrew Messenger, and Robert Heusted had also already come to live in that area. Patrick worked with all of them and talked to the remnants of the local Indians to make a land deal, shown in Figure 33. It was signed on July 18, 1640 by "**Amogerone and Owenoke, Sachems of Asamuck, amd Rammatthone and Nawhorone, Sachems of Patomuck**" (see Figure 33). Since Patrick had already used most of his trade goods in Darien in April, he did not have all that he offered in July. He promised to bring them more red coats later, but those coats were never delivered. The Norwalk settlers, on the other hand, were more considerate of the Tankiteke, possibly because they had remained friendly during the Kieft's War period. Later leaders of Norwalk directed that the shortchanging of their local tribe by Patrick be made up *(38)*.

This Greenwich land lay between the Asamuck Creek (present Laddins Rock Road) and the Patomuck Creek (present border with Stamford). Before this deal was signed, a boatload of settlers arrived from Boston, including the famous **Elizabeth Winthrop Feake**, niece of Governor Winthrop, and Robert Feake, her husband. They were friends of Daniel Patrick from Watertown, near Boston, and had probably financed his purchases. (Elizabeth would later be immortalized by the Anya Seton

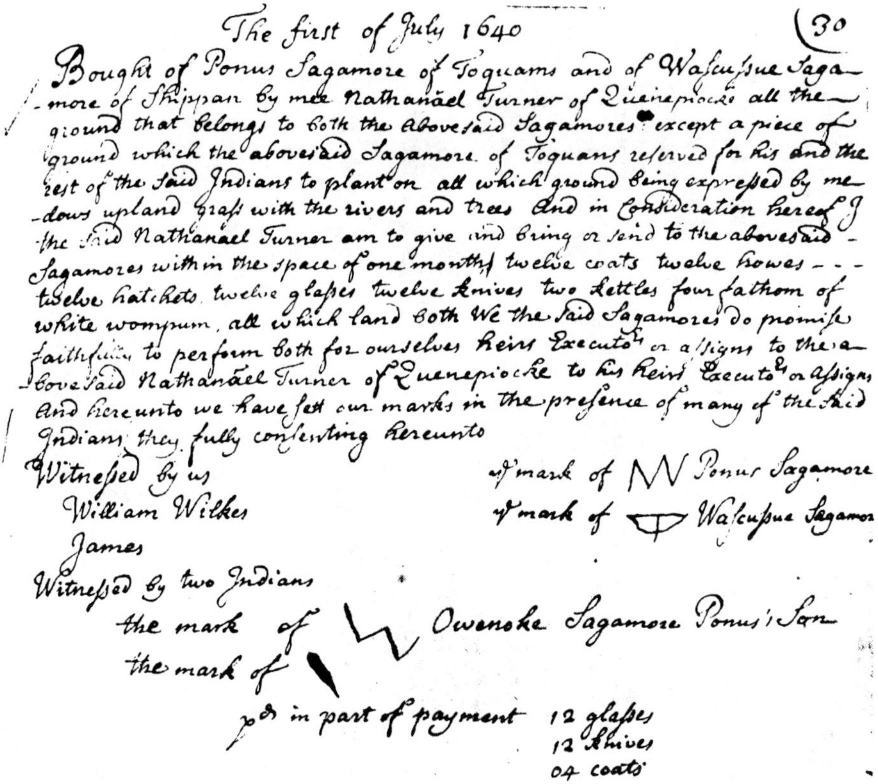

The first of July 1640 (30)

Bought of Ponus Sagamore of Toquams and of Wascussue Sagamore of Shippan by mee Nathanael Turner of Quenepiacke all the
ground that belongs to both the abovesaid Sagamores except a piece of
ground which the abovesaid Sagamore of Toquans reserved for his and the
rest of the said Indians to plant on all which ground being expressed by me
dows upland grass with the rivers and trees And in Consideration hereof I
the said Nathanael Turner am to give and bring or send to the abovesaid
Sagamores within the space of one month twelve coats twelve howes - - -
twelve hatchets twelve glasses twelve knives two Kettles four fathom of
white wompum, all which land both We the said Sagamores do promise
faithfully to perform both for ourselves heirs Executors or assigns to the a-
bovesaid Nathanael Turner of Quenepiocke to his heirs Executors or Assigns
And hereunto we have set our marks in the presence of many of the said
Indians they fully consenting hereunto

Witnessed By us   the mark of M Ponus Sagamore
    William Wilkes   the mark of ▽ Wascussue Sagamore
    James
Witnessed By two Indians
    the mark of ⋀ Owenoke Sagamore Ponus's Son
    the mark of ❱

    pd in part of payment   12 glasses
                            12 knives
                            04 coats

Figure 32

The Toquam and Shippan sell Stamford
July 1, 1640

Stamford Land Records

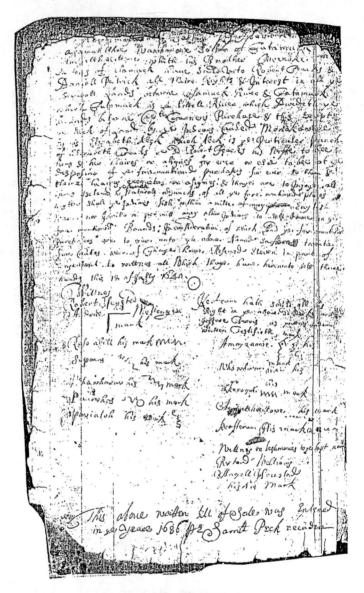

Figure 33

The Asamuck and Patomuck sell Old Greenwich
July 18, 1640

Greenwich Land Records

novel, "The Winthrop Woman.")

There were soon complaints from the Stamford people about the Indians frequenting the house of Daniel Patrick in what is now Old Greenwich. It would therefore seem possible that the second land deal he signed was made around a table in his house there. The earlier settler, Jeffrey Ferris, had probably helped Patrick build the house, as it was on the property that Ferris had acquired the year before.

The fourth Fairfield County land agent to make a land deal was **Roger Ludlow**, who had come from the Connecticut Colony in Hartford. He had previously purchased the Fairfield area from the Pequonnock, who were not Lenape (Delaware), but were allied to the Paugussett and Housatonic. Ludlow probably wanted to expand to the west to stop Daniel Patrick from crossing the Norwalk River to the east. He need not have rushed, as Patrick had run out of trade goods, and he was soon killed in an argument with Dutch soldiers.

On February 26, 1641, Roger Ludlow purchased land for trade goods from the "Indians of Norwake," shown in Figure 34. He claimed all the coastal lands "from the sea a days walk into the country" between the Norwalk and Saugatuck Rivers. He signed the paper with sachem **Mahachemo** and gave his new plantation lands the name "Fairfield." Mahachemo was the same leader who had previously sold west Norwalk to Daniel Patrick. Ludlow was living in Fairfield at the time. He simply extended his holdings west. Actually, the colonial government in Hartford had only given him permission to settle Stratford, but he later told them of the need to move further west to hold back the Dutch incursion.

These four land transfer agreements were the first of which we have records in western Fairfield County. They were the start of a real estate boom that has continued sporadically to the present. The newcomers found the area attractive, because the land was arable, and there were some trees. It was close to Long Island Sound harbors, for fishing and for boat transportation of farm products, and it was an easy commute to Manhattan to meet the traders from all over the world. The Wiechquaeskeck had loved the area and had also found it attractive for exactly the same reasons. Many residents today still have the same reasons for being there.

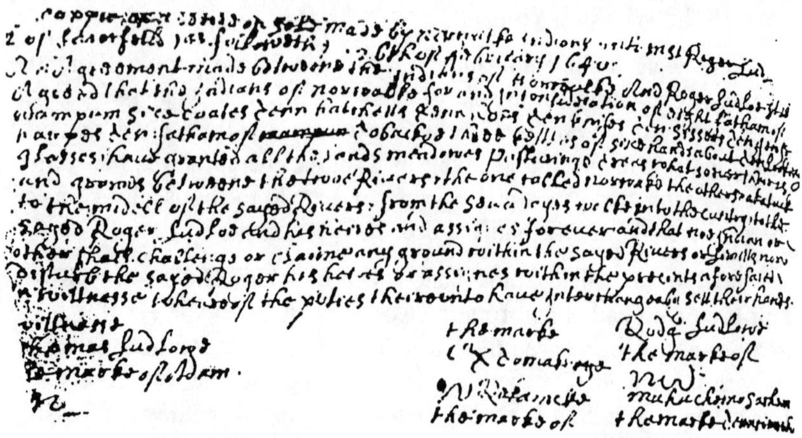

Copy of Original Land Transfer Agreement of Feb. 26, 1640/41

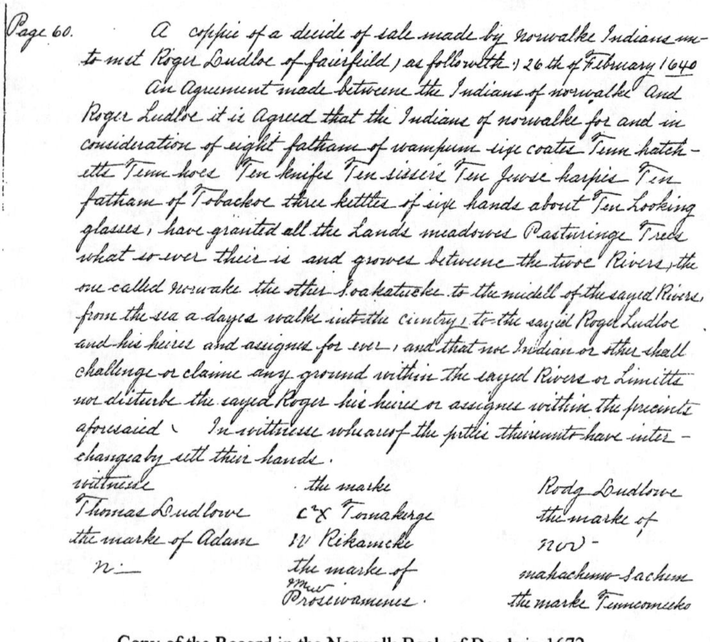

Page 60.   A coppie of a decide of sale made by norwalke Indians unto met Roger Ludloe of fairfield, as followeth, 26 th of February 1640
An Agrument made betweene the Indians of norwalke And
Roger Ludloe it is Agreed that the Indians of norwalke for and in
consideration of eight fathams of wampum six coates Tenn hatchette Tenn hose Ten knifes Ten sissirs Ten Juse harpis Ten
fathams of Tobacke three kettles of six hands about Ten Looking
glasses, have granted all the Lands meadowes Pasturinge Trede
what so ever their is and growes betweene the twoe Rivers, the
one called norwake the other Soakatucke to the middell of the sayed Rivers,
from the sea a dayes walke intothe cuntry, to the sayed Roger Ludloe
and his heirs and assigns for ever, and that no Indian or other shall
challenge or claime any ground within the sayed Rivers or Limitts
nor disturbe the sayed Roger his heirs or assignes within the precincts
aforesaid.   In witnesse whearof the pttie thisuntto have inter-
changaby sett their handes.

witnesse   the marke   Rodg Ludlowe
Thomas Ludlowe   c X Tomakurge   the marke of
the marke of Adam   N Rekamehe   noo -
n   the marke of   mahachmo Sachim
                       noo   the marke Tunnomecko
                       Prosewamines.

Copy of the Record in the Norwalk Book of Deeds in 1672

Figure 34

The Norwalke sell East Norwalk
February 26, 1641

Norwalk Land Records

These land deals accounted for most of western Fairfield County, but there were many small tracts left. There were disagreements with the next generation of Wiechquaeskeck, and a few received consideration in Stamford and Norwalk, although by then there were few of them left *(Appx. C).* Some young Wiechquaeskeck men from Westchester actively raided the area during the next four years *(Chap. 9),* but that was a losing battle for them.

A basic problem with all the land transfer agreements that were made with the Native Americans by the colonists is that the two concepts of land ownership were vastly different. Writing in 1893, Powell *(35: 40)* divided Native American tribal land into three classes: First, the land occupied by the villages; second, the land actually employed in agriculture; third, the land claimed by the tribe but not occupied, except as a hunting ground. He said, "to determine tribal boundaries within accurately drawn lines is in the vast majority of cases quite impossible." Yet, the Europeans came in and drew such lines, and they had Indian leaders sign off on them. In the first half century, the European land transfer documents, which Roger Williams had called for, seemed to be working, but as more Indians died and more settlers arrived, there was less definition of the land that was taken. Finally, the later settlers just took whatever land there was, even if small numbers of Indians were already on it. When the settlers started to push west from the New England states, there was little further consideration of Native American ownership of specific pieces of land. In the first Contact century, however, we have a fascinating series of documents in the land records. They are quite different from the "treaties" that were drawn up with the Natives in the 19th century, usually after a military clash.

These early land transaction documents were written by land agents well versed in English Common Law. There are still copies of many of the agreements that the legally-trained agents wrote. They are not the originals, but transcriptions made in a later century. Figures 31 to 35 are copies of some of these early land deals, and are kept in the Greenwich, Stamford, and Norwalk Town Halls. Possibly, there were many other written deals which were not kept for posterity because those who wrote them did not understand that legal documents should be kept in a safe place for many generations

English Common Law for Land Transactions

In 1636, Roger Williams had established Providence, Rhode Island. He was one of the first to insist that all land deals with the Indians be legally bound by a land transfer document, with a payment of goods, to be legal. These agreements were later recorded by Town Clerks, and then entered into the records as "deeds." Williams had hoped that this would help to make the deals fair to the Indians, and said that these documents should be written to conform to the English Common Law of the time, which has changed little since then. English Common Law was maintained after the American Revolution for land agreements in order not to disrupt continuity of ownership in the new Republic.

Note that these civil land transfer documents were completely different from the military "Indian land cession treaties" that were written across America, mainly in the 19th century. The land transfer documents of the 17th century were civil agreements, although probably only a few of the Native Americans really understood their implications. The later land cession treaties were military field documents.

The leaders of the Colonies followed Williams' advice and were serious about making the Indian land transactions legal according to English Common Law. They simply thrust the laws dealing with property ownership upon the dwindling Wiechquaeskeck. In 1650, the Connecticut General Court directed Roger Ludlow *(Trumbull)* "to take some paynes in drawing forth a body of Lawes for the gouernment of this Common welth." The Code of Laws was adopted in 1650. The codified laws were then sent to England to be printed. Copies, together with copies of the Fundamental Orders, were then sent to all the towns. Around the mid 1650s, it is reported by Trumbull:

> The governor informed the court that there is sent over now in Mr. Garrett's ship five hundred law-books, which Mr. Hopkins hath gotten printed, and six paper books for records for the jurisdiction; with a seal for the colony, which he desires them to accept as a token of his love. The law-books cost, printing and paper, L10.10; the six paper books L2.8. The law-books are now ordered to be divided as followeth: New Haven, 200; Milford, 80; Guilford, 60; Stamford, 70, a part of which for Greenwich; Southold, 50; Brandford, 40. For every of which books, each plantation is to pay twelve pence in good country pay (wheat and pease were propounded) to the governor.

The Wiechquaeskeck and the Tankiteke did not have a chance against this legal juggernaut. They could not even read a simple letter, much less the codified laws. The rapidly encroaching colonists were demanding that the laws be followed down to the last detail. Consider the great number of law-books in each town. America had become "a country of laws" 125 years before the Revolution. The Indians knew nothing about such laws except those few in Massachusetts who had been sent to schools by the Puritans. No one was reported to have given reading and legal training to any Natives in Wiechquaeskeck territory. The Wiechquaeskeck and the Tankiteke had few bargaining chips, and were to spend the next century being manipulated, and slowly ground down, by these laws, that were basically designed to protect the property rights of the English.

It is interesting that the documents that were written then have similarities to the land deeds that are written today *(William Nathaniel Carroll, private communication)*. This is because the English Common Law was essentially unchanged after the Revolution to help maintain legal ownership records in continuity. Some of the phrases in those 1600s documents sound familiar still. A few examples are:

"All their rights and interests in all the several lands"
"Any part or parcel thereof"
"Free said lands from all former sales, gifts, mortgages"
"Give, grant and quit claim all the lands"
"Have sold all our right, title and interest"
"His mark - X"
"In consideration of which are to give unto you"
"Know all men by these presents"
"Lock, stock and barrel"
"To all their heirs, executors or assigns"
"To possess and enjoy their own forever"
"To witness which have hereto set their hand"

The First Three Land Agents

When the land transfer deals were starting with the Wiechquaeskeck and Tankiteke, the Indian leaders had no way of understanding that they were dealing with experienced financiers and leaders with wide backgrounds in commerce and law. The Indian sagamores were intelligent and capable, but they had lived their lives with small Native bands. They had a concept of owning and protecting territory, but absolutely no concept of the permanent ownership of a small plot of fenced land. They understood negotiation of tribal rules, and verbal agreements, but had not heard of the written English Common Law. When the talks started, there was no contest. They dealt with professional, experienced real estate agents, who were also lawyers.

The first land agent to make a deal was not a lawyer, but was a soldier who knew about legal acquisition of land. He was **Captain Daniel Patrick**, who was the epitome of a swashbuckler. He had been trained in the Dutch Army and had served in Holland where he had married a Dutch girl, Anneke. He was hired by the Massachusetts Bay Company as one of the military officers in their private guard force as a Captain, the highest field rank in New England. He had become a "freeman" in Boston in 1631. Patrick had been a leader in the Pequot War *(Mason)*, but had fallen from grace in Massachusetts because, despite the fact that he had an attractive Dutch wife, he was approaching other married woman too often. Governor Winthrop called him "proud and vicious" *(Winthrop)*. The authorities indicated that he and Anneke should leave the Colony. But he was a capable man, so someone in Massachusetts set him up with trade goods to make land deals. This may well have been the Winthrops, since Elizabeth Winthrop Feake had special concessions in Patrick's land deal in Greenwich in 1640. On April 20, 1640, his first purchase was land between the Norwalk and Five Mile Rivers from the Tankiteke Indians of Norwake and Makentouh. Old Greenwich was his second purchase.

The second land agent was **Nathaniel Turner**, who was probably from London. He had become a freeman in Boston in 1632. He was also a Captain in the Massachusetts Bay Colony force, and later became a deputy to the governor. He went to live at Quinnipiac, and represented the New Haven Colony. It was then the most rigid colony in its Puritan beliefs, so the new town of Stamford inherited that thinking.

Roger Ludlow was the third land agent to arrive, representing the Hartford Colony *(Trumbull)*. Ludlow had been high in the ranks of the Massachusetts Bay Colony as an "Assistant." He had owned his own ship, the "Mary and John," and had sailed her with 150 persons from Plymouth, England in 1630. He became a Deputy Governor of Massachusetts. As such, he had directed the settling of Windsor, Connecticut. From there, he went to the Fairfield area to plant a new settlement in 1639. In later years, he moved to Virginia.

When Ludlow saw that Daniel Patrick had a deed to the west Norwalk area, he was probably concerned it would restrict the growth of Fairfield. That was why he went down to Norwalk, and got a land transfer agreement on February 26, 1641, from the **Norwake** for all the land between the Norwalk and Saugatuck Rivers, to join to his earlier purchases. Those lands were most fruitful. By 1650, many settlers, who had moved from the Bay Colony to the Hartford and Wethersfield area, came down to Fairfield to search there for better land.

Ludlow's trade goods were supplied by **William Pynchon,** in his official capacity as Deputy Governor on the Connecticut River. Pynchon and his wife had come over in 1630 with John Winthrop, who was to be Governor of the Colony. Pynchon had money and legal training. He became an important financial figure in the Massachusetts Bay Colony. The Colony was interested in the Connecticut River valley, and sent many settlers overland there, pushing out the Dutch, who had small forts near Hartford and at the mouth of the river, but few settlers. Some Massachusetts settlers went by boat to the Connecticut River, but they had to watch for the Pequot, who tried to prevent their passage. In the Connecticut Colony, Pynchon was on courts and committees with Roger Ludlow. His lengthy financial records in the Massachussetts Historical Society archives show that he assembled large amounts of trade goods for the purchase of land from the Indians. It is probable that both Ludlow from Hartford and Nathaniel Turner from New Haven got their supplies of trade goods through Pynchon.

At the same time, some Dutch settlers were moving east as far as Stamford. Very few went further east, since they had been pushed out of the Saybrook area and the House of Hope, near Hartford, both on the Connecticut River, by the influx of the English from Massachusetts..

17th Century Land Transfer Agreements

The present town boundaries in western Fairfield County were obviously not in existence in 1639. Many of them were formed by the terms of the land purchases from the Wiechquaeskeck in the first few years, and in the following 80 years. Some of the boundaries were along water flows which still exist. A few were marked by trees and physical features which no longer exist. Some were simply compass lines, such as north "a days walke into the country."

Land surveying was elementary when it was done, using only a compass and a "chain" or measuring tape. Thus, western Fairfield County has winding roads that followed old Native and animal paths. They were simply paths of least resistance across the terrain *(Chap. 5)*.

There are still good copies of many land transfer documents that were agreed upon in the 17th century. These "land transfer documents" were simply sales agreements with the Natives, rather than true "deeds" as they are often described. They were bills of sale drawn by experienced lawyers and presented to the Wiechquaeskeck and Tankiteke as a *fait accompli*. They became deeds at later dates, when Town Clerks recorded them legally. For example, the transfer of land in Greenwich on July 18, 1640 was not recorded as a deed until 1686 when "This above bill of Sale was entered in ye Yeare 1686 pr Sam'l Peck recorder." Similarly, Roger Ludlow's land transfer agreement in 1640 from the Indians of Norwalk for all the land between the Norwalk and Saugatuck Rivers was "recorded in the Book of Deeds in the year 1672." It then became a deed that could be referred to in court

An interesting point about the land transfer agreements is that few of them were understood by any of the participants. The Indians did not understand land ownership at first, and could not read the agreements. They were told to put their "marks" on the agreements and did so, some with a flourish. Figure 35, **Indian Marks on a Land Transfer Agreement**, is a particularly good set of Indian marks. It is not the original set of marks, but is a copy made of them by John Copp, the Town Recorder, on February 4th, 1708/09. This set of Indian marks was used for many years by Linnea Greig, in the Norwalk Land Records Office, to show to visiting groups of school children. It is still being used.

These marks have been called their "signatures" because they were distinctive marks indicating identity, but they were not signatures in the normal sense of signing. They were noted as "his mark," or "the marke of" on the documents. The Natives were not alone. More than half of the settlers signed with "his mark," which was commonly an "X" for the illiterate English, but was sometimes an attempt at their initials. Most of the settlers could not read.

Little has really changed in the understanding of legal documents, except that most people can now sign their names. We still trust our lawyers to hand us a document to sign that means what we intend it to mean, even though it is written in words similar to the old English

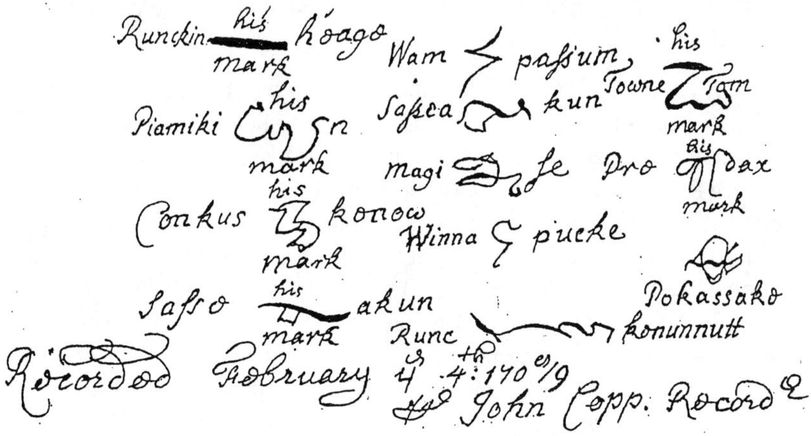

Figure 35

Indian Marks on a Land Transfer Agreement

Norwalk Land Records

On February 15, 1651, these Norwalke Indians sold the present land of Darien and New Canaan to a group of settlers. It was essentially all the land between Capt. Patrick's purchase on the west side of the Norwalk River to the Noroton River. The signers included the famous leaders **Runckinheage** (Runckinhoago) and **Piamikin**. The Natives' "marks," next to their names, are some of the most interesting marks on local records. Note that the agreement was signed in 1651, but was not recorded as a deed until 1778/9. This deed came from the Norwalk Land Records, through the courtesy of Linnea Greig.

Common Law. There was the same trust in the 17th century, also, but frequently the Indians were receiving poorer terms than they had expected. In Greenwich, for example, when they transferred their land by these mysterious documents, they found themselves excluded from their traditional fish traps in Greenwich Cove, on which they had depended for food for centuries. So few of them were left, they could do nothing about it. As even fewer were left, more transfer agreements were thrust before them in the next hundred years which effectively eased them off all the land.

Many of the land transfer documents signed by the Native Americans in the 17th century are readily available in the respective Town Halls and Historical Societies in Fairfield County. Land transfer agreements listed here are from as far east as Southport because there was much interaction between the Wiechquaeskeck, Tankiteke, and Pequonnock Indians. Some of the Tankiteke were possibly Munsee-speaking Delaware Indians, like the Wiechquaeskeck. The Sasqua band of the Pequonnock, in Fairfield, however, were clearly Paugussett, part of the larger group of Natives along the Housatonic, who spoke the Quiripi dialect. They could understand each other, however. They intermingled in the late 17th century as they were pushed out of their ancestral lands by disease, and by the influx of the Europeans. Remnants of both moved north together up the Norwalk River *(Chap. 10)*.

17th Century Land Transfer Agreements in Southwestern Connecticut

The following is not a complete list of the land transfer documents in southwestern Connecticut, but it contains most of the key documents of major historical interest. Chronologically, they are:

1639 - Roger Ludlow's Purchase of Fairfield

Ludlow, representing the Connecticut Colony at Hartford, made an agreement with the Paugussett tribe for Uncoway, which was all the land around Fairfield west to the Saugatuck River. The Paugussett were Algonquian-speakers allied with the Housatonic. They were friendly with the Tankiteke, who were then a connection to the Wiechquaeskeck. This purchase was the first large colonist land acquisition in southwestern Connecticut.

April 20, 1640 - Daniel Patrick's Purchase of West Norwalk

Patrick bought from **Mahachemo** all the land between the Norwalk River and the (now) Five Mile River, "as farr up in the cuntry as an indian can goe in a day, from sun risinge to sun settinge." He called it:

> ... the ground called Sacunyte napucke, allso Meeanworth, thirdly Asunsowis. Fourthly all the land adjoyninge to the aforementioned, as farr up in the cuntry as an indian can goe in a day, from sun risinge to sun settinge; and two islands neere adjoining to the said carabtenayueck, all bounded on the west side with noewanton to the east side to the middle of the River of Norwake . . . for him and his forever .

Patrick agreed to give the Indians:

> . . . of wampum tenn fathoms, hatchetts three, howes three, when shipps come; sixe glasses, twelfe tobackoe pipes, thrtee knifes, tenn drills, tenn needles; this as full satisfaction for the aforementioned lande.

Note that Patrick did not hand over all the promised goods, but reserved some until "when shipps come." The Norwalk people later made this up to the Indians. (Later in 1640, Patrick had a similar reservation of coats that he promised in Greenwich. These were never made up.) The agreement was also signed by **Tomakergo** and **Tokaneke**, and witnessed by **Prosewamemos** *(Fig.31)*. This land today is Rowayton, West Norwalk, and part of Darien *(38)*
(Norwalk Town Records).

July 1, 1640 - Nathaniel Turner's Purchase of Stamford

Nathaniel Turner represented the New Haven Colony at Quinnipiac. Those colonists had just arrived in New Haven and were in no hurry to move again, but they were concerned about Daniel Patrick coming down from Boston and getting land in their area. They were also concerned that Ludlow and the Hartford people had moved into Fairfield, just west of New Haven, and they would not have room for expansion. So Turner went quickly to Stamford and made a deal with the local sagamores. It was called an "Acknowledgement of Sale," and was dated July 1, 1640 *(Fig.32):*

> Bought of **Ponus** Sagamore of Toquams and of **Wascussue** Sagamore of Shippan by mee Nathaniel Turner of Quenepiocke all the ground that belongs to both of the Above said Sagamores:

> except a piece of ground which the above said Sagamore of
> Toquams reserved for his and the rest of the said Indians to plant
> on.

This included most of present Stamford and Pound Ridge, except for some planting land reserved for the remaining Indians, which is now the Cummings Park area around Westcott Cove. Turner had come in a hurry because of the other purchases being made. He had few trade goods, but promised to bring:

> . . . with in the space of one month, twelve coats twelve howes - - - twelve hatchets, twelve glasses twelve knives two kettles four fathom of white wampum.

At the time, "pd in part of payment," he gave them "12 glasses, 12 knives, 4 coats." The agreement was witnessed by two Indians, one of whom was **Owenoke**, the son of Sagmore **Ponus**. Later, Owenoke was not satisfied with the agreement, and another deal was made with him *(Stamford Town Clerk's Office, Book B, p.30)*.

July 18, 1640 - Daniel Patrick's Purchase of Old Greenwich

Daniel Patrick was in west Norwalk, and felt boxed-in by Turner's purchase. He looked for a larger tract of land with expansion possibilities, which was not under the control of the religious New Haven Colony. He knew that the Winthrop group from Boston were on the way in their boat, so he moved swiftly. He had talked to Jeffrey Ferris by this time, in what is now Old Greenwich. He bypassed Stamford and went to Greenwich to make a deal with the Indians. The land agreement was signed on July 18, 1640. It read in part:

> Wee **Amogerone & Owenoke**, Sachems of Asamuck, and **Rammathone**, **Nawhorone**, Sachems of Patomuck, have sould unto Robert Feacks and Daniell Patricke all theire Rights and Interests in all ye severall Lands betwene Asamuck River and Patomuck, which Patomuck is a little River which Divideth ye Bounds betwene Capt. Turner's Purchase & this . . .

This agreement was signed by **Amogerone, Nawthorne** (Nawhorne), **Amsetthehone,** and **Keofferam**. It was witnessed by **Rasobabitt, Saponas, Whonehorone, Pauonohas,** and **Powiatah.** This was the land that is now Old Greenwich from Greenwich Cove and Sound Beach Avenue north of Binney Park, across to the Stamford border. It is interesting that there was a section set aside:

> . . . by ye Indians called Monakewego, by us Elizabeth Neck, which Neck is ye peticaler purchace of Elizabeth Feakes, ye sd Robt Feacks his Wiffe, to be hers & her heaires or asignes for ever . . .

This tract, which was bought for Elizabeth Winthrop Feake, may well be one of the first properties in Connecticut owned by a woman in her own name! The trade goods offered probably came from Governor Winthrop in Boston, or from another of the Winthrop family. Since most of his trade goods had already been used in the Norwalk purchase, Patrick only offered "twentie five Coates, wherof Theye have Reserved eleven in part of payement." There is no record as to whether Patrick, or anyone in Greenwich, ever came up with the promised eleven coats to give to the dwindling Indian group. Since the Dutch attack on the Wiechquaeskeck's central village of Nanichiestawack intervened, and Patrick had been killed by a Dutch soldier, it is unlikely that the reserved coats were ever delivered *(Fig. 33) (Greenwich Town Records)*.

November 4, 1640 – Transfer of Stamford Title to Settlers from Wethersfield

The New Haven Colony had sent Nathaniel Turner to buy the Stamford area, but, since they had only recently "planted" themselves in New Haven, there were evidently no settlers willing to move again so soon. They therefore made an agreement with Andrew Ward and Robert Coe, approved by the New Haven General Court, to transfer ownership of the area to the Wethersfield Men's Plantation. This was an inter-colonist agreement for "Ye sd Town called Toqums," with no Indians involved. *(Stamford Historical Society)*.

26 Feb. 1640/1641 - Roger Ludlow's Purchase of East Norwalk

An agreement made between the Indians of Norwalk and Roger Ludlowe, "for and in consideration of eight fathom of wampum, sixe coates, tenn hatchets, tenn hoes, tenn knifes, tenn sissors, tenn jewesharpes, tenn fathom Tobackoe, three kettles of sixe hands about, tenn looking glasses," granted all the lands between the Norwalk and Saugatuck Rivers, "from the sea a days walk into the country." It was signed by **Tomakergo, Tokaneke,** and Sachem **Mahachemo,** and witnessed by Thos. Ludlowe, **Adam,** and **Prosewamenos** *(Fig. 33) (Norwalk Town Records)*.

This was a move by the Connecticut Colony to extend their Fairfield holdings as far west as possible. In the next century, the remaining Tankiteke merged with the remnant Wiechquaesgeck and slowly retreated north into apparent oblivion *(38) (Chap. 10)*.

NOTE: Around this time, the change from the Julian Calendar to the Gregorian Calendar was reaching America. Under the Julian Calendar, the new year had started in late March. Thus, a 26 February, 1640, Julian date was really in the second month of the Gregorian year of 1641.

Nov. 1641 - Greenwich Boundary Agreed with Stamford

The Greenwich Plantation joined the New Haven Colony, different from Stamford, who were with the Hartford Colony. The two groups established a boundary line between Greenwich and Stamford running north from the "Patomogg Brook." This is still the modern boundary. It states, "Nether will aney of us or shall aney for us object against this agreement upon ye account of ye Indians." Thus the Wiechquaeskeck had been completely squeezed out. It was signed by Daniell Patrick and Robt. Fekes for Greenwich and by Andrew Warde, Robert Coe, and Richard Gildersleve for Stamford *(Greenwich Town Records)*.

March 24, 1645 - Piamikin Sells the Eastern Section of Stamford

"**Piamikin** Sagamore of Roatan & owner of all the Lands lieing between five miles river & pinebrook" gave the lands for unnamed "devers reasons and considerations" to Andrew Ward and Richard Law of "Stanford."

Everyone signed with "markes," including the Englishmen Jerimy Jagger and Georg Slauson. The Indian witnesses were **Piamikin, Wasasary, Paugaton, Mamaiema,** and **Toquatos** *(Stamford Town Clerk's Office. Book A, p.343)*.

July 1, 1650 - Stephen Goodyear Closes Daniel Patrick's Purchase

Two Indians, claiming to be the "surviving proprietors of ther land lyinge on the other side of the Norwalke River" which had been "sold unto Captain Patricke of Greenwich," testified that Patrick had never fully paid for the land. He had failed to pay "twoe Indian coates and fowre fathom of wampum." Stephen Goodyear, a prominent merchant in New Haven, received the deed and gave the Indians the unpaid balance owed on the original sale *(38)*.

February 13, 1651/1652 - Norwalk Shorelands and Islands Transferred to Settlers

There was still a dispute with the Indians about the shorelands and islands around Norwalk. After all, they had been the prime fishing and shellfishing areas for the local Native band. The Indians who claimed that they had not sold away these lands were: **Runckinheage, Piamikin, Towntom, Winnepucke, Pokessake, Cockenoe-de-longe-Island, Magiso, Magushshetowos, Conckuskenow, Wampasum, Sasseaum, Runckenunnutt, Skowkecum, Soanamatum, Prodax,** and **Matumpun.** This agreement confirmed the transfer to the settlers of a number of shorelands and islands on the coast of what is now Norwalk and Darien, possibly together with the rest of Darien and New Canaan between Patrick's purchase and Stamford. It extended north to "Moohakes Country." The marks of those who "signed and delivered" the document are reproduced in Figure 34.

Ray and Stewart *(38: 7)* comment that "This deed may be the first recorded instance of increasing land values in Norwalk's history," for, in 1652, the proprietors paid 'Thirty fathom of Wampum, Tenn Kettles, Fifteen Coates, Tenn payr of Stockings, Tenn Knifes, Tenn Hookes, Twenty Pipes, Tenn Muckes, Tenn needles, considerably more in wampum and useful items than either Ludlow or Patrick had paid a decade earlier for substantially larger areas."

June 9, 1654 – Ward and Law Report on the 1645 Deed from Piamikin

They gave "**piamikee**, in ye presence of other four or five Indians" "one Coat...with some quanity of tobaca" to satisfy a disagreement over the English hogs and cattle spoiling the Indian corn." There was evidently only a handful of Indians left in the area at that time. *(Stamford Town Clerk's Office, book B, p.33).*

1655 – Onax Gets Consideration for Confirming the 1640 Agreement in Stamford

Onax, the son of Ponus, sagamore of Toquams, complained about the 1640 land transfer agreement and was given "consideration" for confirming it. *(Stamford Historical Society).*

March 20, 1656 –Settlers of Fairfield buy Sasqua (Southport) from the Pequonnock

The Fairfield settlers bought marshland around Sasqua (Southport) and Sasquannock, between the Mill River and Sasco River, from the Pequonnock Indians *(28)*. The agreement was signed by **Momechemen, Weenam, Tospee, Quanomscoes,** and **Aucan.**

March 20, 1661 – Fairfield Allowed Land for Indian Farming

Fairfield made an allocation to allow land for the Indians to farm around Sasqua (Southport). It was signed by 11 Indian men and 3 women. They were **Nimrod, Anthony, Panuncamo** (Ponanocamos in 1656), **Musqot** (Muskot in 1656), **Solamorton, Poppoos, Tospee** (also 1656), **Witteren, Wompegan, James (alias), Wotuss, Awatum, Cramheag's squaw, Solamorton's sister,** and **Wissahoes** (a woman) *(28)*.

April 11, 1666 – Continued Purchase of Southport by Fairfield Settlers

The Fairfield settlers firmed up their hold on the east side of the Saugatuck River by purchasing the rest of Sasqua (Southport). The deal was made with both the Norwalk Indians (Tankiteke) and the Sasqua Indians (Pequonnock). The land in question was bounded by Muddy Creek, which the Indians called Muskot Creek. Those who signed were **Momechemen** (Mamachin), **Weenam, Tospee, Quanumscoes,** and

Aucan, all signers of the 1656 agreement. It was witnessed by **Mamachin, Weenam, Ponancamos, Muskot,** and **James** *(28).*

January 7, 1667 – Stamford Confirmation of Deed with Descendants of Ponus

Stamford made a land agreement with **Taphase,** son of Ponus, and Penehay, son of Onax (another son of Ponus). It referred to "Several Trackes of Lande" in Stamford. There was objection to, but confirmation of, some old deeds. It was agreed that those who could live on the purchased lands were: **Taphance** (same as Taphase), his wife and children, **Penehay, Paharron,** and **Nowattonnamanssqua** (an old woman) *(Stamford Historical Society).*

December 25, 1669 – Norwalk North Boundary Settlement

Mamchimons was granted forty coats to settle a controversy over Norwalk's northern boundaries *(Norwalk Town Records).*

1679 – Southport Settlers Agreement with Young Indians

Southport settlers made an agreement with two Sasqua Indians who had been underage when the 1656 land transfer agreement was signed. They agreed to the terms. One was the famous **Chi-Kin Warrups** (Chickens**),** who was a survivor, and had many future dealings with settlers *(Chap. 3).* The other was **Creconoes** *(28)*

May 26, 1685 – Patent Granted to Stamford by Connecticut

The "General Court of Connecticutt" granted to several men in Stamford a Patent for all the lands from Norwalk to Greenwich and from the sea to Bedford, to "be an Intire Township of itself." No mention is made of any Indian claims *(Recorded in Book F, p. 418, Stamford Town Clerk's Office).*

February 1, 1686 – Land Transfer of Horseneck Plantation (Greenwich)

Seven men on a Greenwich town committee made an agreement on Feb. 1, 1686 which said in part:

> Witness these presents, yt whereas, wee to witt, **Kowanonussa** and **Kouko**. **Querrecqui** and **Peattun** and **Pakochero** and **Rumppanus**, we do owne and declare ourselves to be ye true proprietors of all ye land or lands which lyeth or yt is between Mianus River and Biram River and run to New York line...

There is no mention of any payment, possibly because the Native band must hve been reduced to very few people and had little power. The agreement says that they "have received full satisfaction in land to witt, planting land, the which land is fenced in at Cos Cob Neck...about thirtie acres." This land was the "Indian Field" *(Fig. 27)* where there once had been a flourishing Indian fishing and farming village in the summer. It was probably where they were then living. The Indians were soon to learn that they did not even own their fish traps in the Mianus River any more! The agreement describes "four papooses" who were to have the land for their lifetime, after which it would revert to the town. Three of the four were ten years old and the fourth was a year old. The three mothers were **Pakekcho** (Pakochero), **Oruns** (Orems) *(Chap. 3)*, and **Wetorrum**. **Kowanonussa** was a "gran mother." In less than twenty years, this land was taken from the few survivors, if any, that were left.

The agreement was signed by **Wesskum** "who am a sagamore of Wapping," **Karonusso** (Kowanonussa), **Koruko** (Kouko), **Quorrurqui** (Querrecqui), and **Poatum** (Peattun). It was witnessed by **Ruapapanus** (Rumppanus) and **Pakoheharo** (a woman, see above) *(Greenwich Land Records)*.

An interesting part of this agreement is that it was endorsed by "I, Wesskum, who am four score years old and upwards..." He also stated that "ye above sd Wesskum, who am a sagamore of Wapping." It can be presumed that, when he was a young Wapping man, he had married into the local group, stayed with the family, and rose to be a sagamore. This is one of the few written connections of the Wapping (sometimes called "Wappinger") to the Wiechquaeskeck *(Chap. 3)*.

1687 – Stamford Land Transfer by Winbock and his Four Sons

Transfer of land in Stamford by **Winbock** and his four sons **Ompassum, Nacepun, Rockcomp, and Popowompom** (*Stamford Historical Society*).

June 2, 1696 – "Cauk's Purchase" in the Byram River area, Greenwich

Seven Greenwich settlers purchased most of the land in Greenwich between the Byram River and the New York border "in Consideration of a valuable satisfaction" which was not described. The Indian proprietors were listed as **Cranamateen, Nepawhen, Naterchechan,** and **Moshareck.** The agreement was attested by **Waspahing** (John Cauk) and was "Signed, Sealed & Delivered in ye presence of us." **Robbin, John Cauk, Porscome, Keenhotam, Crawamateen, Nepawhen, Naterchehan,** and **Moshareck** (*Greenwich Land Records*).

"John Cauk" was a name given by the English to a leader and survivor, **Waspahing (Waspahin)** of the Sioascauk band who lived near the water in what is now Byram. The site was favorable for both fishing and farming. Cauk also signed later documents (*Chap. 3*).

July 8, 1701 – Confirmation by Catonah of Land Grants in Stamford

To clarify and confirm various previus grants of land from the Indians to the Stamford settlers, including those by **Taphase** and **Penehay** in 1667 and by **Nowatonimons** and others, a legal document was given to **Catona** (Katonah, Catoonah), **Coee,** and others to sign. (Catona was listed as a sagamore, but was then actually the sakima of all the Wiechquaeskeck in the Greenwich, Stamford, and Bedford area.) This document said it "Doth....Conferme all ye sd old Deeds: of **Taphass: ponass** & **penehays** & old **Onax** & also young **Onax**" telling the Indians to "Give Grante & quit Cleame unto all ye Lands meadows Trees feeding Grounds Rivers pooles & other privileges." This forced the remnant of the Wiechquaeskeck in the whole area of Stamford to vacate their lands and move to the Ramapoo area of Ridgefield. It would not be long before they would come under final pressure to move from there as well.

The witnesses who signed by "markes" were probably the last Wiech-quaeskeck men in the area who were not servants or farm laborers. They were **Arecarius,** Sagamore **Catona, Joneye:** alias **John Cauke** (Wespahin from Greenwich), **Mockea, Capt. Monige, Pohornes, Papacuma, Kenhoetam:** alias **Rich Smith** (from Greenwich), **Simon, Wequacumake, Ramhorne, Ahquamaus, Suringo, Aruta,** and **Papiamah**. Samuel Hait, the Justice of the Peace, almost immediately entered the document as a deed, since by that time the offices of the Town Clerks had been well established in each town

(Original deed in the Town Clerk's office, Stamford, Connecticut. Recorded in Book A, p. 375).

December 23, 1701 – Second "Cauk's Purchase" in Byram, Greenwich

The last piece of Indian land in the Byram area was sold "in considera-tion the value of twenty five pound of lawfull money of this collonie." It was "granted bargained sold sett over and delivered" by **Wespahing** (Waspahin) alias **John Cauk,** and **Wohornis** (Wohorness). It was attested by a Native "called of Indians **Kinhotan** by ye English **Richard Smith**" who also signed Catonah's sale of July 8, 1701. He was **Keenhotam** in the 1696 document. It was also attested by **Wallon W.** This was the end of the Sioascauk band of Indians in Greenwich. *(Greenwich Land Records).*

December 18, 1703 – Final Land Transfer of Indian Field, Greenwich

The last three survivors, possibly with children, sold Indian Field *(Fig. 27)* on the east bank of the Mianus River, Cos Cob, Greenwich "for a valuable consideration to the full satisfaction" to a group of Greenwich settlers. The Indians were **Waspahin** (John Cauk**), Aurems** (the mother, Orens, in 1686), and **Paxcanahin**. It was described as in "ye third year of ye Raign of our Soveraign Lady Queen Ann of England Scotland Ierlande." It was recorded immediately by "Samuel Peck Justice of ye Peace" (*Greenwich Land Records).*

September 30, 1708 – The Push of the Indians from Ramapoo

Ridgefield settlers petitioned the General Assembly at Hartford to remove the Indian remnant who were in the Ramapoo area, near Ridgefield. The State bought approximately 20,000 acres for the large sum of one hundred pounds sterling and transferred the land to the "Proprietors of Ridgefield" (*Chap. 10*). The deed was signed for the Indians by **Catoonah** (the sachem), **Waspahchain** (John Cauk, the survivor, again), **Wawkamawwee, Woquacomick, Narranoke (Orencke** in 1715, **Norreneke** in 1721), **Tawpornick,** and **Cawwehorin.** It was also signed by **Gootquas** and **Mahke** *(4)*.

The Indians did not all leave then, as there were subsequent purchases of scattered holdings in the Ridgefield area in 1715, 1721, 1727, 1739, and 1743 *(4)*. The Native Americans had evidently, by then, learned more about the value of real estate.

February 12, 1708/1709 – "A little field" in Greenwich

It was after the 17th century, but it is noteworthy that the last piece of Indian land in Greenwich was sold in February, 1709, by **Waspahing** (again, John Cauk) and **Wohorness** (Wohornis, who had also been involved with Waspahing in the 1701 sale in Byram). It was called "a little field in ye lands of Greenwich" (*Greenwich Land Records*).

By this time, all the lands in Greenwich, Stamford, Darien, and Norwalk had been signed over by the Native Americans or simply taken by new settlers who moved into empty land. Only a few Indians were left living in the area as farm laborers or servants. Some of the Wiechquaeskeck had first fled to the Ramapoo area of Ridgefield. Then most of this good land had been taken away by the Land Transfer Agreement of 1708, but a few Indians remainded independently in the hills. The remnant scattered north and west, some going with **Chi-Kin Warrups** to Kent, Connecticut *(Chap. 10)*. There were still a few areas of land that had not been clearly defined in the deeds. These were soon acquired by the new settlers who got the required papers from the Town Clerks and registered them in the Town Meeting minutes.

Dutch foot soldier of the early 17th century

CHAPTER 9

GOVERNOR KIEFT'S WAR

The situation in New Netherland changed markedly in 1638. The change was to have a devastating effect on the Native Americans. A weak and vacillating governor, Wouter van Twiller, was removed, and a former trader, Willem Kieft, was sent by The Hague to be Director of the Colony. The business climate was shifting dramatically. It was the final year of the Dutch West India Company's monopoly on the fur trade in the Hudson Valley. There were few fur-bearing animals left to catch in the Wiechquaeskeck area.

To increase their profits from fur trading, the West India Company had a policy, for many years, of keeping friendly relations with the Indians and of discouraging colonists. In 1638, they decided that it was necessary to increase New Netherland's low population *(Jameson: 273)*. After Kieft's arrival, anyone could trade with the Indians, and the rules for settlers were eased. Many more settlers moved in. They established farms in Indian territories, and most became traders, also. Contacts with the Natives increased *(34: 169)*. They scattered all around the New Amsterdam area and up the Hudson River valley. The settler population soon doubled, reaching 2,500 by 1645. More ships of many countries came to New Amsterdam to trade. Kieft estimated that ships from 18 nations, from all over the world, were coming to New Amsterdam harbor to get their share of the newly-opened trade *(Brodhead: 198)*.

The Dutch knew that their Fort Goede Hoop, (Fort Good Hope, the future site of Hartford) on the Connecticut River, was becoming untenable because of the influx of English settlers overland from Massachusetts. In addition, some English settlers were moving on from the Connecticut River valley, and were coming down closer to New Netherland, and buying Indian lands *(Chap. 8)*. English farmers began intermingling with the few Dutch settlers around Stamford and Greenwich.

At the same time, the number of Native Americans remaining had shrunk to only a fraction of what they had been when the Dutch traders had first arrived. Over 80 percent of the Natives had been devastated by the new diseases. They were angry, and ready to strike back at the invaders. There were many arguments with the intrusive new farmers. Several remote settlers' homes were attacked and burned. The Wiechquaeskeck lands were in the middle of this maelstrom, and the young Indian men were both frightened, and seething with animosity.

An excellent modern description, and analysis, of the relations between the Dutch and the Indians at5 that time is Paul Andrew Otto's thesis, **New Netherland Frontier: Europeans and Native Americans Along the Lower Hudson River 1524-1664,** Indiana University, June 1995. It is available in the New York State Library, Albany (974.702 N532 99-960) *(34).*

Paul Otto describes how the Dutch had become dependent on the Native Americans, not only for the peltry to trade, but also for much of their food. The Dutch employed Natives for labor and domestic help. Natives were both guides away from Fort Amsterdam and translators, as many had learned the Dutch language. Some Indian women intermarried with the Dutch. The Native Americans still thinly inhabited much of the land. Otto notes the deteriorating relationship between the Dutch settlers of New Netherland and the Munsee-speaking inhabitants of Lenapehocking, "Land of the Lenape" *(26)* in the early seventeenth century. The situation often led to frustration on both sides, and to conflict.

Otto notes *(34: 167)* that as the population grew and trade increased, Dutch farms scattered further, and tensions between the Dutch and the Native inhabitants multiplied. Kieft even imposed a tax on Indian corn and consistently refused to cooperate with the Indians, to the extent that it was difficult for any of the older Munsee leaders to prevent aggressive actions by the angry young men. Kieft pushed on militarily until he had overwhelmed all the Munsee-speaking Delaware.

There was conflict over the use of the land. The Indians depended on their unfenced gardens of corn, beans, and squash. The Dutch let their livestock forage freely in the woods and into the Indian gardens *(34: 171).* The Indians sometimes killed the intruding livestock. The Dutch shot at the Indians near their farms.

Dutch sailors, soldiers, and others, stole furs and wampum from individual Natives who had come to New Amsterdam to trade. Indians stole goods and livestock from Dutch farms. The Dutch were quick on the trigger. The Lenape were quick with arrows and knives. There was great misunderstanding between them.

The Indians were criticized for believing that revenge was justice, an "eye for an eye." But when the Indians killed a few people, the Dutch would move in massively for revenge and destroy a whole village. The Dutch have been criticized for over-reacting to theft. This conflicted with the Indian concept of property in which anything of your friend's that you wanted, you used. The cultural patterns had no mesh.

Most importantly, the Wiechquaeskeck and their neighbors had little more peltry to trade with the Dutch. They had caught nearly all the beaver and other fur-bearers in their area, for trade in the previous two decades. By 1640, most of the Native fur traders who came to New Amsterdam were no longer Munsee. Some were Mahican from several days journey to the North. Most, coming even further, were Mohawk from the Adirondacks. In 1628, the Mohawk had finally defeated the Mahican in the Albany area, and they had free passage on the Hudson River. The Dutch had previously given the Mohawk all the guns they wanted, in order to get their furs. The Mohawk were willing to shoot unruly Munsee at Dutch request, for their own purposes. The Dutch still would not officially sell guns to the Munsee, because they were too close to the settlers. Other traders were selling inferior guns all through the Hudson Valley. The Dutch were soon fighting nearly all the tribes that surrounded New Amsterdam.

The Wiechquaeskeck had little to trade with the Dutch but vegetables, deer, and wampum *(Chaps. 4, 6-C)*. As the English settlers moved down from the east, the dwindling Wiechquaeskeck steadily lost their corn fields and their access to the shore. The remnant were driven into a corner that they did not understand. They were being sold alcohol. They struck back.

The Wiechquaeskeck Clash with the Dutch

There was an open clash with the Wiechquaeskeck in 1641. A young man had waited twenty years to avenge the death of his uncle, who had been robbed of his furs, and killed, as the boy watched. When he was grown, he used a hatchet to kill a man he thought he recognized, an old wheelwright named Claes Swits. Kieft sent a message to the Wiechquaeskeck sakima demanding that the Indians surrender the murderer to the Dutch. The sakima refused, saying that it was legitimate revenge, and told him of his frustration with the Dutch treatment of the Natives. He said that he, "was sorry twenty Christians had not been murdered" *(deVries: 214)* In a few years, this murder would be the Dutch excuse for a mass killing of displaced Indians at Pavonia, New Jersey.

At the same time Pacham *(Chap. 3)*, a Tankiteke sakima, was dealing on friendly terms with the English around Norwalk *(Chap. 8)*. He cooperated with the Dutch and joined some Long Island Indians to attack and kill a few troublesome Raritan. Pacham, who was said to be "great with the governor of the fort," appeared in New Amsterdam. He displayed, "in great triumph . . . a dead hand hanging on a stick, and saying that it was the hand of the chief who had killed or shot with arrows men on Staten Island." He said that he "had taken revenge" for the sake of the colonists "because he loved the Swannekens (as they called the Dutch) who were his best friends" *(vanderDonck: 35)*.

Thus, the Natives of southwestern Connecticut were split between the Tankiteke in Norwalk, who were being friendly with the English and Dutch, and some of the Wiechquaeskeck in Stamford and Greenwich, who had mixed attitudes. The elders could not stop the young men from swooping down to burn and pillage in the area. There were rampaging Indians from The Bronx to Stamford. There was an oral story in Greenwich that "even the stout-hearted lay down in fear and rose up in danger" *(Elizabeth W. Clarke, ed., The First Three Hundred Years, The History of The First Congregational Church, Greenwich, Connecticut, 1967).* Not a farm felt safe. The men took their guns to work in the field. Many houses was attacked and burned,

There is another popular oral story of that time about Cornelius Labden *(31)*. He was a Dutch farmer living in what would become the Greenwich area, with a wife and a sixteen-year-old daughter. One day, the story goes, some Indians pursued him to his house. He ran in the front door and had his wife and daughter hold the bar. He then ran out the back door, jumped on a horse, and fled. When he got to "Laddin's Rock," beside the Asamuck Brook, he rode right over the edge. The story is unclear as to whether he then died. What is often left out is that his wife and daughter were scalped, but Labden is the purported "hero" of the folk tale. It was part of the Dutch-Indian war.

The early settlers, who had come to southwestern Connecticut from New England, starting in 1639, found themselves in an unsettling situation. Some of the Natives nearby were friendly and helpful. Others would emerge from the forest ready to kill and burn. No help was forthcoming from New England against the Wiechquaeskeck. It was too far away, and they were too busy with their own restless Natives. In desperation, a famous

Greenwich settler, Elizabeth Winthrop Feake, went with her friend and neighbor, Captain Daniel Patrick, to the Governor of New Amsterdam for help. Their letter said:

> Whereas, we, Capt. Daniel Patrick and Elizabeth Feake, duly authorized by her husband Robert Feake, now sick, have resided two years about five or six miles east of the New Netherlands, subject to the Lords State General, who have protested against us, declaring that the said land lay within their limts, and that they should not allow any person to usurp it against their lawful rights; and whereas, we have equally persisted in our course during these two years, having been well assured that his Majesty the King of England had pretended some to this soil; and whereas we know nothing thereof, and <u>cannot any longer presume to remain thus, on account both of this strife, the danger consequent thereon, and these treacherous and villainous Indians, of whom we have seen so many sorrowful examples enough.</u> We therefore betake ourselves under the protection of the Noble Lord States General, His Highness the Prince of Orange, and the West India Company, or their Governor General of New Netherlands, promising for the future to be faithful to them, as all honest subjects are bound to be, whereunto we bind ourselves by solemn oath and signature, provided we be protected against our enemies as much as possible, and enjoy henceforth the same privileges that all Patroons of the New Netherlands have obtained agreeably to the Freedoms. *(Underlining added to show feelings)*

> 1642, IXth of April, in Fort Amsterdam
> DANIEL PATRICK
> Witnesses, -   Evararudus Bogardus
>   Johannes Winkleman

Thus, they agreed with Governor Kieft that Greenwich would fall under Dutch jurisdiction and protection because of "these treacherous and villainous Indians, of whom we have seen so many examples enough." The people of Stamford remained under the English, but were cooperative, as they, too, were fearful. They later twice allowed Dutch troops to embark from their town after attacks on nearby Natives.

The next winter, the situation in New Netherland took a turn for the worse. In February, 1643, a group of Mahican had attacked the Wiechquaeskeck, on the Hudson River *(Jameson: 275)*:

> God wrecked vengeance on the Witquescheck without our knowledge through the Mahicanders *[Mahican]* dwelling below Fort Orange, who slew seventeen of them, and made prisoners of many women and children. The remainder fled through a deep snow to the Christian houses on and about the island Manhatens. They were most humanely received being half dead from cold and hunger, they supported them for

fourteen days, even corn was sent to them by the Director. A short time after, another panic seized the Indians which caused them to fly to divers places in the vicinity of the Dutch. This opportunity to avenge the innocent blood *[of Claes Smits, killed by a Wiechquaeskeck]* induced some of the Twelve Men to present to the Director that it was now time, whereupon they received for answer that they should put their request in writing . . . to be allowed to attack those . . . on the Manhatens and on Pavonia, at which place about eighty Indians were killed and thirty taken prisoners.

This massacre by the Dutch at Pavonia (now Jersey City) has been described by numerous writers. Some have called it "The Slaughter of the Innocents." It was a bloodthirsty killing.

At about that time, Kieft learned that there was a Wiechquaeskeck "fort" in the general area of Stamford and Greenwich and sent a force to demolish it. In March, 1643, he dispatched Ensign van Dyke and eighty soldiers on a nighttime expedition to destroy the rumored stronghold *(Fig. 36)*. They landed at Patomuck Brook (now Tomac Creek) in Old Greenwich and asked directions of Captain Daniel Patrick, who lived in the area and spoke Dutch. Patrick was friendly with the local Indians, however, and could have been purposely misleading. He sent the Dutch force, in the middle of the night, across the Mianus River to the summer village complex of Petaquapen (Cos Cob). They tore down and burned some palisadoes, keeping two intact in case they were counterattacked. They then set upon the few longhouses and wigwams in Petaquapen. They killed about twenty old people, women, and young children who were staying there for the winter. The rest of the Natives had all gone many miles back to Nanichiestawack in the hills for the winter hunting, wampum making, training, and festivities.

The Dutch were furious about being misled, and having killed only women and old people. They returned to Stamford, where they argued with Patrick about being fooled. The story is that Patrick spat in the face of one and turned away. He was promptly shot in the back of the head by a Dutch soldier with a hand gun.

A day or two later, Mayn Mayanos *(Chap. 3)*, a sagamore of the Petaquapen area, rushed down to Stamford in a frenzied state *(Fig. 9)*. He was livid that the Dutch would kill old people, women, and children. He walked up to three Dutch soldiers and shot one with his bow. As he was struggling with a second soldier, a third shot him. They then put his head on a pole, and displayed it at Fort Amsterdam.

The timing of this story varies. Jameson *(Jameson: 281)* puts the date of the abortive raid and the killings by Dutch soldiers of both Daniel Patrick and Mayn Mayanos as 1644. That is unlikely, and the confusion probably came from the Julian-Gregorian calendar switch. There appears to have been a year between the abortive attack at Cos Cob and the later successful attack by Captain John Underhill on Nanichiestawack, in 1644.

There were many Dutch forays throughout New Netherland in those years. In March, 1643, a force had marched on Staten Island, confiscating corn, and burning villages. There was fighting with the Hackensack, the Raritan and other Munsee tribes on Long Island *(33)*. To the Dutch, the Wiechquaeskeck were just one of five different tribes that van Kieft was trying to subdue.

Dutch-Native affairs continued to worsen. This was a wild time in New Netherland. On Long Island, some Dutch wanted to kill some Indians, but were refused permission by Director Kieft. Others took two wagons and stole the Indian's corn, killing three men in the process. The Natives retaliated by burning three houses: "The Indians showing themselves afar off, called out – 'Be ye our friends? Ye are mere corn stealers'" *(Jameson:277)*.

Other attacks and murders followed, by both the Dutch and by all the tribes in the New Netherland area. Some settlers even tried to shoot the Director in his own house! Jameson continues:

> In this confusion mingled with great terror passed the winter away, the season came for driving out the cattle, this obliged many to desire peace. On the other hand the Indians, seeing also that it was time to plant maize, were not less solicitous for peace, so that after some negotiation, peace was concluded in May Anno 1643 . . . it was generally expected that it would be durable.

But the peace was ephemeral. Soon both the Europeans and the Natives were being killed at random, and "terror increased over all the land" *(Jameson: 280)*.

The Wiechquaeskeck Go on a Rampage

More Native tribes became involved. Eleven Munsee bands, including the Wiechquaeskeck, now fought an open war against the Dutch. Indian war parties attacked isolated colonists. Dutch settlers deplored that the Indians "killed all the men on the farm lands whom they could surprise . . . they burned all the houses, farms, barns, stacks of grain, and destroyed everything they could come at" *(34: 186)*.

Kieft tried to make peace on Long Island, but soon both the Dutch and the Indians were fighting there again. Kieft also had no success in talking to the Wiechquaeskeck and other Munsee bands. On July 20, 1643, David de Vries reported that one of the Munsee chiefs told him:

> ... he was very sad that there were many of the Indian youths who were constantly wishing for a war against us, as one had lost his father, another his mother, and a third his uncle, and also their friends, and that the presents *[Kieft's]* or recompense were not worth taking up...

The New Haven Colony was aware of what was happening only fifty miles to the west. The "Eight Men" (the leaders) of New Netherland had sent a letter "to the north to our English neighbours, to request an auxiliary force of one hundred and fifty men" to help them. New Haven did not send the men, but took the warning to heart. A General Court held at New Haven for the Plantations on the 6th of July, 1643 proclaimed *(Trumbull)*:

> It is ordered that every male fro 16 yeares olde to sixty, within this jurisdiction, shall henceforth be furnished of a good gun or muskett, a pound of good pouder 4 fathom of match for a match-lock and 5 or 6 good flints for a fyre lock, and four pound of pistol bullets. Or 24 mullets *[rowels, or star wheels]* fitted to their guns and so contine furnished from time to time, under the penalty of 10s fine upon every defect in any of the afore-named particulars.

In the summer of 1643, Roger Williams sailed down the coast to take a ship for England out of New Amsterdam (He was *persona non grata* in Boston). He reported that he could see the fires of English houses burning along the way. He was probably writing about burning houses on both sides of Long Island Sound. One of those fires was the house of his friend, Anne Hutchinson, in New Rochelle. She was a religious reformer and a "chirurgist" or surgeon. She had been banished from Boston for preaching unacceptable beliefs. She and her husband had settled on the island of Aquidneck (now Rhode Island). When he died, she moved to a farm in New Rochelle in 1642, where she "planted" a substantial settlement. There, she became a traveling doctor and healed both European settlers and Natives from the Bronx to Stamford. She would ride with about eight other people and go to towns, farms, and Indian villages, helping everyone. The Hutchinson Parkway is named in her honor.

On August 20, 1643, a party of revengeful young Wiechquaeskeck arrived at her farm. Led by Rampage (or Wampage), they killed everyone there except Anne's 12-year-old granddaughter, whom they took captive. They burned the buildings. Rampage was so proud of this atrocity that he adopted the name "AnneHoeck" or Anne-killer. It is interesting to speculate whether the word "rampage", as in "go on a rampage," came from this incident. The Oxford English Dictionary says that it was first used in 1715 and was of obscure origin. It was thought to be probably Scotch because of the word "ramp," but Rampage's actions were a definition of the word.

Governor Kieft's Military Forces

Willem Kieft had recruited an army of Dutch, English, and other European mercenaries and had them well trained. The Natives were unimpressed. They used guerilla tactics and refused to meet the Dutch in a pitched battle. Despite the strong central force, the Dutch colonists continued to suffer attacks which destroyed isolated houses and farms *(34: 191)*. These occurred as far east as Stamford. The Dutch were hard-pressed to fight back against the widely-dispersed Indians.

Kieft was the Governor of a colony that was still run by the West India Company. It was not an official Dutch colony. For protection, they did not have regular Dutch army forces, but a militia that the Company had recruited and armed. Some of their soldiers had been regular Dutch army troops who had emigrated to New Netherland. The force was not solely Dutch men, however. There were Germans who were veterans of the Thirty Years War in Europe. There were also professional soldiers from England, Sweden, Denmark, Scotland, Ireland, and Switzerland. The force was thus a motley group of nationalities, but their officers were all trained and hardened professionals. They were tough, Dutch-trained officers, and they had access to Dutch arms. It was a formidable group. They were organized and experienced *(9: 496)*.

Most West India Company soldiers in New Netherland were equipped with matchlock muskets. A few carried the arquebus, or heavy musket, which was awkward and needed a support stand. Other soldiers carried the formidable half-pike for close-in fighting. Officers wore swords, and most soldiers carried some bladed weapon, ranging from a saber to a short sword. They were thus very effective in hand-to-hand combat. Many wore the decorated high-crested steel helmets called "morions." Those were not unlike modern army helmets.

At that time, the match-lock musket was relatively new. It was so-called because the firing mechanism required lighting a "match" that led to a primed charge in the gun. The match was a cord, or fuse, of gunpowder, which was placed over a "pan" on the musket. If there was not just a "flash in the pan," the burning would go down to the internal gunpowder charge and explode it, propelling out the musket ball. They were heavy guns and heavy balls. They did great damage when they hit the target.

The Dutch had revolutionized European military tactics with this Donderbus, or "thunder gun." It was a shotgun with a flared top for pouring in the gunpowder and iron pellet charge. It was thick and heavy for handling the large charge. It was short and not very accurate, but they learned to use it well. It was awkward to clean and re-load, however, so they trained their men in a precise maneuver. The soldiers lined up in three rows. After the first row discharged their deafening volley, they stepped to the rear to clean their musket barrels. The next row, which had been kneeling as they had been priming their muskets, cutting "matches" and putting powder in the flash pans, moved forward for the order to fire. The third row had been pouring a charge of gunpowder and an iron ball down the muzzle and tamping it in place. They were highly trained to work swiftly and effectively (9).

The shock effect of the systematic, simultaneous, repeated fire was spectacular. The noise was truly thunder, and the volleys kept coming repeatedly. No one had heard the like of it in the New World. It was no wonder that both the Pequots at Fort Mystic and the Wiechquaeskecks at Nanichiestawack fled or cowered helplessly in their wigwams.

In addition, a truly ferocious system had been adapted from naval experience. Navies had learned that they could take miscellaneous metal pieces, heat them red hot, then tamp them down the barrels of their cannon. When these hot flying pieces hit the rigging of enemy ships, they would cut through ropes, wood and canvas, and set the ships afire. The Dutch army copied this, and would heat musket balls and metal pieces as hot as they could on a camp fire and drop them into the funnel-ended Donderbus. When these hot pieces embedded in the dry wood wigwams, they set them afire. At both Mystic and Nanichiestawack, most of the hundreds of Native deaths came from being burned alive as they shrank in fear and helplessness from the thundering volleys.

At about this time, the awkward matchlock musket was being replaced by the flintlock gun. In the flintlock, all the powder was inside, and the internal flint was hit by a mullet (a steel star-wheel), and the spark set off the charge within the gun. (Evidently the mullet often broke when the charge ignited, and had to be replaced.) The flintlock needed several fewer steps to re-load than did the matchlock, and therefore, fewer men for the same firepower. It was still necessary to "trust in God and keep your powder dry," even though the powder was protected better than it was with the matchlock musket.

Kieft's military force was thus formidably armed as it marched against the Wiechquaeskeck. The Natives would be overawed and stunned by thunder and iron in a way they had not expected. The Pequot and Wiechquaeskeck were not proud as they lay helpless in their wigwams during the Dutch attacks, they were shattered. Even today, soldiers throw plastic grenades into large enclosed spaces, not to kill the people inside, but to stun them into submission. The effect of large, close, explosive noises is indescribable.

In the winter of 1644, some "veteran soldiers under Pieter Cock" and some "English under Sergeant Major Van der Hyl" *(John Underhill)* marched to Maspeth on Long Island, "killing about one hundred and twenty men." *(Jameson: 282)* This was the force that was soon to cross Long Island Sound to attack Nanichiestawack.

The Attack on Nanichiestawack

Captain John Underhill, one of the officers in the Fort Mystik fight against the Pequot, had been called by the English settlers to be the military commander of Stamford, Connecticut, in the spring of 1642. He was living in Boston at that time, with little to do. Because of the Indian fighting in New Netherland, Stamford had been fearful of local Native uprisings. The Wethersfield settlers had just arrived in 1641 *(Chap. 8)*, and about 59 families had settled there. Some of them remembered the Pequot attacks on their Connecticut Valley farms. They had persuaded Underhill to come to lead their defense. The Stamford Town Records of October, 1642, show a grant to "Jo Underhill eight acres." He had been given a house and made a freeman of the Colony. He had also been appointed to act on the local Court, which was auxiliary to the General Court of New Haven. Underhill was well-known, however, so the Dutch approached him. They knew he had been trained in Holland, and they soon had him working with their forces.

On Oct. 17, 1643, Kieft called a meeting of the Council of New Netherland *(8: 26)*, which John Underhill attended. It was resolved "to make

a hostile attack on Mamarunock, chief of the Wiquaskecks, and his tribe."
They were not clear on the organization of the Wiechquaeskeck, but
Mamarunock was well-known as a bothersome war-like sakima. (Actually,
he was the sakima of a more westerly group of Wiechquaeskeck.) After the
meeting, Kieft sent a mission to New Haven to hire more soldiers from New
England. (There were already some English colonists in their force.) The
Dutch were turned down at that time, however, "to be reconsidered in the
spring."

Governor John Winthrop of Massachusetts heard about the request and
wrote in his *Journal* that he regarded the appeal to New Haven as "a plot of
the Dutch Governor to engage the English in a quarrel with the Indians,
which we had wholly declined, as doubting the justice of the cause" *(8:27)*.
Winthrop little realized how terrifying these times were for the Dutch settlers
and traders in New Netherland. They had appealed for help time and again
to Amsterdam, Holland. In one instance, a "Memorial of the Eight Men at
the Manhattans" was addressed in December, 1643 to "Noble, High and
Mighty Lords, the Noble Lords the States General of the United Netherland
Provinces *(Brodhead: 139)*.

> . . . we poor inhabitants of New Netherland were . . . pursued by these
> wild Heathens and barbarous Savages with fire and sword; daily in our
> houses and fields have they cruelly murdered men and women; and
> with hatchets and tomahawks struck little children dead in their parents
> arms . . . or carried them away into bondage; the houses and grain-
> barracks are burnt with the produce; cattle of all descriptions are slain
> or destroyed . . . Almost every place is abandoned. We, wretched
> people, must skulk, with wives and little ones that still survive, in
> poverty together, in and around the fort at the Manhatas, where we are
> not safe. . .
>
> We are . . . powerless. The enemy meets with scarce any resistance.
> The garrison consists of but 40 @ 60 soldiers unprovided with
> ammunition. Fort Amsterdam, utterly defenceless . . .

Kieft's force was nearly always out in the field. There was fierce scattered
fighting all that winter throughout New Netherland. Then, the Dutch force
moved from Long Island to southwestern Connecticut *(Jameson: 282-284):*

> Our forces being returned from this expedition *[to Hempstead, Long
> Island]*, Capt. Van der Hil was dispatched to *Stanford [Capt. Underhill
> to Stamford]*, to get some information there of the Indians. He reported
> that the guide who had formerly served us, and was supposed to have
> gone astray in the night, had now been in great danger of his life among
> the Indians, of whom there were about five hundred together. He

offered to lead us there, to shew that the former mischance was not his fault. One hundred and thirty men were accordingly despatched under the aforesaid Genl. Van der Hil and Hendrick van Dyck, ensign. They embarked in three yachts, and landed at Greenwich *[Tomac Cove]* where they were obliged to pass the night by reason of the great snow and storm. In the morning they marched northwest up over stony hills over which some must creep. In the evening about eight o'clock they came within a league *[3 miles]* of the Indians, and inasmuch they should have arrived too early and had to cross two rivers, one of two hundred feet wide and three deep, and that the men could not afterward rest in consequence of the cold, it was determined to remain there until about ten o'clock. The order was given as to the mode to be observed in attacking the Indians – they marched forward towards the houses, the latter being set up in three rows, street fashion, each row eighty paces long, in a low recess protected by the hills, affording much shelter from the northwest wind. The moon was then at the full, and threw a strong light against the hills. So that many winter days were not brighter than it then was. On arriving there, the Indians were wide awake, and on their guard, so that ours determined to charge and surround the houses, sword in hand. They demeaned themselves as soldiers and deployed in small bands, so that we got in a short time one dead and twelve wounded. They were also so hard pressed that it was impossible for one to escape. In a brief space of time there were counted one hundred and eighty dead outside the houses. Presently none durst come forth, keeping within the houses, discharging arrows through the holes. The general perceived that nothing else was to be done, and resolved with Sergeant Major Van der Hil, to set the huts on fire, whereupon the Indians tried every means to escape, not succeeding which they returned back to the flames preferring to perish by the fire than to die by our hands. What was most wonderful is, that among this vast collection of men, women and children not one was heard to cry or scream. According to the report of the Indians themselves the number then destroyed exceeded five hundred. Some say, full seven hundred, among whom were also twenty five Wappingers, our God having collected together the greater number of our enemies, to celebrate one of their festivals in their manner, from which escaped no more than eight men in all, and three of them were severely wounded.

The fight ended, several fires were built in consequence of the great cold. The wounded, fifteen in number, among whom was the general, were dressed, and the sentinels being posted the troops bivouacked there for the remainder of the night. On the next day, the party set out very early in good order, so as to arrive in Stantfort in the evening. They marched with great courage over that wearisome range of hills, God affording extraordinary strength to the wounded, some of whom were badly hurt, and came in the afternoon to Stantfort after a march of two days and one night and little rest. The English received our people in a very friendly manner, affording them every comfort. In two days they reached here *[Fort Amsterdam]*. A thanksgiving was proclaimed on their arrival.

The route of this attack is diagrammed in Figure 36, **Dutch Attacks on the Wiechquaeskeck.**

The location of Nanichiestawack has been of interest, and several people have proposed different conclusions over the years. The best analysis and conclusion appears to be that of Col. Thatcher T. P. Luquer in his article, *The Indian Village of 1643 (30: 21-24)*. Col. Luquer based his conclusions on his extensive knowledge of the Bedford-Cross River area and on his reading of the above report. He specifically noted the time that the expedition took in their march and the description of the two streams. The only possible river in northern Westchester County with a two hundred foot width and three-foot depth was the Croton River. It matched that description before 1906 when it was submerged in Croton Lake by the construction of the Cornell Dam. Luquer had considerable army marching experience and concluded that, at that time of the year when the expedition took place and the weather being unfavorable, an allowance of 1½ miles per hour would be a reasonable marching rate. Since the march lasted about twelve hours, that would mean a distance of 18 miles, which is the distance from Tomac Cove to Cross River.

I agree with Luquer that his interpretation of the Dutch report should be accepted as correct. However, Luquer had the line of march as starting from modern Greenwich Harbor. No landing existed there at that time. The landing at Tomac Cove was then called "Greenwich." As did Luquer, I have gone along the route, measured it, and observed the landmarks. I went with Chitanikapai (Nicholas Shumatoff, Jr.) who has long worked in the area. He has traced the trails, campgrounds, and the deer pound there. He pointed out that if you drive Route 22 from Bedford to Cross River, you can see the two hills as you cross a bridge just before the Pepsi-Cola building turnoff. Nanichiestawack was on a site that is now under the water to the north of the bridge.

The Conclusion of Governor Kieft's War

Captain John Underhill had delivered what he called "an annihilating blow" to the Wiechquaeskeck. The league of Munsee tribes fighting the

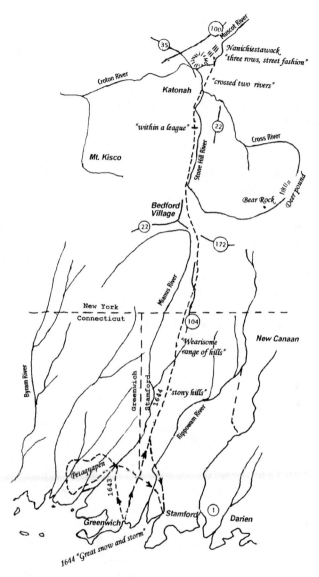

Figure 36

Dutch Attacks on the Wiechquaeskeck

1643 – van Dyke's attack on Petaquapen (Cos Cob)

1644 – Underhill's attack on Nanichiestawack (Cross River)

Dutch was effectively broken. The word got out to all the Hudson Valley, and a group of Native leaders recognized that Underhill was the victor. In April, 1644, Indian leaders turned up in Stamford, "asking Captain Underhill to apply to the Governor of New Netherland for Peace" *(8:32)*. *The Calendar of Historical Manuscripts in the Office of the Secretary of State, Albany* includes an item from the Council Minutes dated April 16, 1644 *(Brodhead)*:

> . . . of the arrival at Stamford of **Mamarunock, Wapgaurin,** chiefs of the **Kichtawanck, Mongochkonnome, Pappenoharrow,** of **Wiquaskeck** and **Nochpeem,** together with the **Wappings,** to solicit Captain Underhill to sue in their names for peace, which is granted on condition that they keep quiet in future.

It is interesting that **Mamarunock** is listed as a chief of the Kitchawanck. He is the same Mamarunock (of Mamaroneck) that was called a Wiechquaeskeck sakima earlier in Kieft's War. **Mongochkonnome** was also a sakima of the Wiechquaeskeck at that time. He was to be followed in line by **Sauwenarack,** who signed a later treaty of peace with the Dutch in 1664. In turn, he was succeeded by **Goharis,** who signed numerous sales of land covering most of Westchester in 1681 to 1684. These three sakimas sold much of the land in Westchester.

In the 1644 document, the Wiechquaeskeck leaders promised, "now and forever to refrain from doing any harm to either people, cattle or houses, or anything else within the territory of New Netherland."

John Underhill presented their appeal to the Director. Director Kieft then sent emissaries to the key Native American leaders from New Jersey to the upper Hudson, and a treaty was drawn up at Fort Amsterdam. It was a formal treaty of peace, with a return of prisoners. It must have been an impressive sight to those who knew the Indian tribes in the Hudson River area. Several Mohawk ambassadors attended as mediators, including **Sisiadego, Claes, Noorman, Oratonin, Auronge,** and **Sesekemas**. The Mohawk were essentially the rulers of the Hudson Valley by that time. They preferred peace with the Dutch to make their fur trade operate smoothly. **"John Onderhil"** was also present. The signatures on the treaty concluded with "Their Sackemakers or Indian Chiefs:"

Oratany, Chief of **Achkinckeshaky** *(Hackensack)*

Sesemus and **William,** Chiefs of **Tappan** and **Rechgawawanck**

Pacham *(Tankiteke),* **Rennekeck** – left power with others

Those of **Onany** and their Neighbors:

Mayauwetinnemin, for those of **Marechkawaick**

Nayeck *(Nyack)* and their Neighbours; together with

Aepjen, in person, speaking for the

Wappinex, Wickquaeskeckxx, Sintsings, and **Kitchawangs.**

The signing included "the mark of **Aepje**," sachem of the **Mahikanders** (Mahican). Aside from the presence of the Mohawk leaders, Aepje (Aepjen) the Mahican, was the chief leader of all the River Indians in the Hudson Valley, which included all the Wiechquaeskeck.

Aepjen's Indian name was **Skiwias** (also Eskuyias, Skiwiaen). "**Aepjen**," meaning "little Ape" in Dutch, was a Dutch name of disrespect for him *(13: 311)*. Obviously, he was short and hairy, but he was the undisputed leader of the Mahican. His wife's name was **Kachkowa**. Skiwias (Aepjen) spoke for all the tribes of the lower Hudson River Valley. Note that on this, and the Stamford document, the Wapping or Wappinex are referred to, not the "Wappingers" *(Chap. 2)*.

Despite this impressive treaty, troubles with the Natives continued in New Netherland. There was a major Indian assault on New Amsterdam in September, 1655, called the "Peach War." It started when a Dutch settler shot a River Indian woman who was picking peaches in his orchard. Also, from 1659 to 1664, the Esopus War raged further up the Hudson Valley around the present site of Kingston. This war probably drove the Rechgawanck south to The Bronx. One result of the 1645 Treaty was the release of **Sauwenaro** (Sauwenarack), a Wiechquaeskeck sakima in Westchester County. He later signed a number of land transfers in Westchester between 1660 and 1666, and a treaty in 1664.

Some Wiechquaeskeck continued to live in Westchester in this period, but many transferred their land formally to the settlers. The few left were steadily moving out of southwestern Connecticut. Their roots had been completely torn up at Nanichiestawack. Some Europeans then increased their sale of liquor to the remnant Natives, to be able to get them in debt, and seize their land. This led to many minor incidents, but there were no further serious complaints of fighting. The big problem for the few remaining Wiechquaeskeck was the rush of new immigrant settlers from Europe looking for land. They exerted great pressure. Finally, every plot of usable farming land in Connecticut was either acquired by a land transfer agreement or simply taken and used because there were no Indians camping on it. The destruction of Nanichiestawack was the beginning of the end for the Connecticut Wiechquaeskeck *(Chap. 10)*.

In July, 1644, heavy Dutch reinforcements arrived at Fort Amsterdam from the West Indies. By then, the expense of the English soldiers was too much for Kieft, so he dismissed Underhill and his English company on July 22. He rewarded Captain Underhill with a large tract of land on Long Island for his services in the war. Underhill was no longer needed in Stamford, so he moved to Long Island. One of his properties was close to Bergen Beach on Jamaica Bay, which is now part of the Gateway National Recreation Area. This land was only about ten miles from Flushing Bay, where Elizabeth Winthrop Feake Hallett had moved from Greenwich. Elizabeth's daughter, also Elizabeth, married John Underhill there. Years before, Underhill and his father had both trained in the Dutch military service in Holland, and he had married a Dutch woman, Helena de Hooch, and had a family when he left Boston. Evidently he was a widower on Long Island. As more English settlers arrived, he became an even more important figure.

Peter Stuyvesant became the Governor of New Netherland in May, 1647, replacing Willem Kieft. Relationships were poor then between the Dutch and the New Englanders, partly because of English settlers pressing closer and closer to New Netherland. Also, the Indians were still restless. Governor Stuyvesant, and his counterpart, Governor Theophilus Eaton of Boston, exchanged letters accusing each other of giving liquor to the Indians and stirring up trouble, but they were polite in their correspondence. Stuyvesant had many problems in New Netherlands dealing with fractious citizens and the increasing sale of both liquor and firearms to the Natives. He strongly suppressed Indian uprisings in 1655, 1658, and 1663, but the few Wiechquaeskeck in southwestern Connecticut had remained subdued.

Willem Kieft sailed for Holland in 1647. His boat was wrecked in a storm off the southwestern coast of England on the way home. All were drowned.

CHAPTER 10

"THE LAST OF THE MOHICANS"

James Fenimore Cooper, already world-famous as a novelist, wrote **The Last of the Mohicans** in 1826, creating the key book in the "Leatherstocking tales." The stories of Natty Bumppo and his Indian companion, Chingachgook, became a true American "myth" which has appealed to all levels of readers. Chingachgook may well have been modeled on Cooper's few Wiechqueskeck neighbors in Mamaroneck.

The stories were based on the intercolonial French and Indian Wars in the first half of the 18th century, when many battles were fought in upstate New York between the British and the French. This was the period when the Wiechquaeskeck had just been pushed out of southwestern Connecticut, and they had moved up the Hudson and Housatonic Rivers to Schagticoke (Kent), Connecticut, Scaghticoke (about 20 miles northeast of Albany) in New York, and Skatekook (Stockbridge), Massachusetts *(7: Mahican, 204)*. Many young Indian men living in those towns volunteered as scouts with the colonial British army, and a large percentage died in the fighting. The majority were Mahican (thus, *The Last of the Mohicans*), but these were towns to which some Wiechquaeskeck had been pushed as well.

Schagticoke, Scaghticoke, and Skatekook have had many spellings over the years. Shirley Dunn *(13)* notes that when Hudson's crew rowed from Albany to Schagticoke in 1610, one spelling was Scaticook. The names of the three sites obviously come from the same root word. It would appear that the early Mahican had been in all three places.

It is believed that Cooper wrote much of the story in an inn on the Boston Post Road in Mamaroneck, New York, which is still standing. For many years in the 20th century, it was called the Fenimore Cooper Inn. (In 2001, it is a restaurant called Down by the Bay.) Cooper had married Susan De Lancey, daughter of a Tory family, and lived there comfortably. Susan's father owned the inn. It is significant that there were probably still a few Wiechquaeskeck around Mamaroneck, and he could have gotten some information from them. He certainly knew that the Mahican federated tribes included the Westchester-Connecticut area, and they were vanishing rapidly from settler expansion and the French and Indian War.

The Wiechquaeskeck are Pushed Out

By 1700, most of the Wiechquaeskeck had left Greenwich, Stamford, and much of Norwalk. On July 8, 1701, the local sakima, Catonah, signed an agreement in the Bedford area *(Chap. 8)* that clarified and confirmed the earlier grants of lands to the settlers throughout the area. The Indians were told to "Give grant & quit Cleame unto all ye Lands meadows Trees feeding Grounds Rivers pooles & other privileges." The witnesses who signed by "markes" led the last Wiechquaeskeck in the area who were not servants or farm laborers. They were from Greenwich, Stamford, and Norwalk. Their retreat into oblivion was beginning. They had lost all their rights to fishing and farming on the coastal lowlands.

The 1701 agreement forced the last of the Wiechquaeskeck, who were more or less staying together as a band, together with a few Tankiteke and others, to vacate their lands and move to the Ramapoo area of Ridgefield. Ramapoo probably means "a rocky place." It is a hilly and rocky area. (The "R" sound was not used by the Lenape, so the name probably came from northeastern tribes). Although the land was good for hunting, it was not suitable for farming, except for small corn, bean and squash patches. As a result, the settlers did not go there at first. The Indians could not go to the coast for fish, but they could hunt in the hills. Game was plentiful, but times were changing rapidly.

England and Scotland were in the start of an agricultural revolution that would change into the Industrial Revolution in a century. Cromwell's Civil War in the middle of the 17th century had essentially combined the economies of England and Scotland and had started the creation of larger armaments factories and woollen mills. It was the start of a century of disarray in Scotland, which began with a major defeat of the Scotch Royalists in 1648. Many Lowlanders went along with the new economic changes, while many Highlanders actively fought them until the battle of Culloden in 1746. The landholders of Scotland saw the new woollen economy coming, and the Highland Clearances were started. These land seizures drove many Scotch to North America. Around 1700, there were still a million people in Scotland, although great numbers had already gone to Northern Ireland, and many more had emigrated around the world, including to New England.

They knew sheep farming and wool production. There was similar emigration of both agricultural and factory people from all over Europe.

Wool production was the "electronics industry" of the late 17th century, in the way that it changed the world. There was an international demand for wool, with the ability to trade worldwide. Even the small, early woollen mills required steady sources of supply. Wool became the obvious use for the land of New England, and it directly affected the Wiechquaeskeck. No longer were the settlers looking only for fertile, manageable, crop farm land. Now, they were eager to get any land that could grow grasses, clover, alfalfa, and oats for their sheep. In the late 17th century, the new colonists moved *en masse* into the hilly areas of New England and New York to raise sheep. Many had been displaced themselves in the Land Clearances, and now they displaced "the Last of the Mohican."

The hills of Fairfield and Westchester were then mostly barren. A great many acres had been burned off by the Wiechquaeskeck during their deer hunting expeditions. The land was poor for any type of farming, even the growing of grasses, because of the myriad stones of all sizes left there by the ice sheet 10,000 years before. The sheep farmers looked at this as an opportunity. With their oxen and horses pulling "stone boats" (large, heavy, flat sleds), they moved the surface stones to their property lines, then made "dry wall" fences and paddocks with them. They were perfect for penning sheep. Where we now have tree-covered hills, they had miles of stone walls snaking over the bare hills. A multitude of sheep covered the hills of Fairfield and Westchester. Many stone walls in Fairfield County date from this time. In Ward Pound Ridge Reservation there are remnants of a large network of stone walls in the woods, which have since sprung up around them. The sectioning of the farms can be vividly seen, and there are still a few of the paddocks, or sheep holding pens, left.

All the remaining land in Fairfield County was completely used for sheep farms by the new immigrants.

The Dispersion of the Wiechquaeskeck

The new settlers that were moving into Ridgefield were unhappy that there were any Natives at all on the land, using it for hunting and their little corn patches. The newcomers soon petitioned the General Assembly at Hartford to remove the Indian survivors that were camped around the lakes in the Ramapoo area. The State of Connecticut bought approximately

20,000 acres for the then large sum of 100 pounds sterling *(Chap. 8)*. The Indian sellers were led by **Catoonah**, the sakima *(Chap. 3)*. The others who signed the agreement on Sept. 30, 1708, were **Gootquas, Wawkamawwee, Wooquacomick, Naraneka, Waspahchain, Tawpornick, and Cawwehorin.** (Waspahchain was John Calk, the survivor from Greenwich who was often in on the land deals. Five months later, he would even be signing another agreement on Feb. 12, 1709, for the last small piece of Indian-held land in Greenwich *(Chap. 8))*. Nearly all the remaining Wiechquaeskeck in southwestern Connecticut had been pushed together.

A few Wiechquaeskeck still held onto small pieces of land throughout the Fairfield County area, and some held on for many more years, while working for the intruding settlers. The new immigrants made scattered deals for land in the hills north of Ridgefield in 1715, 1721, 1727, 1729, and 1743. The little Native groups had probably not wanted to move, but the pressure of the sheep farmers was intense. At least the Indians had evidently learned a little about the value of real estate by then, and the Hartford Assembly insisted upon relatively equitable purchases.

The Wiechquaeskeck were not longer a cohesive tribe at this time. Catoonah's leadership was segmented. The majority of the Wiechquaeskeck who had lived in southwestern Connecticut had moved north to Kent, Stockbridge, and Albany, but there may well have been some who traveled west with other Lenape to Ohio, Wisconsin and Oklahoma. They would have had many problems with the other, new European settlers along the way. A great migration of the New Jersey Lenape to the West had been caught between the armies and settlers of the English and French. It is a complex story, and we do not know if it has any direct relationship to the fleeing Wiechquaeskeck from southwestern Connecticut, who were also Lenape. The flight of the Delawares west is well described by Robert S. Grumet in **The Lenapes** *(21)*.

There is one particular unknown factor that is of interest in following the Wiechquaeskeck from Ridgefield. There is a tribal group that has long maintained their Lenape identity near Mahwah, New Jersey called the Ramapough Lenape Nation, "Keepers of the Pass." They have a Tribal Office at 189 Stag Hill Road, Mahwah, NJ, 07430 (Email: ramapoughnation.org). Their current chief is Walter *(Silent Wolf)* Van Dunk. Their stories go back to the 18th century. They know of no connection between their Ramapough and the Ramapoo of the Ridgefield area. The names are intriguingly similar, since both mean something like "flat rocky area" in Lenape. They cannot be considered as having the same source as the Wiechquaeskeck without some historical proof, however.

We have some stories of the Ridgefield Ramapoo group moving to the Kent, Connecticut, (Schagticoke) area. John W. DeForest *(10: 389-420)* gives information about four Indian groups that had gathered together in northwest Connecticut after many had been evicted from the coastal areas. These Indians came from several tribal groups and "were a clan that never had a distinctive name." They were "a mere collection of refugees and wanderers, who had migrated hither from the southern and eastern parts of Connecticut, to escape from the vicinity of the English settlements." DeForest did not believe that they were very numerous. Then, even as the Ramapoo area was being sold in 1703, and some Wiechquaeskeck went to Kent, European settlers from Milford, on Long Island Sound, moved up to the area. They bought New Milford from the Natives already there, squeezing that remote area. DeForest said that the Scatacook (another spelling of the name) Indians of Kent were formed as a group about 1728, which would agree with the removal from the Ridgefield area. The moves did not take place quickly.

The Kent Scatacooks were a mixed band of refugees who had come from many places, from Massachusetts to southwestern Connecticut. The first founder of the group was actually a Pequot, Gideon Mauwehu, who had brought a small band up the Housatonic. Any displaced Native American was welcomed there. Small groups flocked in from all quarters. In ten years, there may have been a hundred men and their families. But, the "Scatacooks had not enjoyed their happy valley many years before they were disturbed by the arrival of the whites." The settlement of Kent, "commenced in 1738, was prosecuted rapidly" *(10: 409)*. The Moravian missionaries *(Heckewelder)* began to preach to the Scatacooks "and soon effected a remarkable change in the character of the tribe. . . A church was built and a flourishing congregation collected" *(10: 410)*. This infuriated the settlers' rumsellers, however, who were losing customers. They therefore acted in a pattern that was repeated in many locations. The rumsellers first gave free rum, to create a habit, then they charged high prices and pushed their wares on surrounding Natives, getting them into serious debt. They finished by seizing the land in payment of the liquor debts. The commercial and liquor interests also persuaded the authorities to drive out the Moravian missionaries and to open the tribal areas to their liquor sales. The Indians, without leaders, "sank into intemperance, and began to waste away. In this mournful manner ended the most promising, and, for a time, the most successful religious effort that was ever commenced among the aborigines of Connecticut" *(10: 411).*

Despite this slow destruction of the tribal group, the white authorities were anxious to keep them on their side. During the French and Indian War in 1744, Governor Clinton of New York sent to them commissioners from both Connecticut and Massachusetts, and pleaded with them to stay at peace or to join in the fighting on the English side. The group was well received by the Scatacooks, who even presented the visitors with a belt of wampum and three marten skins. We know that a number of the young Indian men did join the English forces, and many were killed in the fighting. Since they were used as scouts, a higher proportion of them was killed than of the regular troops.

The pressure of the surrounding Europeans was tremendous on the small band in Kent. Brasser said that, even "by 1700 Mahican society was being undermined by all the negative aspects of the colonial frontier." *(7: Mahican 206).* Brasser continues, "the Indians complained 'that many of our people are obliged to hire land of the Christians at a very dear rate, and to give half the corn for rent, and the other half they are tempted by rum to sell.'" The settlers managed, with their legal grasp on the Indian lands, to squeeze the Natives. In fact, "in 1775 the Assembly ordered that the lands of the Scatacooks should be leased to pay their debts and defray their expenses" *(10: 417).* Then, we have word from one of the families from southwestern Connecticut *(Sect 3 – Chi-Kin Warrups).* "Thomas Warrups, probably a son of the old Sagamore of Reading, was allowed to sell thirty acres of land to pay his debts and provide for his family. The old squaw of Chickens was still living; she was blind, however, and had lately been sick." Brasser gave a detailed account of the trials and tribulations of the Mahican, beset by the settlers, through the 18th and 19th centuries. It is probable that there were a few Wiechquaeskeck caught up in the relentless removal that he described.

A later reference *(10: 419)* to the coastal Indians at Scatacook says, "An honorable exception to the prevailing intemperance and idleness of the Scatcooks seems to have existed in Benjamin Chickens, a descendant of the old sachem, Chickens." He built a house, and fenced and cultivated his lands. He sold his lands and developed others more than once. Finally, the Chickens family apparently moved to New York.

Chi-Kin Warrups and his family were not Wiechquaeskeck, however. They wereTankiteke from the Southport area. They are of interest here because of their intersection with the remnant Wiechquaeskeck in their retreat north along the Norwalk and Housatonic Rivers.

Finis

DeForest said *(10: 359)*, " The Indians of Greenwich, Stamford and Norwalk, seem to have melted away unnoticed: a great part of them probably moved to other homes, and one portion appears to have settled for a time in what is now Ridgefield. We learn from the census of the Connecticut Indians, taken in 1774, that there were then only eight natives remaining in Greenwich, nine in Norwalk, and not one in Stamford." It appears that most of the few Wiechquaeskeck in the Ramapoo (Ridgefield) area in the early 18th century were finally pushed into oblivion, north along the Housatonic River. It is possible that some of them left in other directions and headed west with other Lenape. There is no known record.

Hardy was the last-known full-blooded Wiechquaeskeck to live in Greenwich. He was probably the last in southwestern Fairfield County. He worked as a farm laborer. He died in 1861. His unmarked gravestone is on the west side of Round Hill Road in Greenwich, in the vicinity of Fort Hills Lane, north of the Howe family burying ground.

CHAPTER 11

ARCHAEOLOGICAL STUDIES IN SOUTHWESTERN CONNECTICUT

There are a number of windows through which we can see the past dimly. Geology, biology and other sciences show us how the landscape was formed and how vegetation and animals came to the area. Anthropology and paleontology analyze the movements and changes of humans and animals over time. History allows us to read documents and records of what happened in historic time. Archaeology relates to all these disciplines to discover and interpret the material remains of man's past. The body of archaeological conclusions often illuminates the life of the past.

Archaeology is the extension of history into the unwritten and unrecorded. It digs into the structures and detritus of the past to give us more information on understanding our people, our nation, and ourselves. It is a dirty, back-breaking, intellectual pursuit that should be highly appreciated by anyone who wants to know who preceded them.

Archaeology is based on factual interpretation, with some art thrown in. Its practitioners use the scientific method of theorizing, gathering data, interpreting their findings, then analyzing the results, before reaching conclusions. Archaeology has become an important part of our understanding of the world around us. Scientific archaeological methods give us information that is both interesting and enlightening.

This introduction is a plea to the reader to respect any old objects or artifacts that are found in the course of ordinary living. If you find an "arrow head" (projectile point) or anything else that looks like it was worked by a human in the past, please report your find to a professional or amateur archaeologist. Only they are in a position to look at your finding and to say whether it is of interest to Science, and possibly even of importance.

A major place in western Fairfield County for the reporting of archaeological finds (such as "arrowheads") is the Archaeology Department of Norwalk Community College. Contact Ernest A. Wiegand, Professor of

Archaeology, Norwalk Community College, 188 Richards Avenue, Norwalk, CT 06854. Phone (230) 857-7377. He trains and works with both amateur and professional archaeologists.

If you find interesting material and simply want to talk to a local person, contact your town's historical society, museum or archeology association. Your find may hold the key to a piece of the history of your community. There are state and local laws that are an attempt to preserve archaeological findings. They only work, however, if interested people cooperate with the archaeologists.

Despite this, there is always an interest by amateurs in "pot hunting" or digging recklessly in an ancient site to get a souvenir. This is an understandable feeling, but it cannot match the thrill of advancing knowledge.

Some Archeological Terms

Archaeology is a science, and archaeological terms have specific meanings. A few which are useful to this story are:

Archaeology - Archaeology is the systematic recovery and study of material evidence remaining from past human life or culture. It has become a science rather than an art. A substantial body of technical literature has been written.

Artifact – An artifact is an object showing human workmanship or modification.

Focus – The convergence of artifact types found with previously-dated artifact types, to determine the date of artifacts.

Historical Archaeology – The combination of professional archaeological analysis with information gathered from written records.

Horizon – Horizon is a geological term referring to the deposits of a particular time indicated by the presence of known fossils in a stratum (layer of stone). In archaeology, it refers to dated artifact types in a level of a dig.

Sequence – Sequence is the order of time succession of artifacts in a dig, based on their shape, technology, and art. Most of the deposited earth is shallow in the Wiechquaeskeck area, and thus the sequence of artifacts is often not obvious. In Middle America, there may be deposited layers twenty or more feet deep in the great river flood plains. In the Carolinas, where the Native Americans were closer to those lived in Connecticut, the soil is also deep, as the land was untouched by the Ice Sheets. When the artifacts are carefully removed, layer by layer, from deep digs, they give a picture of the march of technology over time. Some of these known sequences, from deep soil elsewhere, can be applied to finds in southwestern Connecticut.

Site – A site is a particular plot of land which archaeologists pick to do research. They record it first by a field survey and surface checks. They then document the dig with detailed maps, sketches, forms, and notes.

Tradition – Tradition is the passing down of elements of a culture from generation to generation, by artifact design and by oral communication.

A good introduction for the amateur to American archaeology can be found in: Louis A. Brennan, **Beginner's Guide to Archeology**, Dell Publishing Company, New York, 1973.

A. ARCHAEOLOGICAL STUDY SITES AND FINDINGS

The following are summaries of some of the archaeological reports about southwestern Connecticut that have been published in professional journals. They are arranged chronologically because there is a time value of one report building on others. Newer archaeological methods are employed in more recent digs.   Figure 37, **Some Archaeological Studies in Western Fairfield County**, roughly locates 21 dig sites. These studies are discussed because they have been reported in the scientific literature.   There are hundreds of other sites that have been worked on by Norwalk Community College, archaeological associations, professional archeologists and historical societies. Also, because of the State law requiring archaeological studies of possibly historic sites, there are many more studies in private files of land ownership.

The relevant published archeological papers for southwestern Connecticut are:

(ARCH1) 1956 Robert Carl Suggs, "**The Manakaway Site, Greenwich, Connecticut**," *Bulletin of the Archaeological Society of Connecticut*, (28), New Haven, 1956.

This is a site on the southeast corner of Greenwich Point, which juts into Long Island Sound. Many of the artifacts were Bowmans Brook and

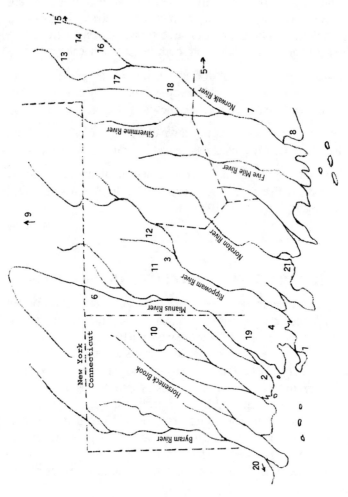

Figure 37

Some Archeological Studies in Western Fairfield County

1 Manakaway	8 Spruce Swamp	15 D'Aulaire
2 Indian Field	9 Bear Rock Petroglyph	16 Turner Ridge
3 Hunting Ridge	10 Babcock	17 Wolfpit
4 Laddins Rock Rd	11 Bear Rock Complex	18 Perkin Elmer
5 Samp Mortar Res.	12 Rockrimmon Complex	19 Dundee Rkshelter
6 Mianus Gorge	13 Indian Rock House	20 Rye Marshlands
7 Bitter Rock	14 Split Rock	21 Cove Island

Adapted from Ernest A. Wiegand, **Rockshelters of Southwestern Connecticut: their Prehistoric occupation and use**, p. 7, Norwalk Community College Press, 1983.

Clasons Point focus, dating around 1200 AD. There was a predominance of late, triangular projectile points. It was a summer fishing and shellfishing site, occupied intermittently over short periods of time. There was little evidence found of wampum making at the site,

The shells of a dozen varieties of marine mollusks were found, most of which are still common there. Some levels showed a ratio of 200 clams to 1,000 oysters, showing modern tastes! They identified the animal skeletal remains, in order of frequency, of: deer, racoon, puma, wildcat, bear, beaver, squirrel, chipmunk, skunk, fox (?), dog, mouse, and bison (?). There were many sherds of pottery.

(ARCH2) 1956 Julius Lopez and Stanley Wisnieski, **"Discovery of a Possible Ceremonial Dog Burial in the City of Greater New York,"** *Bulletin of the Archaeological Society of Connecticut*, (28), New Haven, 1956.

The remains of two dogs were found buried on Flushing Bay, across from LaGuardia Airport. This find is included because it shows that the local Natives of the time had affection and regard for their dogs. It is believed that the dogs were killed and buried near their dead human companion. They were interred in much the same fashion as human corpses. The grave was evidently enclosed by a ring of posts, and a fire was burned over it. Formal canine burials were frequent in New York State, and were common throughout America.

(ARCH3) 1958 Bernard W. Powell, **"Preliminary Report on a Southwestern Connecticut Site,"** *Bulletin of the Archaeological Society of Connecticut*, (29): 12-19, New Haven, 1958.

This coastal site, called Indian Field *(Fig. 27)*, is along the west bank of Cos Cob Harbor in Greenwich. There was a thin marine shell midden and numerous shell pits. A variety of incised and cord-marked pottery was found, dating from about 1000 AD to Contact. They included the Windsor and East River Traditions, and East River ceramics. The many projectile points were mixed, about half being the more recent triangular and half being the older stemmed, side-notched, and other forms. There has been more recent professional digging at this site.

(ARCH4) 1959 Bernard W. Powell, "**A Ceramic Find at Hunting Ridge, Connecticut**," *Bulletin of the Massachusetts Archaeological Society*, 20 (3): 43-45, Attleboro, 1959.

This inland site was a findspot for 66 potsherds and a small chipped quartz knife. Powell thought that the pottery bore resemblances to the Owasco Tradition in New York, dated there between 1,000 and 1,400 AD.

(ARCH5) 1961 Bernard W. Powell, **Some Connecticut Burials**, Massachusetts Archaeological Society, 23 (2): 26-32, Attleboro, 1962.

There were finds of three purported Indian burials near U.S. 1 in the Stamford-Greenwich border area. A child's burial on Acosta Street had sketchy evidence. A possible burial near Laddin's Rock Road in Old Greenwich was brought to the attention of P.G. Howes, Curator of Bruce Museum, but by the time he reached the site, it had been disrupted and used as road fill. He did find a human cranium and other bones, however.

The most significant find was under the front entrance of the bowling alley which was being built in 1958. (It is now a furniture store.) Powell was able to get there only after foundation concrete had been poured. A smart workman showed him where the bones were under the concrete, and he dug them out from under the fresh cement. He found an intact skull, which he believed was Native American.

(ARCH6) 1962 Bernard W. Powell, "**An Aboriginal Quartz Quarry at Samp Mortar Reservoir, Fairfield, Connecticut.**" *Bulletin of the Archaeological Society of New Jersey*, (22), 1962.

This site is north of Fairfield near the Samp Mortar Reservoir. It is included here because it showed that the Natives of this area worked quartz outcroppings in gneissic rock, possibly starting 5,000 years ago. Quartz is extremely hard. The Natives could only chip, flake, or spall it with hammerstones made of quartz. As primordial molten quartz flowed up through cracks in the gneiss (metamorphic rock) in "dykes," some of the molten quartz lava would flow into small side cracks and harden. These branches were prized by Native artisans, as they could readily make them into uniface flakes.

(There were many such quartz quarries and chipping stations throughout southwestern Connecticut. It is mentioned in Chapter 2 that Don Walton found a quartz chipping station just east of the Old Greenwich Civic Center on Harding Road, and retrieved many pieces of projectile points. That site has now been covered by a large building. The concrete floor has been poured, and the archaeological site is forever lost.)

(ARCH7) 1964 Bernard W. Powell, "**The Mianus Gorge Rock Shelter**." *Pennsylvania Archaeologist*, 142-148, 1964.

Powell found evidence of Archaic occupation in a rock shelter in the Mianus River Gorge. There was long occupation from a pre-ceramic to a ceramic horizon. He was able to look at many layers of artifacts. The projectile points progressed in sequence from lozenge, to stemmed, to side-notched, to triangular. There were a variety of scrapers. Fortunately for archeological history, the area abounds in poison ivy and copperheads, both of which repel "pothunters."

(ARCH8) 1964 Bernard W. Powell, "**Bitter Rock Shelter: A Stratified Connecticut Site**", *Bulletin of the Massachusetts Archaeological Society*, (26): 53-63, 1964.

The Bitter Rock Shelter lies at the foot of a high cliff in the Winnipauk section of Norwalk. The earliest levels appear to be Late Archaic, with some occupancy through Woodland times. Six types of projectile points were found. There were stone axes, celts, needles, knives, scrapers, pendants, etc.. There was a variety of potsherds (ceramic fragments), including stamped, cord-impressed, notched, and incised, with and without shell temper.

Unfortunately, there was considerable "pot hunting" at the site over the years, as it was a prolific site. One local resident had found a full-grooved, polished, greenstone axe about six inches long.

(ARCH9) 1964 Bernard W. Powell, "**A Curious Scratched Design on a Connecticut Paintstone**," *American Antiquity*, 30 (1): 90-100, Salt Lake City, 1964.

From the Spruce Swamp Site *(ARCH10)*, Powell compared a "curious scratched design on a hematite paintstone" to motifs of the Southern Cult. This could indicate long-distance trading, or "it could be explained on the basis of indigenous development." Also at the site, however, was an artifact made from green plasma, a bright green quartz that came from Alabama or Georgia, probably traded from there. Unfortunately, a purported "burial mound" had been destroyed previously.

(ARCH10) 1965 Bernard W. Powell, "**Spruce Swamp: A Partially Drowned Coastal Midden in Connecticut**," *American Antiquity*, 30, (4): 460-469, April, 1965.

This archaeological complex was discovered when a boat basin was dredged in a creek near the Norwalk River. The site had been known, and several sizable local collections of artifacts had been taken from it before it was examined by professional archaeologists. Ted Jostrand, a local amateur archaeologist, helped considerably in cataloging his collection by location and making it available for study.

The area looked at is part of a very large shell midden area from in the water to Sasqua Hill in Norwalk. It is at least 300 feet wide and 350 feet long. It is now partly submerged in Long Island Sound, but it had probably been used for about 3,000 years. There were many projectile points found, from the Archaic Lamoka types to the late Woodland Levanna type.

(ARCH11) 1971 Bernard W. Powell, "**First Site Synthesis and Proposed Chronology for the Aborigines of Southwestern Connecticut**,"*Pennsylvania Archaeologist*, 1971.

Bernard W. Powell, of Wilton, CT, published about ten papers on local archaeology between 1958 and 1965. In this paper, he summarizes these and other studies, comparing artifact types, excavated features, and stratigraphy. He shows relationships to a cultural chronology proposed earlier for nearby coastal New York.

*(ARCH12) 1972 Nich*olas A. Shoumatoff, "**The Bear Rock Petroglyph Site**," *The Bulletin of the New York State Archaeological Association*, 55: 1-5, July, 1972

This remarkable petroglyph rock is in Ward Pound Ridge Reservation *(Fig. 43)*. It has 12 clearly pecked-and-rubbed designs of bear, deer, and other figures. It may be the only such site existing in Westchester County. Information about it can be obtained from the Trailside Museum. Caution must be taken regarding its location until efforts are made to protect it from possible vandalism.

(ARCH 13) 1972 Frederick W. Warner, **"The Foods of the Connecticut Indians,"** *Bulletin of the Archaeological Society of Connecticut,* (37): 27-41, November, 1972.

In this comprehensive report, Warner assembles the findings from 22 archaeological sites from Greenwich to Bridgeport. He lists evidence of:

- 21 different mammals, including black bear, beaver, bobcat, mink, moose, and wolf.

- 9 different fish, including barracuda, grouper, shark, and sturgeon.

- 14 different shellfish, mostly Virginia oysters, quahogs, and clams.

- 19 different wild vegetable products.

- 4 different cultivated vegetable products.

He discusses the hunting, gathering, fishing, and agricultural activities of the Indians along the Connecticut shoreline.

(ARCH14) 1993 Ernest A. Wiegand, **"Rockshelters of Southwestern Connecticut: Their Prehistoric Occupation and Use,"** Norwalk Community College Press, 1983.

This book reviews the excavation and analysis of 13 rockshelters in Southwestern Connecticut, discussing their stratigraphy, the artifacts and remains found, and the methodologies used. Wiegand discusses and interprets each. It is highly recommended to anyone interested in the Native Americans of southwestern Connecticut.

(ARCH15) 1985 Stuart J. Fiedel, **"The Dundee Rockshelter, Greenwich,"** *Bulletin of the Archaeological Society of Connecticut,* (48): 31

The Dundee Rockshelter is located in a public park in a residential area of Greenwich. Over the years it has been extensively pothunted, and the stratigraphy was badly disturbed. Fiedel found eight complete, or nearly complete, projectile points, knives, scrapers, and burins (flint tools for incising pottery), many preforms, and much lithic debitage (chips of worked stone). There were many potsherds and bone fragments. The shelter was apparently visited most frequently between 2500 to 1700 BC, with little middle Woodland or later material *(Fig. 2)*.

In 1989 there was a concerted attempt in Greenwich to dedicate the area for permanent preservation. It is now called the Edward R. Schongalla Park.

(ARCH16) 1985 Ernest A. Wiegand II, **"The Prehistoric Ceramics of Southwestern Connecticut: An Overview and Reevaluation,"** *Bulletin of the Archaeological Society of Connecticut*, (50): 23-42, 1987.

Wiegand reviews the reported ceramics from 15 sites in Southwestern Connecticut. He discusses the paste characteristics, the temper and surface treatments of ceramic vessels, such as interior and exterior cord-marking, the lip-notched decorations, and the dentate stamping of the vessels found. He describes the problems of assembling sherds into a single vessel. The cord marking and other attributes allow the analysis of the Tradition of particular areas. The Wiechquaeskeck area has a mixture of the Windsor Tradition and the East River Tradition in Early and Late Woodland times. Wiegand quotes Snow *(46: 330)* as suggesting the gradual movement of prehistoric Munsees into the area "where the indigenous population was absorbed rather than replaced by the dominant immigrant communities."

(ARCH 17) 1988 Stuart J. Fiedel, **"Orient Fishtail Points from the Rye Marshlands Conservancy,"** *Bulletin of the Archaeological Society of Connecticut*, (51): 111-124, 1988.

Fiedel found 28 complete Orient Fishtail points, as well as numerous point fragments, by a surface collection in the Rye Marshlands Conservancy. The name comes from the Orient Point Culture at the east end of Long Island, dated between 1043 BC and 763 BC. The fate of the people who made these broad spears is unknown. Their artifacts resemble the Adena type, suggesting "some kind of participation by Northeastern populations in the Adena interaction sphere." (the St. Louis area along the Mississippi.)

(ARCH18) 1992 Lucianne Lavin and Laurie Miroff, **"Aboriginal Pottery from the Indian Ridge Site, New Milford, Connecticut,"** *Bulletin of the Archaeological Society of Connecticut*, (55): 39-61, 1992.

This site is to the east of the Wiechquaeskeck and Tankiteke area, but relates to it. The pottery examined "indicates the presence of extensive earlier Woodland components, which appear to belong to the Point Peninsula ceramic tradition . . . in interior New York State." For the earlier Woodland times, at least, "it suggests that west-central Connecticut was populated by Indian groups whose cultural affiliations – possible even roots – lie to the west in the Hudson Valley societies."

(ARCH19) 1998 Ernest A. Wiegand, "**A Unique Prehistoric Vessel from Stamford, Connecticut**," *Bulletin of the Archaeological Society of Connecticut*, (61): 21-25, 1998.

There is a small, intact prehistoric clay pot, in the collections of the Stamford Historical Society, that was found in the Cove Island, Stamford, area. The pot is unique in that it has two pairs of holes just below the rim. They were made by punching in the wet clay. They allow the vessel to be suspended in a level manner. The vessel is small, with a capacity of only 200 millilitres (about 7 ounces), and was probably used for dry storage of special herbs. Its compact paste and round base are characteristic of late Woodland pottery. It is very similar to a pot from the Manakaway site, in the Bruce Museum, Greenwich.

(ARCH20) **WorldWideWeb**. On the Internet, there are two major sources of archeological information. The most specific for understanding many aspects of Wiechquaeskeck life in the area is **http://www.nativetech.org**. **NativeTech** is an educational website that covers topics of Native American technology and emphasizes the Eastern Woodlands region. It is dedicated to disconnecting the term 'primitive' from peoples' perceptions of Native American technology and art. It was developed by Tara Prindle, and contains hundreds of pages. Note that much of its information is about more northern people, and about central Connecticut people of the **Windsor Tradition**. The Wiechquaeskeck were Lenape of the **East River Tradition**, and there are a number of differences. The neighboring Paugussett were closer to the Windsor Tradition, so there are many overlaps.

ArchNet, at **http://www.archnet.asu.edu**, is hosted by the Archeological Research Institute at Arizona State University. This WWW Virtual Library – Archeology is a major web source of archeological information, with millions of pages. To study the Wiechquaeskeck, searches should be made on the

Lenape (Delaware), and on the **East River Tradition**.

ArchNet was founded by Thomas Plunkett, and Jonathan Lizee, then at the University of Connecticut, 1993-99, so it contains considerable information on archeological discoveries in Connecticut. In a brief review, it also apparently emphasizes the Windsor Tradition archeological findings for Connecticut. In searching **ArchNet** for information that is applicable to the Wiechquaeskeck, look for the New York City area, Long Island, and the lower Hudson Valley, again, on the Lenape and the East River Tradition.

In addition to these published archaeological reports, there are a great many contract archaeological reports that have been filed in the Town Offices of the area. Those reports have been produced because they are legally required if any new construction might impact a possible archaeological site. The reports have detailed the discovery and interpretation of dozens of local sites.

B. DATING INDIAN ARTIFACTS BY THEIR TECHNOLOGY

Artifacts found at Native American sites can often be dated by their technology. In prehistoric times, whenever intelligent individuals developed a useful new tool, container, or projectile point, the idea soon spread by diffusion over the whole continent. When we find an Indian artifact, we can often tell by its technology, roughly within a century, when that type of artifact was in use. The dating comes from highly-stratified sites that have been studied.

Stratigraphic dating is difficult in Wiechquaeskeck territory because the whole area was scoured by the great Ice Sheet, and it is still recovering from the effects. The soil is not thick enough to show us clear strata over time. The Carolinas, however, were untouched by the vast Laurentian Ice Shield. There are good layered deposits in other parts of the Southeast, in New York State, and areas in the mid-Atlantic region. Layering (stratification) occurred wherever floods or organic deposits covered over the artifacts and detritus of one group of people, and let the next group of people build over it. Many archaeological digs can slice down twenty feet or more and expose layer after layer of Native American artifacts. These layers exhibit and sequence the progression of artifact technology over time.

It is believed that diffusion of ideas was rapid enough so that we can take the archeological Time Line given to us in other areas of eastern America and translate it to the Northeast. All innovations did not diffuse, of course, and there were intelligent, inventive Natives in local Connecticut areas as well, but there will be observed similarities. Thus, archaeologists look where there was sedimentation, particularly over prehistoric campsites, with enough stratification so that a reasonable succession of technologies can be observed, and compare previously studied successions to the observations in southwestern Connecticut.

There is also the advantage today of being able to analyze the atomic structure of carbon for the dating of organic materials, because carbon from living organisms contains radiocarbon, C-14, which breaks down over time to C-12, at a known rate. In this process, archeologists can get very good dates of site occupation by analyzig the ratio of C-12 to C-14. If a projectile point, or other lithic material, is found beside charcoal fragments, a date can be determined for the lithic material from the organic (containing carbon) charcoal that is present. This can only be done in an undisturbed site.

Powell *(ARCH11)* gives an analysis from radiocarbon dating of archaeological periods and cultural sequences for coastal New York. From a practical viewpoint, this process allows us to give reasonable, approximate dates for Native American projectile points that are discovered by the hundreds in this area.

Once again, if anyone discovers projectile points or other Native artifacts in good condition, it is of great scientific importance that they report their finds to an archaeologist. Only then can it be determined if the Indian artifact is of scientific importance, or is common to the area. This is particularly important for Clovis Fluted points *(Fig. 38)*, which are very ancient.

Figures 38, 39 and 40 show a few of the more common projectile points that may be found in the Wiechquaeskeck area. They are not full size on the page, but their relative sizes are shown. Projectile points are identified by their shape, because there is great variability in their sizes *(40, ARCH1, ARCH3, ARCH4, ARCH15, ARCH17, ARCH20)*.

Figure 38, **Paleo-Indian and Early Archaic Projectile Points**, shows some typical examples of that period. The Clovis point is always of considerable interest because of its age. Most were large points to be fastened to a spear. Some points were quite small. The point is named after a site where it was first dated in Clovis, New Mexico. It has since been

Figure 38

Paleo-Indian and Early Archaic Projectile Points

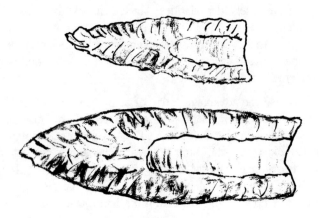

Clovis Fluted Point
stemless, lanceolate spear points

Paleo-Indian Period, ca. 12,000 to 8000 BC

Report finding any Clovis Point to an archeologist!

Bifurcate Base Point   **Neville Point**
straight stemmed

Early Archaic Period, ca. 6000 to 5000 BC

found in many parts of the continent. That was the period of roaming Native bands with no fixed habitation, and some of them found their way to the Northeast. The Paleo-Indian Period was from ca. 10,000 to 8000 BC in the Northeast. The Early Archaic Period was from ca. 8000 to 6000 BC.

Figure 39, **Middle and Late Archaic Projectile Points**, shows a selection of a few types of such points. They are spearheads because bows were not used until the Middle Woodland period. There are many variations, depending on the stone available to be used, and the intended prey. The Archaic was followed by a Terminal (or Transitional) Period from ca. 1700 to 1000 BC, with many new design variations of the projectile points.

Figure 40, **Woodland Projectile Points**, shows the kinds of points that are most frequently found in southwestern Connecticut. The Woodland Period was from about 1000 BC to the time of European Contact. The later arrow points were efficient and well-designed. They were in use in America into the 1800's. These triangular points sometimes had thong lashings simply tied around the stone point rather than in a notch. The point may have been inserted in the top of a split shaft, and held in place by resin. Lashing was around the shaft. The stone arrow points of this Period had a fine balance and could be shot accurately. They were smaller than the previous points because most of the game then hunted was smaller. They were still effective for killing a deer or a bear because they were sharp and penetrated well.

Further Study

Those illustrated are a selection of common points that have been found in the Wiechquaeskeck area. For further study, an excellent book is: William A. Ritchie, **New York Projectile Points – A Typology and Nomenclature**, Bulletin 384, New York State Museum, 1971, rev. 1997. Albany, New York *(39)*. It was written for New York, and some of the projectile points described have not been found in Connecticut, but most of them are applicable, and the technologies point to their age.

Other Artifacts

There are many other types of Native American artifacts that have been found. Many were made by the early Wiechquaeskeck, and were in use in the 17th century. After trade for peltry started in the 16th century, however, metal woodworking and agricultural tools soon began replacing those made of stone. Metal pots and other cooking vessels were soon found to be

Figure 39

Middle and Late Archaic Projectile Points

Brewerton Point   **Sylvan Point**   **Vosburg Point**
ear-notched   left barb broken   corner-notched
reworked as a scraper
Middle Archaic Period. ca. 5000 to 2000 BC

Beekman Triangle Point Normans Kill Point Wading River Point
no stem   side-notched   stemmed
Late Archaic Period ca, 2000 to 1000 BC

Figure 40
Woodland Projectile Points

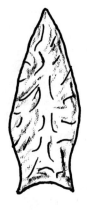  

Orient Fishtail Point   **Meadowood Point**   **Rossville Point**
lanceolate blade   medium to large   lozenge shape

Transitional and Early Woodland Periods, ca. 1000 to 400 BC

Jack's Reef Point   **Levanna Point**   **Madison Point**
corner-notched   as broad as long   small, thin, triangular

Middle and Late Woodland Periods, ca. 900 to 1800 AD

superior to the breakable clay vessels. Even tomahawks and arrowheads were soon made of metal, when they could get hold of it. Sometimes Contact Indians would trade for a brass metal kettle, then break it up, drill holes in it, and use the pieces to make projectile points, fishhooks and tools. The old stone tools and clay vessels long had a place, however. A few of them are pictured in the following figures.

Figure 41, **Stone Axe, Celt, Scraper and Drill**, shows examples of these Native tools. They all came in many sizes and varied shapes, up to 20 pounds weight. An **axe** had a groove for hafting or lashing to a handle. Axes were usually convex on both sides, and were single-bit, or with one cutting end. Marks from usage sometimes show that the other end was used as a hammer. The sharp bit was first chipped by pecking with a very hard stone then fine-ground, possibly using a piece of sandstone, as a whetstone. Axes were usually made from an igneous rock, such as quartz, or a dense metamorphic rock. Sometimes, rocks with less hardness were used because they would still cut wood and were much easier to make. They would become blunt more quickly, of course. Because axes have been found from crude to highly polished, it is known that an axe would first be shaped by pecking then finally shaped by grinding.

Celts are ungrooved axes, or wedges. They tended to be long, and wider at the cutting edge than the base. They could have been hammered against a log to split planks. Smaller celts may have been used as heads for tomahawks, or as chisels or gouges for shaping dugout canoes or trimming wood structures. When polished smoothly, they are as elegant a tool as any produced by the Indians.

Scrapers were round, flat stones with a sharpened edge. They were used by the women, mainly for fleshing hides or for scraping both the meat and fat from one side and the hair from the other side of the hide. There is little to distinguish stone knives from scrapers. They both varied in size from sharp flakes to hand-sized. They were evidently a general household tool, used for leatherwork, small woodwork and pottery work, as well as for cutting food.. Any sharp-edged stone could find a use among the many chores of the women.

Drills look like narrow projectile points. They are characterized by a thin narrow pointed end, and came in many shapes. Some were of a shape for turning with the fingers. Others were shaped for hafting, so they could be

Figure 41

Stone Axe, Celt, Scraper, and Drill

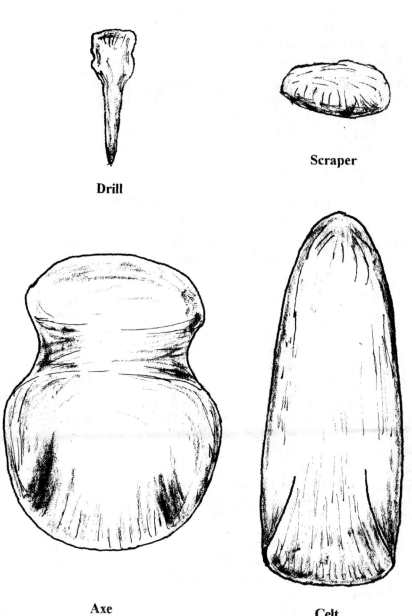

Drill

Scraper

Axe

Celt

lashed to a rod, which could then be turned between the palms, or with a small bow. They could have been used on wood, soft stone, or leather. Very narrow drills were used to make the holes in the shell for making wampum beads. After the Europeans arrived, the Indians soon learned to smash and grind bits of metal, like small saws, to make good drills. Hardened-steel European drills and needles were very desirable to obtain.

The artifacts shown in Figures 38 to 41 are among the more common that are found in this area, but there are many other tools and decorations that may be unearthed. The many types of tools include adzes, atlatl weights, awls, bannerstones (which gave momentum to projectiles), burins (engraving tools), chisels, choppers, fishhooks, gorges (fishhooks to be swallowed), harpoons, gravers, plummets, and netsinkers. (Some hammerstones were even used for cracking the very hard walnuts in the area.) Other stone artifacts were decorations such as discs, effigies, and gorgets, and practical mortars and pestles (for grinding corn and beans).

An **adze** is a tool with the cutting edge at a right angle to the handle, like an axe with the head on sideways. It was used for shaping wood, such as for forming a dugout canoe, creating decorative posts, and for making planks from logs.

An **atlatl** was a device for throwing a spear. It had been developed throughout the world in ancient times. It was essentially an extension of the forearm, giving extra leverage for propelling a spear or dart. One end was carved, or lashed, so that the atlatl would not slip out of the hand. The other end had a notch or projection to fit the base of the spear as it was thrown. An **atlatl weight** was a stone fitted in the middle of the atlatl to give extra momentum to the throwing, producing added velocity and impact. Some atlatl weights were drilled lengthwise. Others were center-drilled and are called **bannerstones**. Some were bipennate, or winged. Only soft stones could be used for working and drilling atlatl weights because they needed a great deal of working, and had to be carefully balanced. Thus, they were often made of slate, steatite, catlinite, and other stones with a Mho's hardness of 2 or 3.

A **burin** was an engraving or scoring tool with a single cutting point, usually made of quartz, because of its hardness. A **graver** was a similar tool with a wider blade. They were used to decorate clay pots, wood effigies, and softer stones.

C. CLAY POTTERY AND WEAVING

Ceramics were introduced into the Northeast in the early Woodland Period, so the Wiechquaeskeck had over a thousand years for development of the ceramics-making process. Algonquians made useful clay pots of various sizes that could be set upright in a campfire, and would withstand the wood flames. They had also learned to make necks and collars so that the pots could be suspended over the fires, from forked sticks or from the tops of wigwams.

Fig. 42, **A Typical Wiechquaeskeck Clay Cooking Pot**, is a generic drawing of the clay pots that came in many sizes and shapes. This figure shows a late Woodlands shell-tempered clay pot, as it is very well shaped. It shows a few characteristic, stamped impressions *(ARCH1, ARCH16)*. In most pots, the stamped impressions were carried around the whole circumference. The pot pictured has a typical pointed base for stability in a wood fire when used for cooking. The point came from the making of the pot. The artisan dug a hole in smooth soil, then shaped the hole by turning a stick around in a conical way in the hole. The prepared clay was then rolled out in a rod-like shape and coiled in the conical hole, building up the round pot. (This forming method took the place of the pottery wheel that had long been used in Europe for shaping.) The vessel was then taken out of the hole, smoothed by hand or wet leather, and possibly edge-decorated and engraved. It was then fired as hot as could be done on an open fire without bellows.

For a good description and classification of such Native ware, see Ernest Wiegand's **The Prehistoric Ceramics of Southwestern Connecticut: An Overview and Reevaluation** *(ARCH16)*. Wiegand discusses the paste characteristics, temper and surface treatments of ceramic vessels, such as interior and exterior cord-marking, lip-notched decorations, and dentate stamping of the vessels found in this area. He notes that the cord marking and other attributes of the ceramics that are found by archaeologists can be used to analyse the Tradition of particular areas. Southwestern Connectcut is archaeologically in the East River Tradition *(search ARCH20)*. This Tradition was typically Lenape.

Glossaries of Ceramic Attributes, which discuss technological attributes, morphology, surface treatment, and stylistic attributes of Native ceramics, are described also in both NativeTech and ArchNet on the Web. Note again, that most of the Web material for Connecticut describes the Windsor Tradition of most of Connecticut, including the Housatonic Basin. There are

Figure 42

A Typical Wiechquaeskeck Clay Cooking Pot

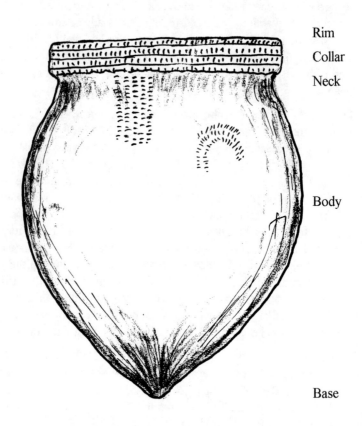

Rim

Collar

Neck

Body

Base

Shell-tempered clay pot
Often decorated with tool or rope impressions
These (partial) designs are from the Manakaway site *(ARCH1)*

Cooking pots had a pointed base to set in a wood fire
Some had a neck for rope suspension over a fire

Diameter at rim from 12 to 25 cm. (5 to 10 in.)
Height of pot from 20 to 35 cm. (8 to 15 in.)

a number of differences between the Windsor Tradition and the East River Tradition of the Wiechquaeskeck, which Wiegand describes. There was, of course, considerable overlap from trading between the Lenape and the Housatonic peoples.

Weaving

In the NativeTech Website *(37)*, Tara Prindle also gives a fine overview of Native American cordage and weaving, including the sources and methods of making cordate, and the types of weaving done by the Woodland People. The Web address is: http://www.nativetech.org/ cordage/cord.html. (2000).

The Wiechquaeskeck made cordage from many natural materials such as bark fibers, plant stalks, grasses, and deer sinew. William Wood reported on the Native cordage in 1634 *(Wood: 107, 108)*:

> Before [*they got English hooks and lines]* they made them of their own hemp more curiously wrought of stronger materials than ours, hooked with bone hooks...They made likewise very strong sturgeon nets with which they catch sturgeons of twelve, fourteen, and sixteen, some eighteen foot long...

> Their cordage is so even, soft, and smooth that it looks more like silk than hemp. Their sturgeon nets be not deep, nor above thirty or forty foot long, which in ebbing low waters they stake fast to the ground where they are sure the sturgeons will come, never looking more at it till the next low water.

Wood was talking about Massachusetts Natives, but the same technology had probably reached the Wiechquaeskeck. This strong, excellent cordage was difficult and time-consuming to make, however, and Wood also reported that "Since the English came they be furnished with English hooks and lines." Steel hooks had an obvious advantage over bone hooks.

We also know that the Natives did some simple weaving before the Europeans arrived. They were pleased to be able to trade with the Europeans for coarse cloth, however, and soon learned how to make clothing from it. The trade cloth, like Duffel's cloth, was much wider than any cloth they had made before the Contact Period.

The northeastern Indians did not have any looms, such as had been developed in the southwest, where animal hair was more abundant. The Wiechquaeskeck did basic "finger weaving," which is well-described by Prindle *(37)*. Essentially, this meant that they warped a limited number of cords to a tree or post, then woofed them (cross threads) with other strands to weave them together. In this way, they made many sashes, belts and straps for around the waist, over the shoulder, or around the head. They also wove straps for bags *(Figs. 29 and 30)*. By the middle of the 17th century, probably the few Wiechquaeskeck who were left had a great mixture of clothing, with some European clothes, some made in their own style from the European broadcloth, some skins and pelts, and a variety of their woven belts and sashes.

Technology was transferred over vast distances, taking a very long time, in ancient days. In the New York Times of Dec. 13, 1999, Natalie Angier reports on the findings of the archaeologists Olga Soffer, James M. Adovasio, and David D. Hyland. They analyzed the distinctive markings and patterns on a number of European figurines from Paleolithic times. They found that there is evidence that the Paleo-women wove "plant fibers into cloth, ropes, nets and baskets." They had linen-like string skirts and elaborate hats and snoods in 23,000 BC! There is a likelihood that, in over 20,000 years, many weaving, braiding and plaiting ideas diffused around the world.

In the 17th century, the Wiechquaeskeck traded with the Dutch for "Duffels cloth," a coarse woolen cloth with a thick nap, made in Duffel, The Netherlands *(Chap. 7)*. The Wiechquaeskeck immediately knew what to do with the Duffels cloth. They threw it over their shoulders, and fastened it with belts. They also used it for men's breech cloths and for women's wrap-around skirts.

We do not know if the Wiechquaeskeck used fiber (linen) cloth for clothing before the Historic Period. They had fiber string for fish lines and wove it into nets. Some nets were so light that they threw them over flocks of feeding birds to catch them. They pressed cord markings into clay pots to make a design *(ARCH16)*. They had woven bags and baskets. It is therefore possible that some of the items that the Wiechquaeskeck wore in preContact times were woven from plant fibers. The pieces would have been narrow and hand-woven *(37)*. Since woven cloth would have all decomposed long ago, however, the only hard record we have is in the woven cloth patterns impressed on their clay pots. There are also Verrazano's descriptions *(Verrazano: 136-138)*, but few of those are very specific.

PETROGLYPHS OR ROCK CARVINGS

Petroglyphs are designs and figures incised, pecked, or scored into the surface of large rocks. In some parts of America, there are many petroglyphs, but they are mostly carved into soft sedimentary stone. Few examples of petroglyphs have been found in the Wiechquaeskeck area, for several reasons. Primarily, the early settlers used all the stones they could move to make stone walls for their sheep, and for building foundations. They cared little whether there were obscure carvings on the stones. Another factor is that the Ice Sheet ground away a great deal of the sedimentary rocks in the area, leaving only the very hard metamorphic and igneous rocks for artisans to use as canvases. Also, petroglyphs are usually on exposed rock surfaces. The weathering over the centuries could have obliterated simple carvings.

Petroglyphs were probably not produced as aesthetic objects, but rather as symbols of clan information, hunting magic, or shamanism. We can look with wonderment at a petroglyph of a bear, but we have no information as to whether it was pictured for admiration, or to overcome it in the hunt.

Fig. 43, **Petroglyphs**, shows the one rock carving that has been described academically in this area *(ARCH12)*. Nicholas Shoumatoff, Jr. was working at Ward Pound Ridge Reservation, near Cross River, NY, in 1972, and found that local families were quite familiar with the petroglyphs that are now called Bear Rock. No one had documented them before. They are a remarkable sight on a large granite rock about 9 feet high beside a well-used trail. Information about the location and a map can be obtained at the Trailside Museum in the Reservation. Bear Rock is on the Dancing Rock Trail. The Dancing Rock is a large balanced flat rock that is also unexplained, but appears to be on a rock area that could have been used for ceremonies. It is important to preserve these artifacts, so the sites should not be widely advertised.

Shoumatoff describes the Bear Rock Petroglyph as having twelve clearly pecked and rubbed designs, with pecking up to 0.5 inches deep. The bear is the clearest and finest design, with its bulky shape, rounded ear, and profile, which strongly suggests to most observers a reclining bear looking over its left shoulder. The other designs appear to indicate a twin deer-bear profile, a wild turkey or grouse, and many elliptical and other designs placed over the rock. Few other reported petroglyphs

Figure 43
Petroglyphs

Bear Rock Petroglyph
Granite rock about 9 feet high
Ward Pound Ridge Reservation, Westchester County, New York

Erratic metamorphic stone,
about three feet high.
Balanced on ledge rock.

Pecked-and-rubbed carving.
About 18 inches high.

Possible Petroglyph
Valleywood Road, Cos Cob, Connecticut

compare closely to these. Digging near the site uncovered abundant Archaic artifacts, with few or none from Woodland Period times. This would indicate that the petroglyphs, and the use of the site in ceremony, are ancient.

Petroglyphs are quite rare in the Wiechquaeskeck area. There is another possible petroglyph on private property on Valleywood Road in Cos Cob *(Fig. 43)*. It is a pecked-and-rubbed carving about 18 inches high on the face of an erratic metamorphic stone about 3 feet high and 8 feet long that is balanced on the edge of a ledge rock. This petroglyph has not yet been reported academically, so no attempt has yet been made to compare the shape of the carving with other petroglyphs, or to decypher it. It is exceedingly old, and the hard metamorphic stone has deeply cracked and weathered over the many centuries. This vast exposure has possibly obscured other carving. The partial design shown in Figure 43 appears to be pecked and rubbed, however, which is a good indication that it was made by humans. The pecking (probably with a hard quartz stone) is clear, and up to 0.5 inches deep.

APPENDIX A

AMERICAN-EUROPEAN TIME LINE - 1492 to 1700

In the European migration to America, traders, fishermen, settlers, and soldiers came and displaced the Native Americans by sheer numbers, sometimes fighting them. To understand the wider conditions at the time of the European takeover, it is helpful to place them in the framework of events in Europe in the same period. When the explorers arrived, it became One World then as much as it is today. There was essentially free trade between all the continents at that time, although the trade was frequently interrupted by continent-wide wars.

The English, Dutch, French, Spanish, Portugese, Swedes, Danes, and Germans were all fiercely fighting each other, in changing combinations, throughout the 16th, 17th, and 18th centuries, and beyond. Along the eastern seaboard of America, the forts first built by the European immigrants were erected facing the sea as protection against the ships of other European countries. Only simple wooden walls were raised for protection from the Native Americans, and they usually had open gates.

The following **American-European Time Line – 1492 to 1700** indicates a few of the interrelationships between events in Europe and events in America in those two centuries.

1490's
1492 - Christopher Columbus sailed from Spain to the Bahamas.
Caribbean Arawaks tried to kill the invaders.
Spanish slaughtered many Native Americans.
1497 - John Cabot sailed from Bristol to Newfoundland.
English War of the Roses, a devastating civil war, ended.

1500's
Breton and Basque fishermen sailed to the Grand Banks for fish.
Portugese followed Cabot's route. Seized some Natives as slaves.
Time of Copernicus and Leonardo da Vinci.
King Henry VIII ruled in England.

1510's
Spain and France were at war. Spain took over The Netherlands.
Many European fishermen sailed regularly to the Grand Banks.
Indians had contact along the coast with both fishermen and traders.
English longbow was still used as their main infantry weapon.
Luther started the Reformation in Europe.
Michelangelo completed painting the Sistine Chapel.

1520's
Verrazano explored the eastern coast of America for the Dutch.
Cortes conquered the Aztecs in Mexico. DeSoto landed in Florida.
Magellan sailed around the world.

1530's
Spanish discovered the Mississippi River for Europe.
Spanish conquered the Incas in South America.
European taking of Native Americans as slaves continued.

1550's
First infantry muskets developed in The Netherlands.
Spanish Inquisition started. Spain and France were at war
English aided the uprising in The Netherlands against Spain.
Queen Elizabeth helped English pirates seize Spanish treasure ships.

1560's
Forty years of war between Catholics and Protestants in France.
Sweden and Denmark waged a ferocious war.

1570's
Over 350 European fishing boats sailed yearly to the Grand Banks.
Great religious struggles throughout Europe. Thousands were killed.

1580's

Spain seized Portugal. There was "hideous oppression" of peasants.
The Spanish Armada sailed to defeat England, but floundered.
Spain had a bloody war with the Moors from Africa.
Galileo lectured on geometry in Florence.

1590's

France and Spain were still at war.
Great wealth in Spain from the New World's gold and silver.
Spain had introduced potatoes and corn from the New World.
William Shakespeare wrote plays.

1600's

1602 - Gosnold attempted a colony in Massachusetts.
1607 - English settlement succeeded in Jamestown, Virginia.
1608 – Champlain settled French in Quebec.
1609 - Henry Hudson arrived, looking for the Northwest Passage.
English army fought in Ireland. England made peace with Spain.
Sweden was at war with Russia, Poland, and Denmark.
Widespread plague and epidemics devastated much of Europe.
Shakespeare wrote Hamlet, King Lear, and Macbeth.
Galileo constructed an astronomical telescope.

1610's

Adriean Block mapped the coast of New York and Connecticut.
The Wiechquaeskeck built palisades as defence against the Pequots.
1617-1619 - Devastating smallpox epidemics in New England.
Massachusetts Native population dropped from 30,000 to 300
    (Josselyn1: 89)
Smallpox was pandemic in both Europe and America for decades.
Van Tweenhuysen Co. started a trading post on Hudson River.
Dutch traded for furs from Delaware to Connecticut Rivers.
1619 – Dutch ship brought first slaves from Africa to Virginia.
Beginning of the Thirty Years War that engulfed central Europe.
Coffee first arrives in Netherlands from the Near East.
Francis Bacon wrote philosophy in England.
1611: King James Bible, Authorized Version, was published.
William Harvey, in London, discovered the circulation of blood.

1620's
1620 - Pilgrims arrived at Plymouth, Massachusetts.
Dutch West India Company got a charter for New Netherland.
1624 – Large hurricane struck New England.
1626 - Dutch purchased Manhattan, and built Fort Amsterdam.
Dutch colonists settled around New York area
1624-28 – Mohawk-Mahican War, both had traded for guns.
England and Holland were at war with Spain.
Velasquez was made the court painter to Philip IV of Spain.

1630's
Plagues, smallpox and another hurricane in New England.
1630 – John Winthrop arrived in Boston with 1,000 Puritans.
The Great Migration of English Settlers started to the Boston area.
1633 - Fort Good Hope (Hartford) established by the Dutch.
1636 – Thomas Hooker's group moved from Boston to Hartford.
1636 – Roger William's group moved to Rhode Island
1636 - New England started war with Pequots.
1638 - Pequot War finished at New Haven and Fairfield.
1638 - Kieft became New Netherland Governor.
1638 – Earthquake struck across most of New England.
Harvard College founded in Cambridge, Massachusetts.
Puritans set up a strict colony in New Haven.
Dutch migration into the Hudson River valley increased.
First printing press started in New England.

1640s
New England settlers migrated to western Connecticut.
1641 – Stamford named as a town
1642 – Greenwich settlers asked to be under Dutch protection.
1642 – Pascal invented the first calculating machine.
1642 – Cromwell's Civil War in England halted the Great Migration.
1643 – Anne Hutchinson and family killed by the Wiechquaeskeck.
1643-44 - Gov. Kieft's war against the Wiechquaeskeck.
1644 – Underhill and Dutch destroyed Nanichiestawack.
1645 – Peace treaty signed between Dutch and Indians (Aepjen).
The Unified Colonies of New England federated.
1648 – Cromwell sent 500 Welsh and Scots prisoners to America.
Discipline emphasized in European armies. Firearms used.

1650s

Smallpox was pandemic in both America and Europe.
1656 – Greenwich came under jurisdiction of New Haven
1656 – Huygens invented the pendulum clock.

1660s

French and Dutch declared war on England.
Smallpox epidemic throughout England.
Smallpox epidemic sweeps through Indians in northeast.
1662 – Connecticut granted a Charter by Charles II.
1664 - English fleet seized New Amsterdam.
1665 – Town of Greenwich given patent by State.
1665 - The Great Plague of London, 20 percent killed.
1666 - Newton discovered calculus and the laws of gravity.
1668 – Hugenots established settlement at New Rochelle.
1668 – Newton invented the reflecting telescope.
Footbridge built over the Mianus River.
Coffee introduced into North America.

1670s

King Philip's War devastated large part of New England.
Stockades built around houses in Greenwich and Stamford.

1680s

1685 – Patent granted to Town of Stamford.
1688 - Hugenots came to settle around New Rochelle.
1689-1697 – King William's War in North America (English vs. French).
William Penn's sons signed treaty with Delaware Indians in Pennsylvania.
William of Orange brought English and Dutch together.
Start of modern British Army, with training and drills.
Bubonic plague epidemic throughout Europe.

1690s

1690 – First North American newspaper published in Boston.
1697 – Town of Ridgefield received patent from State.
Smallpox and malaria widespread among Delaware Indians.

1700s

Missionaries founded Indian refugee town at Stockbridge, Mass.
Spain was bankrupt, partitioned, and nearly depopulated.
Johann Sebastian Bach was an organist in Germany.
Sweden was fighting Russia, Poland and Denmark in a long war.
Newton, Leibnitz and the Bernoullis advanced mathematics.
1725 – Wolves eliminated in the Wiechquaeskeck area.

APPENDIX B

SOME MAPS AND CHARTS OF THE 17th CENTURY

WIECHQUAESKECK REFERENCES – B, **Seventeenth Century Maps in Chronological Sequence**, lists 16 maps from the 17th century and two later maps that contain some helpful, unique information. These maps were drawn in either Holland or England. Most were based on information from the log books of the early explorers, and of expeditions specifically sent out to map the coast line. Logs of reputable captains were written in a structured format that allowed others to interpret from them.

Figure 44, Willem Janszoon Blaeu's map of 1635, **Nova Belgica et Anglia Nova**, was the basic 17th century map that described the New York area and southern New England. Blaeu was the official cartographer of the Dutch company. Details and illustrations on many of the subsequent maps, particularly the Dutch maps, were copied directly from this Blaeu map.

The many illustrations on these maps and charts are interesting, but there is a central problem with them. It is unlikely that many of them would have been in the dated and located entries in the log books. It is possible that some of the illustrations were drawn by artists on the ships, but most were drawn in Europe. There was no way that the exact locations of the illustrations could have been determined by the distant map makers in The Hague, Amsterdam, and London. Therefore, there are some obvious anomalies on the maps. For example, there are fine drawings of Natives in small birchbark canoes in New Amsterdam. These canoes are those of the Abenaki Indians in Maine, however. It is very likely that more than one such canoe was taken back to Europe and examined there. They were sometimes placed on the maps in southern New England or New York harbor, however, because the draftsmen did not have documentation of their origin. Another example is the picture of a Pequot "beaked" canoe. They must have been intriguing to the map makers. They match the brief descriptions that we have of Pequot war canoes of the time, but they were placed at random on the maps. A third problem is that the drawings of New Amsterdam were not always exact,

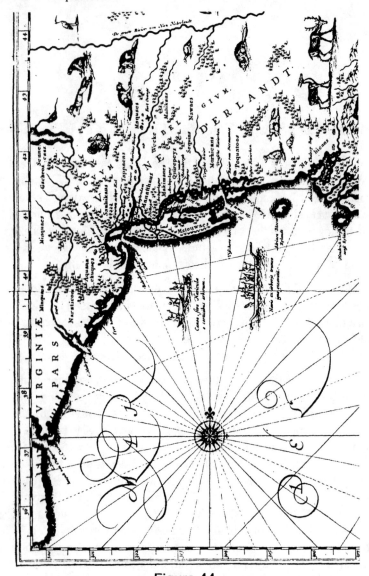

Figure 44
Willem Janszoon Blaeu's Map of 1635

This map by Willem Janszoon Blaeu, *Nova Belgica et Anglia Nova*. Was one of the earliest maps that showed the Long Island Sound area reasonably accurately. It was subsequently copied, with embellishments, by many other map makers. From the Collections of the Library of Congress, Maps Division.

although they gave good representation of the buildings and structures.

There has been modern criticism of Figure 5, **Earliest View of New Amsterdam.** There are certainly problems with the exact location of the fort, the shape of Manhattan Island, and the size of the river on Long Island. It is a remarkable picture to be published by 1651, however, and we can learn much from it. The Dutch ships, large and small, and the Dutch houses are good representations. There is a problem with the two Abenaki canoes and the two Pequot canoes in the harbor, however. As noted above, the map maker obviously did not know the provenance of those canoes, that had probably been brought back to Holland for exhibit.

Figure 45, **Adriaen van der Donck's Map of 1656**, is from the Collections of the Library of Congress, Rare Books Division, LC 918589. It is a facsimile of the original in Adriaen van der Donck's, *Deschryvinge van Nieuw-Nederlant . . . 1656.* It was published in Stoke's, *The Iconography of Manhattan*, vol.1, pl. 6. It was drawn in Holland by E. Nieuwenhoff. It has an illustration of "New Amsterdam on Manhattan Island," with several features such as the large church, a windmill, and a gallows.

Van der Donck's map shows considerable knowledge of New Netherland, the Connecticut River area, and settlements along the Delaware River. Van der Donck had seen these areas himself. Note that he has placed the Manhattans in Westchester County as well as on Long Island. He does note the village of Wichquaskeck, the village of Nanichiestawak, the fort of Betuckquapock, and the settlements of Groebis (Greenwich) and Stantfort (Stamford). He has little understanding of the territory above Fort Orange (Albany) and the Colony of Rennselaerswyck, showing "Quebecq" as very close. Van der Donck was one of the first to wrongly label the Indians of this area as the Siwanoy. This name was then repeated on many subsequent maps. The map shows the Indian village of Heemstee (later Hemsted and Hempstead) on Long Island which Underhill and the Dutch destroyed just before marching against Nanichiestawack in 1644.

Figure 46, **Seller and Price Map, Showing Compass Mapping, 1675**, is from the Collections of the Library of Congress, Geography and Maps Division, LC 915610. It is a small part of *A Chart of ye Coast of New England New York and Long Island from Cape Codd to Sandy Point by Jer. Seller & Cha. Price at the Hermitage Stairs in Wapping. London, 1675.* It is a navigation chart, and shows Wisquaskeck, Grenwich, Shepan Point, Stanford, Newark Islands, Newark, and Fairfield.

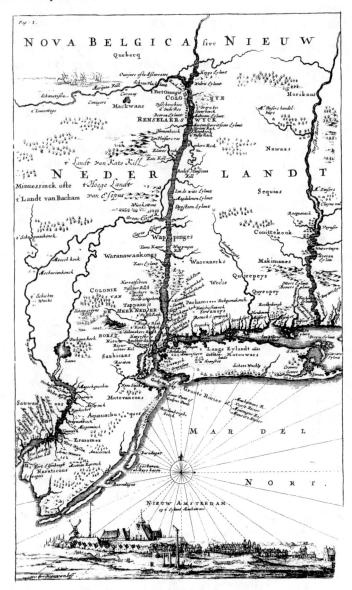

Figure 45
Adriaen van der Donck's Map of 1656

The original map was published in Adriaen van der Donck's *Deschryvinge van Nieuw-Nederlant . . . 1656.* It was later published in Stoke's *The iconography of Manhattan,* vol. 1, pl. 6. From the Collections of the Library of Congress, Rare Books Division, LC 915859.

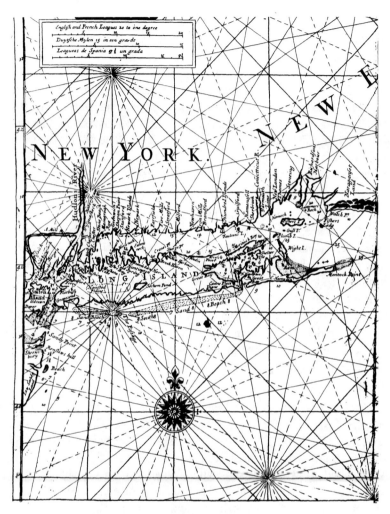

Figure 46

Seller and Price Map, Showing Compass Mapping, 1675

From *A Chart of ye Coast of New England New York and Long Island from Cape Codd to Sandy Point* by Jer. Seller & Cha. Price at the Hermitage Stairs in Wapping, London, 1675. From the Collections of the Library of Congress, Geography and Maps Division. LC915610.

Compass mapping takes many bearings from a single base point, and estimates distances. Some of the observation points and bearings were obviously simulated, but the map was reasonably accurate.

Technically, a **map** is a representation of an area on a flat surface. A **chart** is an outline map for the use of navigators. Compass mapping is done by taking many compass bearings from a single base point. In the early maps, some of the observation points and bearings were obviously simulated, but the maps were reasonably accurate. In the Fig. 46 chart, real compass bearings were taken near Long Island and on the east side of Hudson's River. The other compass roses were calculated to help fix intersections that would give a good shape to the chart. On such charts, one compass rose was always drawn with a large magnetic north symbol, with degrees indicated, to make it look like the compass cards that were being used on the ship.

Compass mapping appealed to sailors because it was their view of the area. It was useful because the navigators at that time did not know their longitude, except by estimation. Accurate chronometers, needed for longitude, had not yet been invented. They knew their latitude accurately by sighting the angle of the North Star with a sextant. Thus, there is a latitude scale on the left side of the Seller & Price chart that is very good. They approximated the lines of position of their observation points fairly well, so their charts were quite usable. Note that they also took many soundings and entered the depths in fathoms. It is doubtful that they knew much about magnetic deviations caused partly by varying amounts of iron in the land masses, but they had probably observed magnetic anomalies as they sailed along shore lines.

Figure 47, **John Speed's Map,** *The Theatre of the Empire of Great Britain, 1676,* is from the Collections of the Library of Congress, Geography and Maps Division, LC915610. It is a map of New England and New York sold by Tho.Bassett in Fleet Street and Richard Chiswell in St. Paul's Church Yard, London. This map shows the change to English spellings of place names, after the English ships had seized New Amsterdam. Lange Eylandt became Long Island, Godyns Bay became Goodwins Bay, etc. Most Indian names remained the same.

Figure 47 is only a portion of John Speed's map. The full map shows two vast rivers, called The Grand River of Canada and the Great River of New England, just north of Albany, joining just before the Great Fall to become the St. Laurent River. Lake Champlain, called Lake of Irocoisen, is very large on the map.

Figure 47

John Speed's Map, *The Theatre of the Empire . . .,* 1676

From John Speed, *The Theatre of the Empire of Great Britain, 1676.* A map of New England and New York sold byt Thom. Bassett in Fleet Street and Richard Chiswell in St. Paul's Church Yard, London. From the Collections of the Library of Congress, Geography and Maps Division, LC 915610.

Figure 48, **Nicolaum Visscher's Map,** *Novi Belgii Novaeque Angliae nec non partis Virginiae Tabula multis in locis emendata per Nicolaum Visscher, 1685,* is from the Collections of the Library of Congress, Geography and Maps Division. It goes back to the Dutch spellings of the place names. Long Island Sound is called the Oost (East) River. English settlements on Long Island are called Jorck (York) Shire. The map lists all the other names that the Hudson River has been called: Groote River, Manhattans River, Noort River, Montaigne River, and Maurits (Mauritius) River. It shows the fort of New Amsterdam, and it labels many Indian villages.

Figure 48

Nicolaum Visscher's Map, *Novii Belgii . . .*, 1685

From *Novii Belgii Noavaeque Angliae nec non parties Virginiae Tabula multis in locis emendate per Nicolaum Visscher*. From the Collections of the Library of Congress, Geography and Maps Division.

WIECHQUAESKECK REFERENCES

A. SEVENTEENTH CENTURY DOCUMENTS

NOTE: Some of these 17th century books are in many university and public libraries. Those listed here were used by the author, and are simply noted for the convenience of other readers, particularly in Connecticut. The Yale University Library has a particularly large collection of the majority of these listed books. They have sent fine copies of many of their books that refer to Native Americans in New England to the Mashantucket Pequot Library, Ledyard, Connecticut, where they are also readily available. The Beinecke Library, at Yale, has original and early editions of some of these books, which can be reviewed there.

(Bradford) Bradford, William, **Bradford's History "Of Plimoth Plantation",** From the Original Manuscript, Wright & Potter Printing Co., Boston, 1899. (Greenwich Library, American Heritage Center in Laramie, Wyoming, Yale University Library, Mashantucket Pequot Library)

> Reprinted as, **Of Plymouth Plantation 1620-1647 William Bradford,** The Modern Library, New York, 1981.

(Brodhead) Brodhead, John Romeyn, **Documents relative to the Colonial History of the State of New York, procured in Holland, England, and France,** E. B. O'Callaghan, ed., Weed, Parsons, and Company, Albany, reprinted 1856 (Connecticut State Library, Hartford)

(DonBartholomew) Don Bartholomew de las Casas, **"An Account of the First Voyages and Discoveries made by Spaniards in America,"** J. Darby, London, 1649. (Tappan Rare Book Library, American Heritage Center, University of Wyoming, Laramie)

(Gookin) Gookin, Daniel, **Historical Collections of the Indians in New England**, Arno Press, New York, reprinted 1972. (Stamford Ferguson Library, Mashantucket Pequot Library, Yale University Library et al.)

(Hariot) Hariot, Thomas, **A briefe and true report of the new found land of Virginia**, Frankfort, 1550. (Library of Congress F229.H27 1590)

(Heckewelder) Heckewelder, John, **A Narrative of the Mission of the United Brethren among the Delaware and Mohegan Indians**, 1740-1808. The Barrows Brothers Co., Cleveland, reprinted 1907. (refers to 17th century) (Tappan Rare Book Library, American Heritage Center, University of Wyoming, and Beinecke Library, Yale University)

(Jameson) Jameson, J. Franklin, ed, **Narratives of New Netherland 1609-1664**, Original Narratives of Early American History, Facsimile reproductions for American Historical Association, Charles Scribner's Sons, New York, 1909. (Connecticut State Library, Greenwich Library, Yale University Library, et al.) Also reprinted by Barnes & Noble, Inc., New York. Within this book are the following separate narratives:

(deLaet) de Laet, Johan, The New World, 1625, 1630, 1633, 1640.

(deRasieres) de Rasieres, Isaack, Letter to Samuel Blommaert, 1628.

(deVries) de Vries, David Peterz, Korte Historiael Ende Journaels Aenteyckeninge, 1633-1643.

(Journal) Journal of New Netherland, 1647.

(Representation) The Representation of New Netherland, 1650.

(vanMeteren) van Meteren, Emanuel, On Hudson's Voyage, 1610.

(vanWassenaer) van Wassenaer, Nicholaes, Historich Verhael, 1624-1630.

(Johnson) Johnson, Edward, **Wonder-Working Providence of Sions Saviour in New-England (1654)** and **Good News from New England (1648)**, facsimile reproduction, Scholars' Facsimiles and Reprints, Delmar, NY 1974. (originals in Beinecke Library, Yale University Library, Mashantucket Pequot Library)

(Josselyn1) Josselyn, John, **Colonial Traveler, A Critical Edition of Two Voyages to New England,** reprinted by University Press of New England, Hanover, 1988. (Yale University Library, Beinecke Library,

Mashantucket Pequot Library)

(Josselyn2) Josselyn, John, **New Englands Rarities Discovered**, printed in London, 1672, reprinted by Massachusetts Historical Society, Boston, 1972.

(Mason) Mason, Major John, **A Brief History of the Pequot War in 1637**, S. Kneeland & T. Green, Boston, 1736, facsimile reproduction by Readex Microprint Corp., 1966. (Stamford Ferguson Library, et al.)

(Morton) Morton, George, **New English Canaan**, printed in London, 1624. (Stamford Ferguson Library, et al.)

(Mourt) Mourt's **Relation, A Journal of the Pilgrims at Plymouth**, edited by Dwight B. Heath from the original text of 1622, Applewood Books, Bedford, Mass. (Yale University Library, Mashantucket Pequot Library, et al.) **Mourt's Relation** and **Bradford's History** have been chronologically combined with other original Colonial documents in Willison, George F., **The Pilgrim Reader**, Doubleday & Co., Inc., Garden City, New York, 1953.

> NOTE: "Mourt" is probably a printer's error for George Morton, a Pilgrim Father. "G. Mourt" appears as a signature on a document. "Relation" is simply the recounting of a story.

(O'Callaghan) O'Callaghan, Edmund Burke, ed., A Brief and True Narrative of the Hostile Conduct of the Barbarous Natives towards the Dutch Nation, 1643, New York Colonial Manuscripts, Albany, NY 1863. (Beinecke Library, Yale University)

(Purchas) Purchas, Samuel, **Henry Hudson's Voyages, from Purchas His Pilgrims, 1625**, March of America Facsimile Series, University Microfilms, Inc., Ann Arbor, Michigan. (Stamford Ferguson Library, et al.)

(Smith) Smith, John, **The Generall Historie of Virginia, New England, and the Summer Isles**, March of America Facsimile Series, University Microfilms, Inc., Ann Arbor, Mich. (Stamford Ferguson Library, et al.)

(Stam) Stam, Jacob Frederick, **New England Canaan**, or New Canaan, containing an Abstract of New England, Amsterdam, 1637. (Tappan Rare Book Library, American Heritage Center, University of Wyoming, Laramie)

NOTE: "Canaan" is a Biblical reference to the Israelites entering the Promised Land, just as the Pilgrims were then entering New England. The term is used by other writers, also.

(Trumbull) Trumbull, J. Hammond, transcriber, **The Public Records of the Colony of Connecticut, prior to Union with New Haven Colony**, May, 1665. Published by the Connecticut Historical Society, Hartford, Conn., 1850

(vanderDonck) van der Donck, Adriaen, **A Description of the New Netherlands**, Thomas F. O'Donnell, ed. (Yale University Library, Mashantucket Pequot Library, et al.) Reprinted by Syracuse University Press, Ithaca, New York, 1968.

(Verrazano) Wroth, Lawrence C., ed., **The Voyages of Giovanni da Verrazzano 1524-1528**, Yale University Press, New Haven, reprinted 1970. (Yale University Library, Beinecke Library, Mashantucket Pequot Library, et al.)

(Williams) Williams, Roger, **A Key into the Language of America**, Gregory Dexter, London, 1643. Reprinted in **Collections of the Rhode Island Historical Society**, Vol. I, John Miller, Providence, 1827. (Rhode Island Historical Society Library, Providence) Reprinted by Applewood Books, Bedford, Massachusetts.

(Williamsletters) Williams, Roger, **The Correspondence of Roger Williams**, Vol. 1, 1629-1653, Glen W. Fantasie, ed., Brown University Press, Hanover, 1988.

(Winthrop) **Winthrop Papers**, manuscript accumulations, v.2. 1623-1630, v.3. 1631-1637, Massachusetts Historical Society, Boston, Mass. 1929. (Massachusetts Historical Society, Boston)

(Wood) Wood, William, **New England's Prospect**, University of Massachusetts Press, Amherst, 1977.

NOTE: Willison, George F., **The Pilgrim Reader**, Doubleday & Co. Inc., Garden City, New York, 1953, is a chronologically collated version of several colonial manuscripts, in their original language. It includes **Bradford's History, Colonial Papers, Mourt's Relation, Good Newes from New England**, and other material intermixed.

B.   SEVENTEENTH CENTURY MAPS IN CHRONOLOGICAL SEQUENCE

Block, Adriaen, and Cornelis Doetz, **Map of New Netherland,** Algemeen Rijksarchief, The Hague, The Netherlands, facsimile of VEL 519, 1613/1614. (The earliest known map of, and the first use of the name, New Netherland)

Hendricksen, Cornelius, map of the Hudson River area, (based on Block) Submitted to the States General of the Netherlands, 1616.

Map of the Hudson River area, c. 1630, (Harrisse Collection, Geography and Map Division, Library of Congress)

Blaeu, Willem Janszoon, Nova Belgica et Anglia Nova, 1635 (Library of Congress)

> NOTE: This is the basic 17th century map of the New York area. Details and illustrations on many of the subsequent maps in the 17th century were copied from this Blaeu map.

Van der Donck, Adriaen, Deschryvinge van Nieuw-Nederlant ..., 1656 (Library of Congress)

Connecticut and New Haven Colonies, 1635 – 1660. (Library of Congress)

Hack, Gulielmus, England in America, 1663. (not copied from Blaeu) (Library of Congress)

Goos, Pieter, Pas carte van Nieu Nederlandt en de Englische Virginie, van Cabo Cod tot Cabo Canrick, 1667. (Friends of New Netherland, Albany, NY, Mashantucket Pequot Archives)

Montanus, Arnoldus, Die nieuwe en onbekende weereld: of beschryving van America, Amsterdam, 1671. (Library of Congress)

Ogilvie, Novi Belgii, 1671. (Mashantucket Pequot Archives)

Allardt, Carolus, Restitutio Map and View, Holland, 1674. (Museum of the City of New York)

Seller, Jer., & Cha. Price, A Chart of ye Coast of New England NewYork and Long Island from Cape Cod to Sandy Point, 1675. (Library of Congress)

Speed, John, The Theatre of the Empire of Great Britain, 1676. (Library of Congress)

Visscher, Nicolaum, **Novi Belgii, Novaeque Anglia nec non, partis Virginiae Tabula**, 1685. (probably represents 1656 information). (Library of Congress - sold commercially)

Morden, Robert, map 1687 (Mashantucket Pequot Archives)

Danckers, Justo, **Novi Belgii**, 17th century (Mashantucket Pequot Archives)

Eighteenth century maps referring to 17th century with unique information

West Chester under the Mohegan Indians 1609, compiled for Bolton's History of West Chester, Miller & Boyle's Lith., N.Y.

The Hudson River Region 1609 - 1770, prepared for the Chronicles of America under the direction of W.L.G. Joerg, American Geographical Society.

C. ARCHEOLOGICAL REPORTS

(ARCH1) Suggs, Robert Carl, **"The Manakaway Site, Greenwich, Connecticut,"** *Bulletin of The Archaeological Society of Connecticut*, No. 29, pp 21-47, New Haven, 1956.

(ARCH2) Lopez, Julius, and Stanley Wisniewski, **"Discovery of a Possible Ceremonial Dog Burial in the City of Greater New York,"** *Bulletin of The Archaeological Society of Connecticut*, No. 29, New Haven, 1956.

(ARCH3) Powell, Bernard W., **"Preliminary Report on a Southestern Connecticut Site,"** (Indian Field, Greenwich), *Bulletin of The Archaeological Society of Connecticut*, No.29, pp 12-19, New Haven, 1958.

*(ARCH4)*Powell, Bernard W., **"A Ceramic Find at Hunting Ridge, Connecticut,"** *Bulletin of the Massachusetts Archaeological Society*, Vol.20, No.3, pp. 43-45, Attleboro, 1959.

(ARCH5) Powell, Bernard W., "**Some Connecticut Burials**," (U.S.1, Greenwich-Stamford Town Line), *Bulletin of the Massachusetts Archaeological Society*, Vol.23, No.2, pp 26-32, Attleboro, 1962.

(ARCH6) Powell, Bernard W., "**An Aboriginal Quartz Quarry at Samp Mortar Reservoir, Fairfield, Connecticut**," *Bulletin of the Archaeological Society of New Jersey*, No. 22, 1962.

(ARCH7) Powell, Bernard W., "**The Mianus Gorge Rock Shelter**," *Pennsylvania Archaeologist*, Vol. 33, No. 3, pp 142-148, 1964.

(ARCH8) Powell, Bernard W., "**Bitter Rock Shelter: A Stratified Connecticut Site**," (Norwalk, Connecticut), *Bulletin of the Massachusetts Archaeological Society*, No. 26, pp 53-63, Attleboro, Massachusetts, 1964.

(ARCH9) Powell, Bernard W., "**A Curious Scratched Design on a Connecticut Paintstone**," *American Antiquity*, Vol.30, No.1, pp 90-100, Salt Lake City, 1964.

(ARCH10) Powell, Bernard W., "**Spruce Swamp: A Partially Drowned Coastal Midden in Connecticut**," *American Antiquity*, Vol. 30, No.4, pp 460-469, 1965.

(ARCH11) Powell, Bernard W., "**First Site Synthesis and Proposed Chronology for the Aborigines of Southwestern Connecticut**," Pennsylvania Archaeologist, 1971.

(ARCH12) Shoumatoff, Nicholas, "**The Bear Rock Petroglyphs Site**," The Bulletin of the New York State Archaeological Association, Vol. 55, pp 1-5, 1972.

(ARCH13) Warner, Frederick W., "**The Foods of the Connecticut Indians**," *Bulletin of The Archaeological Society of Connecticut*, No.37, pp 27-41, New Haven, 1972.

(ARCH14) Wiegand, Ernest A., "**Rockshelters of Southwestern Connecticut**," Norwalk Community College Press, Norwalk, Connecticut, 1983.

(ARCH15) Fiedel, Stuart J., "**The Dundee Rock Shelter, Greenwich**," *Bulletin of the Archaeological Society of Connecticut*, No. 48, pp 31-33, New Haven, 1935.

(ARCH16) Wiegand II, Ernest A., **"The prehistoric ceramics of Southwestern Connecticut: An overview and reevaluation,"** *Bulletin of the Archaeological Society of Connecticut,* No.50, pp23-42, Bethlehem, CT, 1987.

(ARCH17) Fiedel, Stuart J., **"Orient Fishtail Points from the Rye Marshlands Conservancy,"** *Bulletin of the Archaeological Society of Connecticut,* No.51, pp111-124, Bethlehem, CT, 1988.

(ARCH18) Lavin, Lucianne, and Laurie Miroff, **"Aboriginal Pottery from the Indian Ridge Site, New Milford, Connecticut,"** *Bulletin of the Archaeological Society of Connecticut,* No.55, pp39-61, Bethlehem, Connecticut, 1992.

(ARCH19) Wiegand, Ernest A., **"A Unique Prehistoric Vessel from Stamford, Connecticut,"** *Bulletin of the Archaeological Society of Connecticut,* No.61, pp21-25, Meriden, Connecticut, 1998

(ARCH20) WorldWideWeb sites. Prindle, Tara, NativeTech, http://www.nativetech.org, and ArchNet – WWW Virtual Library – Archeology, http://archnet.asu.edu.

C. OTHER DOCUMENTS THAT ILLUMINATE THE SEVENTEENTH CENTURY

1.   Aldrich, Samuel Ray, **Fertilizers and Manures**, Encyclopaedia Britannica, Vol. 9, 1961.

2.   Atwater, Edward A., **History of the Colony of New Haven to its Absorption into Connecticut**, printed for author, New Haven, Conn., 1881.

3.   Ayres, Harral, **The Great Trail of New England**, Medaor Publishing Company, Boston, 1915.

4.   Bedini, Silvio, A., **Ridgefield in Review**, The Ridgefield 250th Anniversary Committee, Ridgefield, Connecticut, 1958.

5.   Bolton, R.P., **Indian Paths in the Great Metropolis,** Contributions from the Museum, 23, Museum of the American Indian, Heye Foundation, New York, 1922.

6. Bragdon, Kathleen J., **Native People of Southern New England, 1500-1650**, Univerity of Oklahoma Press, Norman, Oklahoma, 1996.

7. Brasser, T. J., **Early Indian-European Contacts**, and **Mahican**, in Bruce G. Trigger, ed., **Northeast**, Volume 15, **Handbook of North American Indians**, Smithsonian Institution, Washington, D.C., 1978.

8. Carder, Robert Webster, **Captain John Underhill in Connecticut, 1642-1644**, Bulletin of the Underhill Society of America, Greenwich, CT, Dec. 1967.

9. Cooke, Jacob Ernest, ed., **Encyclopedia of the North American Colonies**, Charles Scribner's Sons, New York, N. Y.

10. DeForest, John W., **History of the Indians of Connecticut from the earliest known period to 1850**, Connecticut Historical Society, Wm Jas Hammersely, Hartford, Conn., 1852.

11. Dornbusch, William F., **Captain John Underhill**, The Westchester Historian, Quarterly of the Westchester County Historical Society, Vol. 49, No. 3, Summer, 1973.

12. Driver, Harold E., **Indians of North America**, The University of Chicago Press, Chicago, Illinois, 1969.

13. Dunn, Shirley W., **The Mohicans and Their Land 1609-1730**, Purple Mountain Press, Fleischmanns, New York, NY, 1994.

14. Flint, Richard Foster, and Morris M. Leighton, **Pleistocene Epoch**, Encyclopaedia Britannica, Vol. 18, 1961.

15. Galinat, Walton C., **The Evolution of Corn and Culture in North America**, Economic Botany, Vol. 19, No. 4, Oct-Dec, 1965.

16. Galinat, Walton C., **The Evolution of Sweet Corn,** Research Bulletin 591, University of Massachusetts-Amherst, College of Agriculture, Agricultural Experiment Station, May, 1971.

17. Galinat, Walton C. and Gunnerson, James H., **Spread of Eight-Rowed Maize from the Prehistoric Southwest**, Botanical Museum Leaflets, Vol.20, No.5, Harvard University, Cambridge, MA, May 1963.

18. Galinat, Walton C., **The Origin of Maize: Grain of Humanity**, Economic Botany Vol. 49, No. 1, pp. 3-12, The New York Botanical Gardens, Bronx, NY, 1995.

19. Goddard, Ives, **Delaware**, in Bruce G. Trigger, ed., **Northeast**, Volume 15, **Handbook of North American Indians**, Smithsonian Institution, Washington, D.C., 1978.

20. Grumet, Robert Stephen, **Native American Place Names in New York City**, Museum of the City of New York, New York, 1991.

21. Grumet, Robert S., **The Lenapes**, Chelsea House Publisher, New York, 1989.

22. Halls, Lowell K., **White-Tailed Deer: Ecology and Management**, The Wildlife Management Institute, Stackpole Books, Harrisburg, Penna.

23. Huden, John C., **Indian Place Names of New England**, National Museum of the American Indian, Smithsonian Institution, New York, 1962.

24. Hyde, George E., **Indians of the Woodlands**, University of Oklahoma Press, Norman, Oklahoma, 1962.

25. Johannessen, Sissel, and Christine Hastorf, eds., **Corn and Culture in the Prehistoric New World**, ISDN-0813383757, Westview Press, Boulder, Colorado, 1993.

26. Kraft, Herbert C., **The Indians of Lenapehoking**, Seton Hall University Museum, South Orange, New Jersey, 1985.

27. Kraft, Herbert C., **The Dutch, the Indians, and the Quest for Copper**, Seton Hall University Museum, South Orange, New Jersey, 1996.

28. Lacey, Charlotte Alvord, **An Historical Story of Southport, CT**, The Fairfield Historical Society, 1927.

29. LaFantasie, Glenn W., ed., **The Correspondence of Roger Williams, Volume1, 1629-1653,** Brown University Press, Hanover and London, 1988.

30. Luquer, Thatcher P., **The Indian Village of 1643**, The Quarterly Bulletin of the Westchester County Historical Society, Vol. 21, No. 2, April-July, 1945.

31. Mead, Spencer P., **Ye Historie of ye Town of Greenwich**, The Knickerbocker Press, New York. NY, 1911.

32. Moeller, Roger W., **6LF21 – A Paleo-Indian Site in Western**

Connecticut, Occasional Paper No. 2, American Indian Archeological Institute, Washington, Connecticut, 1980.

33. Morison, Samuel Eliot, **The European Discovery of America - The Northern Voyages A.D. 500-1600**, Oxford University Press, New York, NY, 1971.

34. Otto, Paul Andrew, **New Netherland Frontier - European and Native Americans along the Lower Hudson River, 1524 - 1664**, PhD Dissertation, Indiana University, Bloomington, Indiana, 1995.

35. Powell, J.W., dir., Tenth Annual Report of the Bureau of Ethnology to the Secretary of the Smithsonian Institution, 1888-89, Washington, D.C., 1893.

36. Prescott, William H., **History of the Conquest of Mexico and History of the Conquest of Peru**, 1856, reprinted by The Modern Library, New York.

37. Prindle, Tara, **Woven Wampum Beadwork**, NativeTech, http://www.nativetech.org/NativeTech/wampum/war, 1999.

38. Ray, Deborah Wing and Gloria P. Stewart, **Norwalk**, Norwalk Historical Society, Inc., Phoenix Publishing, Canaan, NH, 1979.

39. Ritchie, William A., **A Typology and Nomenclature for New York Projectile Points**, New York State Museum, Bulletin No. 384, Albany, NY, 1961, rev. 1971.

40. Rockwell, George L., **The History of Ridgefield, Connecticut**, privately published, 1927.

41. Ruttenber, E. M., **History of Indian Tribes of Hudson's River**, facsimile reprint of 1872 book, Hope Farm Press, Saugerties, NY, 1992.

42. Salwen, Bert, **Indians of Southern New England and Long Island: Early Period**, in Bruce G. Trigger, ed., **Northeast**, Volume 15, **Handbook of North American Indians**, Smithsonian Institution, Washington, D.C., 1978.

43. Sheets, Payson, and Tom Sever, **Arenal Region**, in Trombold *(48)* and http://www.ghcc.msfc.nasa.gov/archeology arenal.html. (1999)

44. Short, Nicholas M., **The Landsat Tutorial Workbook,** NASA Reference Publication 1078, NASA Scientific and Technical Information Branch, Washington, DC, 1982, also http://www.ghcc.msfc.nasa.gov/archeology (1999).

45. Skinner, Alanson, **Indians of Manhattan Island and Vicinity**, American Museum of Natural History, Guide Leaflet No. 41, 1921.

46. Snow, Dean R., **The Archeology of New England**, Academic Press, New York, NY, 1980.

47. The Carolina Dog Association, **The Carolina Dog**, http://www.carolinadogs.org. (2000)

48. Thoreau, Henry David, ca. 1860, **Wild Fruits,** W.W. Norton & Company, Inc. New York, 2000.

49. Trombold, Charles D., ed., **Ancient road networks and settlement hierarchies in the New World**, Cambridge University Press, Great Britain, 1991.

50. Weinstein, Laurie, ed., **Enduring Traditions: The Native Peoples of New England**, Bergin & Garvey, Westport, Connecticut, 1994.

51. Wiegand, Ernest A., **Rockshelters of Southwestern Connecticut: their Prehistoric occupation and use**, Norwalk Community College Press, Norwalk, Connecticut, 1983.

52. Wiegand, Ernest A., **Unpublished reports,** Norwalk Community College, Norwalk, Connecticut.

53. Wilson, Lynn Winfield, **History of Fairfield County Connecticut 1639-1928**, The S.J. Clarke Publishing Company, Hartford, 1929.

54. Wright, John Kirtland, **Map**, Encyclopaedia Britannica, Vol. 14, 1961.